EDUCATION FOR MINISTRY

Reading and Reflection Guide, Volume B

Living Faithfully in a Multicultural World

EDUCATION FOR MINISTRY

Reading and Reflection Guide, Volume B

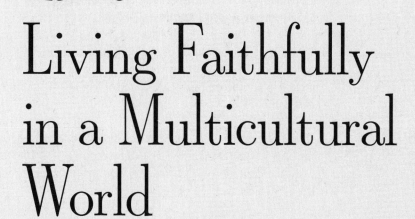

Living Faithfully in a Multicultural World

Morehouse Publishing

NEW YORK

Used by permission:
Still Listening: New Horizons in Spiritual Direction © 2000 by Church Publishing Inc.,
   New York, NY 10016
Beyond Colonial Anglicanism: The Anglican Communion in the Twenty-first Century
   © 2001 by Church Publishing Inc., New York, NY 10016
Constructive Theology: A Contemporary Approach to Classic Themes © 2005 by Augsburg
   Fortress Publishers, Minneapolis MN 55402.
"Believing" from *Christianity After Religion* by Diana Butler Bass © 2012 by Diana
   Butler Bass by permission of Harper Collins Press.

Morehouse Publishing, 4785 Linglestown Rd., Suite 101, Harrisburg, PA 17112
Morehouse Publishing, 19 East 34th Street, New York, NY 10016
Morehouse Publishing is an imprint of Church Publishing Incorporated.
www.churchpublishing.org

Cover design by Laurie Klein Westhafer
Typeset by Beth Oberholtzer

Library of Congress Cataloging-in-Publication Data
A catalog record of this book is available from the Library of Congress.

ISBN-13: 978-0-8192-2919-9

Printed in the United States of America

Contents

PART I: THE GUIDE

Unit One: Spiritual Autobiography and Listening

Unit Two: Theological Reflection as a Life Skill

First Interlude Unit: Developing a Multicultural Community

Unit Three: Developing a Sustaining Spirituality

Unit Four: Attending to the Gaps—Integrating Belief, Behavior, and Doctrine in a Multicultural World

Second Interlude Unit: Globalization, Gender, and Interfaith Dialogue

Unit Five: Vocation—Hearing and Responding to God's Call

PART II: RESOURCES

Supplemental Readings in the Christian Tradition

Resources for Spiritual Autobiography and Listening

Resources for Reflecting Theologically

Resources for Community Life

Acknowledgments

A revision by definition is not *sui generis*. Although this series of Reading and Reflection Guides may look different from previous editions of EfM materials, although it may be organized differently, it is nonetheless built on a framework that has evolved over the nearly forty years of Education for Ministry. Those who have some years of acquaintance with the program will recognize what the new format owes to components developed for its predecessors, among them parallel guides, common lessons, and the many variations of EfM's central discipline of theological reflection.

The developers of those foundational components are by now nearly legion and include not only founder Charles Winters and succeeding leaders like John de Beer and Edward de Bary, but also the many EfM coordinators and trainers whose work with mentors all over the globe and over time has shaped the program.

The principal author of Reading and Reflection Guide, Volume B: *Living Faithfully in a Multicultural World,* the second in the cycle of four guides, is Rick Brewer, who has a long history of writing and curriculum design in EfM. Other contributors to this volume include Angela Hock Brewer and Karen M. Meridith. In addition, several of the essays and resources included in this *Guide,* some adapted, others left as originally published in the previous edition, have long been a part of the EfM program, designed and written by a number of contributors over the years. We are grateful for their work and know that we can look to the future of EfM only because we stand on the shoulders of giants.

Karen M. Meridith, series editor
Executive Director of Education for Ministry
Sewanee, Tennessee
March, 2014

About the Author

Richard E. Brewer (Rick) is a retired Episcopal priest who served in parochial ministry and in adult Christian formation for forty years. A graduate of The University of the South and General Theological Seminary, he has lived in Oklahoma most of his life and served as priest and educator in Tulsa and Stillwater Episcopal churches. Additionally, he developed and directed the Deacon Formation Program for the Episcopal Diocese of Oklahoma.

Rick first learned about EfM in 1975 from Dr. Charles Winters, the originator and first director of the program. He has been a trainer since 1978, a coordinator, a mentor, and interim assistant director for the EfM program. He conceived and edited the Common Lesson series for the first revision of the materials. He coauthored the Parallel Guides and numerous common lessons with the Reverend John de Beer. He, along with Angela Hock, co-wrote *Practically Christian: A Guide to Practical Christian Prayer, Action, and Reflection*. They co-directed Opportunities for Adult Christian Education and Spirituality (OACES), Inc. which developed a variety of adult Christian formation learning guides and a comprehensive ministry formation program for the Episcopal Diocese of Nebraska. For over a decade he participated in the Progoff Intensive Journal program. Rick brings this extensive experience in adult Christian formation to the revision of the new materials for EfM.

Program Overview

The Education for Ministry (EfM) program is a four-year study and group reflection process for the formation of Christian ministry through the development of knowledge, attitude, skill, and identity as Christians. Published texts and essays provide the primary knowledge content in the study of the Christian tradition.

The first year studies the Hebrew Scriptures (Old Testament). The second year offers a study of the New Testament. Year Three provides study of Christian (church) history. Theology, ethics, and interfaith encounter constitute study in the fourth year.

Texts for Each Year

- **Year One:** *A Short Introduction to the Hebrew Bible* by John J. Collins. *The Holy Bible*, Old Testament and Apocrypha.

- **Year Two:** *Introducing the New Testament* by Mark Allan Powell. *The Holy Bible*, New Testament.

- **Year Three:** *Christianity: The First Three Thousand Years* by Diarmaid MacCulloch.

- **Year Four:** *Theology for a Troubled Believer* by Diogenes Allen. *The Christian Moral Life: Practices of Piety* by Timothy F. Sedgwick. *My Neighbor's Faith* edited by Jennifer Howe Peace, Or N. Rose, and Gregory Mobley.

Note: The most recent Oxford Annotated edition of the New Revised Standard Version of the Bible is recommended, but any translation may be used as long as it includes the Apocrypha. Paraphrased Bibles are not recommended for study.

The Interlude Texts for Volume B

- *The Bush Was Blazing but Not Consumed* by Eric H. F. Law.

- *Globalization, Gender, and Peacebuilding: The Future of Interfaith Dialogue* by Kwok Pui-lan.

Reading and Reflection Guide

A *Reading and Reflection Guide* provides weekly reading assignments, reflection questions, and additional supportive resources for the group.

- The entire group uses the same *Guide* each year—Volume A, B, C, or D. Each volume has a particular focus: Volume A, "Living Faithfully in Your World," works with the contexts of a person's life; Volume B builds on "Living Faithfully in a Multicultural World"; Volumes C and D explore Christian maturity and *theosis*, our journey into deeper relationship with God, respectively.

- Each volume contains **Part I**, the reading and reflection assignments, and **Part II**, supporting materials, such as examples of spiritual autobiography and theological reflection.

- Five primary units in each volume have six sessions each.

- Two interlude units in each volume have two sessions each.

- An organization session at the beginning and a closing session at the end bring the total to thirty-six sessions in a year.

Focus of the Reading and Reflection Guide Units in Volume B

The first session of each primary unit is either an essay or other material for all in the group to read to help set the stage for the focus of the unit. In Volume B these are:

- **Unit One**—telling our stories and listening to the stories of others in order to explore identity and meaning (individual, corporate, and historical);

- **Unit Two**—theological reflection as a life skill that informs our orientation to prayer, worship, and spirituality;

- **First Interlude**—developing a multicultural community through dialogue and liturgy;

- **Unit Three**—spirituality, prayer, and worship;

- **Unit Four**—integrating behavior and belief into a congruency that supports faithful living;

- **Second Interlude**—how globalization and gender relate to interfaith dialogue;

- **Unit Five**—vocation: hearing and responding to the call and passion of our lives in relation to God.

PART I

The Guide

Week One: Orientation and Planning for the Year

Mentors often begin the seminar year with an orientation session to distribute materials; begin to get acquainted; make decisions about leadership roles such as worship/devotional leaders, on-board leaders, discussion leaders, and the like; orient all to the seminar format and to the *Reading and Reflection Guide*; and other aspects that mentors and groups want to include. The following components are suggestions that can be adapted or discarded. Online groups will have some differences, but the basic ideas of planning the group's organization, orienting to the *Reading and Reflection Guide* for the year, and beginning to get to know the other group members are the same.

Welcoming

Introductions of each person, using a simple template such as name, year in EfM, how long they have lived in their current location, or any way that someone has used and found helpful for initial connection in a group.

Worship

GOD OF MANY NAMES

Leader	God of a thousand names,
	You come to us in many forms—manna to the hungry
Responders	**water to the parched**
Leader	embrace to the grieving
Responders	**rainbow to the despairing**
Leader	champion of the oppressed
Responders	**defender of the exploited**
Leader	friend to the lonely
Responders	**rescuer to the lost**
Leader	rest for the weary
Responders	**shock to the comfortable**
Leader	peace to the restless
Responders	**gift to the joyful**

| Leader | mystery to the knowing |
| **Responders** | **revelation to the seeking** |

Leader manna, water, embrace, rainbow, champion, defender, friend, rescuer, rest, shock, peace, gift, mystery, revelation . . . In silence, let us reflect on what God's name is for us at this moment . . .

(Silent reflection)

Let us give thanks to God.

ALL **God of many names and still the one, true God,**
You reveal Your name to us in our need,
yet remain beyond our control or understanding.
You are God and we are Your people.
In trust and love, we commit ourselves to exploring
  and discovering
who You are and whose we are. Amen.[1]

Check-in

Each participant responds to one of the following:

- Describe a moment of joy this past week.

- Describe a moment of challenge this past week.

- Describe a moment when someone ministered to you this past week.

 Or use some other way to open up awareness of one another and what is happening in each other's lives.

Organizing

Distribute materials for the year.

- **All Years:** EfM *Reading and Reflection Guide, Volume B. The Bush Was Blazing but Not Consumed*, Eric H. F. Law. *Globalization, Gender, and Peacebuilding*, Kwok Pui-lan.

- **Year One:** *A Short Introduction to the Hebrew Bible*, John J. Collins. *The Holy Bible*, Old Testament and Apocrypha.

- **Year Two:** *Introducing the New Testament*, Mark Allan Powell. *The Holy Bible*, New Testament.

---

1. The Revs. Norma and John Brown, from "God of Many Names," *Mission Prayer Handbook*, Uniting Church Assembly (Australia), http://www.ncca.org.au/departments/ youth/over-this-violence-thing/197-uca-mission-prayer-handbook

- **Year Three:** *Christianity: The First Three Thousand Years*, Diarmaid Mac-Culloch.

- **Year Four**: *Theology for a Troubled Believer*, Diogenes Allen. *The Christian Moral Life: Practices of Piety*, Timothy F. Sedgwick. *My Neighbor's Faith*, Jennifer Howe Peace, Or N. Rose, and Gregory Mobley, editors.

Look through the *Guide* to get a sense of how the weeks and units are laid out. A chart of the year's assigned readings is in Part II, pages 205–208.

- Discuss, ask/answer questions about the *Guide*.

- Returning participants may offer suggestions for study and preparation.

Learning Goals and Needs

Participants identify what they hope to do as part of their participation in EfM this year.

Covenant/Norms

Use any way that works for you to establish an agreed upon set of norms or standards for how the group members will relate to one another during their year together.

Questions to consider when forming norms:

- What environment will best facilitate your goals for this year?

- What commitments will you make to your fellow travelers on this journey?

One possibility is to use Eric Law's Respectful Communication Guidelines (page 286 in Part II of this Guide) as a baseline covenant to which additions may be made as desired by the seminar group.

Seminar Calendar

Look over the thirty-six seminar weeks.

Sign up to lead/provide (as customary for your group):

- Worship

- Spiritual Autobiographies

- Theological Reflection

Note holiday breaks.

Is there anything else that needs to be scheduled?

Our Stories: A Way to Deepen Personal Connections

The spiritual autobiography encouraged for this seminar year helps participants to get in touch with the pattern of diversity that has shaped and continues to shape each person. Beginning in the preparation for Week Two, each will have the opportunity to explore those life dimensions and decide what to share openly with the group at the agreed upon time.

Read the following excerpt from Unit One, Week Two (page 13):

[This year's *Reading and Reflection Guide* volume] invites participants to notice the different cultures present in their lives. These cultures have distinctive qualities and features that differentiate one from another. A people's mores, assumptions, values, sciences, artifacts, and philosophies work together to form their culture. Culture refers to the patterns that order the social interactions ranging from the economic and political interests to educational and family concerns. In short, a group's ways of being in relationship to other people and groups. Culture includes the physical environments and the ways of relating to the geographic conditions.

Language, dress, food, celebrations, rituals, music, stories, myths, and religious practices distinguish a person's ethnic background–a background that is lived out within a cultural ethos. People from very diverse ethnic backgrounds come together creating diverse features of a common society.

Take a few moments to recall stories or information your family has told you about their history, or perhaps information you have discovered through some kind of ancestry research. If, for a variety of reasons, little is known of one's family history, recall the environments in which you have grown up and what the cultural contributions are from those arenas.

Make notes identifying multicultural threads that have contributed to your identity.

Share and listen to one another extend these beginning offerings of personal experience.

Closing Prayer

> All: God of history and God of all nations,
> you have called us to be in relationship with one another
> and promised to dwell wherever two or three are gathered.
> . . . We are a diverse people;
> called to live together
> from many different places and cultures.
> We are amazed by your wondrous deeds
> in creating different cultures, languages, and faces.
> Open our hearts that we may boldly search out
> and celebrate the treasures of diversity among us.
> In the name of Jesus, lover of all, we pray. Amen.[2]

All begin the reading and reflection according to the Guide *directions for Week Two.*

---

2. From the bulletin *Worship for Multiculturalism Sunday*, Canadian Multiculturalism Day, United Church of Canada, 1. http://www.united-church.ca/files/planning/theme/intercultural_service.pdf

UNIT ONE

Spiritual Autobiography and Listening

Week Two

The purpose of Volume B is to build knowledge and skills for living authentically as a committed Christian in a world where multiple cultures live in close proximity. Each unit of the *Reading and Reflection Guide* supports elements of the ministry formation process: autobiography, theological reflection, spiritual maturity, personal theology, and vocation. Unit One focuses on sharing our own stories and listening deeply to the stories of others.

ALL YEARS

Read

Part One—Living in a Multicultural World

Sometime in the latter half of the twentieth century in Manhattan, New York, Carolyn A. Rose composed a collect that expressed a vision for humanity. Anyone living in New York City as she did in the 1950s and '60s experienced refugees and immigrants flooding into the city and knew firsthand the tensions and pressures present whenever people from diverse cultures interact. The prayer likely emerged from the pressures of plurality she felt.

> O God, who created all peoples in your image, we thank you for the wonderful diversity of races and cultures in this world. Enrich our lives by ever-widening circles of fellowship, and show us your presence in those who differ most from us, until our knowledge of your love is made perfect in our love for all your children; through Jesus Christ our Lord. Amen.[3]

The primary petition of the collect envisions a dynamic world in which "ever-widening circles of fellowship" reveal God's love. Decades later, in South Africa, a vision of God fueled the passions of a people who were emboldened to abolish an oppressive apartheid system. Archbishop Desmond Tutu promoted the vision that guided people into a new world. He extended his ongoing commitment to the vision in his book *God Has a Dream*:

> Dear Child of God, before we can become God's partners, we must know what God wants for us. "I have a dream," God says, "Please help Me to realize it. It is a dream of a world whose ugliness and squalor and poverty, its war and hostility, its greed and harsh competitiveness, its alienation and disharmony are changed into their glorious counterparts, when there will be more laughter, joy,

---

3. Collect "For the Diversity of Races and Cultures," *The Book of Common Prayer* (New York: Church Hymnal Corporation, 1979), 840.

and peace, where there will be justice and goodness and compassion and love and caring and sharing. I have a dream that swords will be beaten into plowshares and spears into pruning hooks, that My children will know that they are members of one family, the human family, God's family. My family.[4]

Bishop Tutu continues,

In God's family there are no outsiders. All are insiders. Black and white, rich and poor, gay and straight, Jew and Arab, Palestinian and Israeli, Roman Catholic and Protestant, Serb and Albanian, Hutu and Tutsi, Muslim and Christian, Buddhist and Hindu, Pakistani and Indian—all belong.

A gap occurs between vision and reality; between what is desired and what currently exists. The gap creates a tension that seeks resolution. Either the vision atrophies and dissolves into merely a notion or the current situation moves toward realizing the vision. A vision that is loved can provide motivation and energy to transform current realities into the vision.[5] Ministry occurs in the gap between vision and reality. Carolyn Rose's heartfelt prayer for "ever-widening circles of fellowship" and Desmond Tutu's dream of an inclusive world create lenses through which learners can recognize the knowledge, skills, actions, and attitudes needed to realize the vision. Once people fall in love with God's dream, they enter into a partnership with God.

One way to understand ministry is to see it as the participation with God realizing God's dream. Ministry happens among and within the complexities of the world. Clearly, contemporary life is complex and fast-paced, filled with multiple encounters with ethnic diversity. *Education for Ministry* brings people together by forming a reflecting community of colleagues committed to helping one another to know better what it means to live as an adult Christian in an increasingly pluralistic world.

The Reading and Reflection Guide: Volume B is built on the theme "Living Faithfully in a Multicultural World." Advancements in travel have brought races and cultures together geographically in unprecedented ways. Technology, especially in the advancement and use of communication satellites, has shrunk our world into what Marshall McLuhan aptly described in the 1970s as a "global village." All of humanity has been brought into an awareness of the "wonderful diversity of races and cultures." While all may not celebrate the diversity, the fact of great cultural and racial diversity is undeniable. The following excerpt from Diana Eck's *A New Religious America* sets the stage for the work ahead as she describes the current reality of the contemporary religious scene.

---

4. Desmond Tutu, *God Has a Dream: A Vision of Hope for Our Time* (New York: Image Books Doubleday, 2005), 19–20.

5. Robert Fritz has worked extensively on structural tensions and has written several books on how the tension, once established, brings visions into life. http://robertfritz.com

The huge white dome of a mosque with its minarets rises from the cornfields just outside Toledo, Ohio. You can see it as you drive by on the interstate highway. A great Hindu temple with elephants carved in relief at the doorway stands on a hillside in the western suburbs of Nashville, Tennessee. A Cambodian Buddhist temple and monastery with a hint of a Southeast Asian roofline is set in the farmlands south of Minneapolis, Minnesota. In suburban Fremont, California, flags fly from the golden domes of a new Sikh gurdwara on Hillside Terrace, now renamed Gurdwara Road. The religious landscape of America has changed radically in the past thirty years, but most of us have not yet begun to see the dimensions and scope of that change, so gradual has it been and yet so colossal. It began with the "new immigration," spurred by the Immigration and Nationality Act of 1965, as people from all over the world came to America and have become citizens. With them have come the religious traditions of the world—Islamic, Hindu, Buddhist, Jain, Sikh, Zoroastrian, African, and Afro-Caribbean. The people of these living traditions of faith have moved into American neighborhoods, tentatively at first, their altars and prayer rooms in storefronts and office buildings, basements and garages, recreation rooms and coat closets, nearly invisible to the rest of us. But in the past decade, we have begun to see their visible presence. Not all of us have seen the Toledo mosque or the Nashville temple, but we will see places like them, if we keep our eyes open, even in our own communities. They are the architectural signs of a new religious America. . . .

We are surprised to find that there are more Muslim Americans than Episcopalians, more Muslims than members of the Presbyterian Church USA, and as many Muslims as there are Jews—that is, about six million. We are astonished to learn that Los Angeles is the most complex Buddhist city in the world, with a Buddhist population spanning the whole range of the Asian Buddhist world from Sri Lanka to Korea, along with a multitude of native-born American Buddhists. Nationwide, this whole spectrum of Buddhists may number about four million. We know that many of our internists, surgeons, and nurses are of Indian origin, but we have not stopped to consider that they too have a religious life, that they might pause in the morning for few minutes' prayer at an altar in the family room of their home, that they might bring fruits and flowers to the local Shiva-Vishnu temple on the weekend and be part of a diverse Hindu population of more than a million. We are well aware of Latino immigration from Mexico and Central America and of the large Spanish-speaking population of our cities, and yet we may not recognize what a profound impact this is having on American Christianity, both Catholic and Protestant, from hymnody to festivals. . . .

In the past thirty years massive movements of people both as migrants and refugees have reshaped the demography of our world. Immigrants around the world number over 130 million, with about 30 million in the United States, a million arriving each year. The dynamic global image of our times is not the so-called clash of civilizations but the marbling of civilizations and peoples. Just as the end of the Cold War brought about a new geopolitical situation, the global movements of people have brought about a new georeligious reality.

Hindus, Sikhs, and Muslims are now part of the religious landscape of Britain, mosques appear in Paris and Lyons, Buddhist temples in Toronto, and Sikh gurdwaras in Vancouver. But nowhere, even in today's world of mass migrations, is the sheer range of religious faith as wide as it is today in the United States. Add to India's wide range of religions those of China, Latin America, and Africa. Take the diversity of Britain or Canada, and add to it the crescendo of Latino immigration along with the Vietnamese, Cambodians, and Filipinos. This is an astonishing new reality. We have never been here before.[6]

Reading and Reflection Guide Volume B, *Living Faithfully in a Multicultural World* invites participants to notice the different cultures present in their lives. These cultures have distinctive qualities and features that differentiate one from another. A people's mores, assumptions, values, sciences, artifacts, and philosophies work together to form their culture. Culture refers to the patterns that order the social interactions ranging from the economic and political interests to educational and family concerns: in short, a group's ways of being in relationship to other people and groups. Culture includes the physical environments and the ways of relating to the geographic conditions. Often a person's physical features mark the culture out of which he or she comes.

Language, dress, food, celebrations, rituals, music, stories, myths, and religious practices distinguish a person's ethnic background—a background that is lived out within a cultural ethos. People from very diverse ethnic backgrounds come together, creating diverse features of a common society. Increasingly, ethnic identity has become marbled as different cultures interact.

Focus

List the four or five greatest challenges you have experienced in the face of the information provided above. What image, picture, or metaphor expresses life in a multicultural world?

Part Two: Listening as an Act of Ministry

An ellipse is a figure with two foci that create the elliptical shape. The work in *Unit One: Spiritual Autobiographies and Listening* has two points of focus. One centers the work of constructing a narrative of one's life, especially from the viewpoint of living among several cultures. The other focus works with listening as an act of receiving the story of another. Attending to another's life requires deep, compassionate listening. A primary skill for ministry is listening. The following essay was taken from *9 Skills for Listening to Life* by Geoffery Caine, providing a profile of the features of listening and the various attitudes and skills necessary for effective listening.

---

6. Diana Eck, *A New Religious America* (San Francisco: HarperSanFrancisco, 2002), 1–4.

Why Listen?

Life is messy. Life is noisy. Life is rushed. That means that while life is rich with possibility, it is also full of missed opportunities, problems big and small, miscommunication, and mistakes. So the more tools we have for dealing with the demanding aspects of life, the better.

One set of tools, lying right under our noses, is the underutilized and surprising power of listening.

I gained a fresh understanding of listening when I left Australia and came to live in the United States many years ago. You might say that I'm an accidental immigrant. I came to visit someone. Seven days later we were married. Four days after that I discovered that I was going to immigrate. Life can be like that. And this was quite a shock for someone who used to pride himself on taking the time to think things through. I'm thrilled that I immigrated, but it was difficult. I landed in California. Others may think that California is laid back, but the people here do things fast! They speak more quickly than I do, jump from this to that, and have a whole set of references that meant nothing to me when I first arrived. So finding the right way to jump into an everyday conversation, let alone getting a feel for what people were talking about, was tough for me. All that, and I also needed to find a way to earn a living! I had no choice but to adapt and learn to live here. That forced me to listen in an entirely new way.

In this constantly changing world, most of us are immigrants in some way, and we can all benefit from deeper and more powerful listening. People move from state to state, relationship to relationship, job to job, project to project. Then there's the online world. Writer Mark Prensky talks about the online world in terms of digital natives and digital immigrants—people at home with the world of information technology and others who are just dipping their toes in the digital water. If ever you want to see a failure to communicate, you can see it between many of the citizens of those two worlds. One of the most basic tools available to all of these immigrants is the power of listening.

It's not that most people have suddenly stopped listening. It's just that as everything about the world speeds up, and as the tsunami of online opinions heats up, and as the urgency to make instant decisions flares up, listening tends to get trampled underfoot.

This is unfortunate because listening and thinking are soul mates. If we don't—or can't—listen, then the odds are that we are not doing enough thinking. That's a disaster-in-waiting for everything from marital peace, to making good business decisions, to getting a genuinely great education. . . .

As educators, managers, parents, and others, we have to realize that the people with whom we live and work passionately love and want to feel heard. And so do we. Being heard in and of itself enhances motivation, builds relationship, encourages cooperation, and contributes to better results.

Listening and being listened to are great gifts, and they can be freely available everywhere. We do have to work for them, however.[7]

5 Pillars of Great Listening

> Listen: to pay attention to sound <listen to music>,
> to hear something with thoughtful attention:
> give consideration <listen to a plea>
> —*Merriam-Webster Online Dictionary*

Listening, like any other skill, needs to be built on firm foundations. Some may be obvious, some are surprising. The interesting thing about the foundations of listening is that we have access to all of them because they are literally second nature to us. And yet they are often so much a part of us that they have become invisible.

For instance, as we see in the definition above, good listening often calls for thoughtful attention. But paying attention involves more than just intellect and thought. In order to listen with full attention, many elements of the body, brain, and mind need to work together. There needs to be a blend and a balance of thought, feeling, physical posture, and relationship. So it pays to be aware of, and to strengthen, the foundations upon which good listening are built. It's a little like preparing the soil before planting a garden or strengthening the immune system as the basis for good health. Let's look at five pillars that together form a solid foundation for good listening.

1. We listen with our bodies as well as with our minds

Reflect for a moment about what your body does when you listen to someone tell a story, or when you're at a fantastically interesting conference, or even caught up in a dispute at work. It's not a matter of being right or wrong, but just of noticing what you do.

- When listening to that story with interest, do you find yourself leaning forward, focusing hard, and breathing more heavily? Or do you lean back out of boredom, wish that you could close your eyes, and find yourself adopting a pattern of breathing that resembles falling asleep? (Did you know that when people are bored their brains release a chemical that is just like an anesthetic?)

- When listening to music, are you jazzed up and excited as your head keeps time, or do you sit back with eyes closed as the gentle sounds waft over you?

- When engaged in a dispute, do your fists clench, your shoulder muscles tighten, while your stomach churns? Or, as one alternative, are you firmly centered, well balanced, and alert for whatever might come next?

---

7. Geoffrey Caine, *9 Skills for Listening to Life* (Livingston, NJ: Funderstanding, 2013), Kindle location 10–32.

Musician Steven Halpern calls the body a "human instrument." We can improve listening by taking charge of our breathing, posture, and how relaxed we are. (Research shows that when we are extremely stressed, parts of the brain associated with planning and effective decision making are bypassed and we revert to automatic and very primitive responses such as fight or flight. That state doesn't make for very good listening!)

Listening is also coupled with our other senses. The behaviors, movements, reactions, and context that we notice with our eyes always color the meanings that we discern with our ears.

2. We listen to both thoughts and feelings (even if we are unaware of it)

My wife and I regularly talk, sometimes vigorously, about our finances. Now I used to be a lawyer. (I left the profession many years ago but some aspects of lawyering have become part of my DNA.) When the issue gets intense, I act like a lawyer again. I get formal. I want specifics. I formulate my words and arguments with rigorous clarity and precision. I look for that formal clarity in others. And it drives my wife nuts. She, apart from having been a professor of education, has a background in therapy, and is very sensitive to the tone that people use. When I get overly formal, she feels that relationship is being lost, and has no desire to listen to my words.

We may want to be in the same conversation, but we're not. I am focusing on the facts; she is focusing on the relationship. And until the twain meet, we don't go anywhere.

All communication operates at these two levels: the content of the message and the emotional pull and tug underneath. Almost all people respond to the emotional tug first. Marketers, politicians, and radio and TV shock-jocks all rely on this fact. So does every media outlet where new items are framed in terms of stories, with a setting and characters and drama. As Krishnamurti said,

> . . . when you are listening to somebody completely, attentively, then you are listening not only to the words, but also to the feeling of what is being conveyed, to the whole of it, not part of it.

Some people are very good at communicating at both levels. It is equally important to be good at hearing at both levels.

Perhaps the most important aspect of the social, emotional, and physical nature of listening, as mentioned in Chapter 1 (*Why Listen?*), is the sheer joy and satisfaction of feeling heard. We all love and need to feel heard. This applies to children feeling heard by their parents (and vice versa), spouses feeling heard by each other, employer and employees, students and teachers, colleagues at work, customers, clients, and more.

3. Listening is interactive

Every one of us, even the loners among us, is a social being. Our worlds, and the ways in which we make sense of things, are shaped by interacting with others. Current research in social neuroscience, for instance, shows that there are neuro-cognitive (brain-mind) systems that link what one person feels while doing something to what another feels while observing the action.

From the perspective of listening, this means that our words and actions contribute to what others perceive and how they speak and behave. Have you ever been to a gathering and found yourself talking to someone whose eyes were constantly surveying the room in a search for someone more interesting (or influential or useful) to talk to? Or found yourself talking to someone who appears to be totally unresponsive? Did you feel listened to? Did you feel like continuing the conversation? Compare that with how it feels to be the focus of someone's attention, to have that person authentically and enthusiastically respond to you, and fully share a moment in time with you.

Listening is almost always a dynamic interplay between people. Someone chooses the topic. Some people are more enthusiastic than others. Some responses seem approving and others disapproving. These differing reactions can send a conversation along very different paths. The bottom line is that what we do and say, and how we respond in a conversation, has an enormous impact on what other people say and how they say it. To a very great extent, listeners shape what they hear.

Even no response at all is a response. Imagine that someone is holding forth and has taken over a conversation. The silence of the listeners contributes to the space that the speaker fills with his or her words. And we may or may not want to be there listening. That's why author and consultant Harrison Owen coined the phrase "the law of two feet" as one of the attributes of what he calls "open space technology." People can stay. Or they can leave.

4. Listening is selective

At any point in time, there is always more going on than we can possibly absorb. Sometimes we are attuned to what a particular person is saying, and we automatically listen more fully to that which interests us. Our attention can be grabbed by people who seem to share our beliefs, but also by people who seem to be criticizing what we believe. Every one of us has a nonsense index, and we usually dismiss or ignore things that don't seem to make immediate sense to us.

These are just some of the ways in which each and every one of us filters input and selectively makes sense of the mass of words and sounds and activities that surround us. We can't help but be selective, because we all have biases, preferences, expectations, and ways of seeing and making sense of the world. So to a large extent people do not hear where others are coming from; they hear where *they themselves are coming from.*

We can, however, become more aware of our own tendencies. We can make a point of listening to things with which we do not immediately agree or that do not immediately make sense. Good listeners work to get on the same page and enter into the same stories. We cannot avoid being selective, but we do have a choice about what we actually select.

5. We are always listening to life

Hearing and listening are key components of everything that we do and everything that interests us. We listen in varying ways to the news, to our friends (and, sometimes, our enemies), to teachers, to bosses, to lovers, to passers-by. We listen to and contribute to gossip about neighbors, celebrities, and others. We hear the cheers and jeers of fans at a football match or any other sporting event. We listen to the wind and the rain and the sounds of birds, planes, and traffic of all kinds.

Indeed, sometimes it can seem as though we are afraid of silence. Nowadays the sounds of TVs, radios, and canned music fill the air in restaurants, airports, malls—almost everywhere people congregate. And every movie has a soundtrack intended to stimulate emotional responses to the movie. Life expresses itself though sound. And so hearing and listening matter everywhere.

How do we become better listeners?

The goal is to be willing and able to listen deeply, effectively, and naturally in many different circumstances. The process is developmental. It is a matter of building a scaffold of skills and practices. Ultimately, as these skills become integrated, the scaffold begins to fall away and deeper listening follows naturally.[8]

ALL YEARS: PREPARING FOR THE SEMINAR

Respond

PART ONE:

How have your inherited culture and your experience with interacting with other cultures influenced your view of God, faith, religion, worship, and your deep desires and loves?

PART TWO:

How have you experienced the five pillars of listening? When have you felt listened to? When have you been the listener?

---

8. Caine, Kindle location 106–381.

Which of the five pillars do you do well? Which remain for you to develop further?

How might the process of developing skills in listening as expressed above in Caine's image of building a scaffold of skills and practices apply in general to developing all skills?

Practice

A design in six parts for constructing your Spiritual Autobiography as shaped by living in a multicultural world.

An Image

The old Navaho woman sits silently in front of her loom weaving as generations before her have done. Outside her hogan, she works with the upright loom swiftly forming the natural yarn into a sacred rug pattern. Her rug seemingly forms by itself. She has done this for so many years that routine, not thought, guides her hands. The familiar actions quiet her mind thereby allowing images to form within her. The images carry her thoughts into a daydream: "Our lives are like this rug. We are formed by the Cosmic Woman who makes this world on her loom. Each of us becomes as she weaves us into her Earth Rug. The various colors and textures interrelate to form the world. Each different thread has a place. Each contributes to the whole. Nothing is unintended. All have purpose. Everything belongs."

The Earth Rug image reflects your work within this program. You are striving to know the traditions of God's people so that you can find your place within the intercultural worlds.

The following exercises may guide you in reflecting on your personal history. Such reflection is for your private consideration. Later, you will be asked to decide what you are willing and ready to share with members of your seminar. The story you share within the seminar might be part of what you discover as you do the exercise. However, your seminar preparation is separated from this exercise to encourage you to reflect privately first.

As you reflect on your experiences, you may encounter thoughts and feelings that you are not ready to share. Often, events in our lives need to be protected from outside judgments. Paul Tournier tells of the importance of having privacy. "A creative work is a very fragile thing while it is being produced. It needs secrecy. It can die away, lose its impetus and its conviction by being divulged prematurely. . . . A criticism, a comment, even praise, can disrupt the creative impetus."[9] Your life is a creative work. The experiences and events that form you need the same initial protection that any creative activity needs. Without allowing you to have the protection of secrecy, the new life emerging within may "lose its impetus and its conviction by being divulged prematurely." He continues, "Yes, a certain secrecy, to just the right

---

9. Paul Tournier, *Secrets: Revealing Insights Into the Instruments of Mature Emancipation* (Atlanta: John Knox Press, 1977), 20–21.

extent, ought to enclose every precious thing, every precious experience, so that it can mature and bear fruit." You may wish to maintain a diary or journal to provide a private place where you can write your reflections, memories, and discoveries.

Over the course of the four years of EfM, you will be asked to consider your personal history from several perspectives, as if you are constructing several autobiographies of your life, each from a different standpoint. This year's exercise is designed to enrich your self-awareness and assist you in knowing yourself more fully with reference to living in a multicultural world, using concepts and categories to assist in understanding the multicultural dimensions and dynamics within a person's life and among those with whom that person lives and works.

Each of us begins life in the midst of "givens." Identify the givens present in the beginning of your life and trace your journey through time: family structure, where you were born and lived, rituals of the family, religious world, political events of the time you were born and since, and so forth. Consider how you presently understand where you come from, who your people are, and who you are. The work of constructing an autobiography includes identifying the inherited self that has been shaped, described, and defined by a given culture. Identifying one's cultural identity and how that identity shapes knowing the holy, God, and meaning is a beginning point for the autobiographical work this year. Each person is embedded in a nexus—a web of interconnections and relationships with other people and social institutions. Institutions, while being products of human creativity, become entities that transcend the individuals who created them. Institutions embody cultural values and transmit those values to subsequent generations.

1. Write a brief paragraph that describes your inherited self. For example:

   I am a white Anglo-Saxon heterosexual male whose family of origin were Episcopalians for several generations. I only speak English although I have studied Spanish and German. My family of origin consists of pioneers who settled the United States from Scotland, England, and Ireland. My paternal roots came out of the hills of Tennessee, while my mother's heritage stems from Pennsylvania and Iowa.

   Another example:

   I am second generation Asian-American. I am a lesbian woman whose family came to the United States in the nineteenth century as construction workers on the railroad. My first language is Mandarin Chinese. I grew up in a Buddhist household. In my adulthood I became a Christian through encounters with the Roman Catholic Church in Los Angeles.

2. Construct a description of your personal experience of interacting with other cultures and how they have influenced your understanding of the world, society, humanity, religion, and God. Additionally,

in contemporary society there is an intracultural diversity within each person. The intrapersonal diversity creates an eclectic identity that impacts how God, humanity, nature, and the self is experienced and understood.

Primary question: How has your experience with different cultures shaped your identity and your spirituality?

3. Begin with recalling the various experiences, events, and interactions you may have had with people from cultures different from your own. Awareness of their difference may have come in hearing a different language, seeing people dressed in different clothing, tasting different food, experiencing different religious ceremonies, or listening to music markedly different from your own. You may have heard someone speaking about different groups of people using the third-person plural pronoun "they." As you recall conversations or comments, notice what feelings were associated with them. Was the "other" spoken about in fear, fascination, or affection?

   Interaction with people from different cultures often occurs whenever a person moves into a different geographic area. Or perhaps refugees from war or persecutions brought people from different ethnic backgrounds and cultures into your neighborhood. Other contact may have occurred when traveling on vacation or business.

   Record twenty or twenty-five different experiences or impressions of different cultures.

4. Select five or six memories, then write a short paragraph consisting of no more than three or four sentences. For example:

   As I child, I remember being hurriedly ushered into our house because "a band of gypsies" had come into our yard. They were scavenging anything that was not anchored. I recall peeking out of the window and seeing a woman in a long, dark dress hold a pot that I had been playing with in the dirt. The adults around me were excited and fearful.

   I recall when our school was racially integrated and for the first time, blacks and whites were in school together. The Dunbar School was closed and we all attended classes and played sports together.

   While attending school in New York City, I encountered Hasidic Jews on the subway. It was my first time seeing the way they dressed. Their suits and full beards, their locks of hair wrapped around their ears, barely visible under that black hat, distinguished them from the other passengers on the subway. Before that, my only knowledge of the existence of a Hasidic Jew was from a passing reference to Martin Buber as a member of the ethnic and religious group.

5. Consider different decades of your life in light of your awareness of different cultures. Express how your experiences have shaped who you are and contributed to your spiritual formation. You might create a narrative or story from these various experiences or treat your encounters as if they were small pieces of material from which you could create a collage or mosaic that communicates something about you and your spirituality.

6. Prepare a ten- to fifteen-minute presentation that tells of your experience of living in a multicultural world. Include in it how your sense of self, God, truth, belonging, compassion, and/or justice has been shaped by your multicultural experiences.

Week Three

An authoritative resource for broadening and deepening biblical study is the Oxford Biblical Studies Online Internet site, which has articles, maps, timelines, a variety of biblical translations, illustrations, and numerous other items. Articles on biblical interpretation are particularly supportive for participants in Years One and Two. Some articles, maps, and timelines may be helpful to those in Years Three and Four. Also, notice that the site contains the *New Oxford Annotated Bible*. All EfM participants have access as subscribers through the DuPont Library at the University of the South (Sewanee).

Reach the site with the following internet address:
  http://www.oxfordbiblicalstudies.com
  The login ID is **efm-sewanee** and the password is **ministry**.

YEAR ONE

Read

Collins, Preface; Introduction; Chapter 1, "The Near Eastern Context"; and Chapter 2, "The Nature of the Pentateuchal Narrative"; pages 1–35

Focus

Notice unfamiliar terms and names such as anthropomorphic, Torah, Pentateuch, Julius Wellhausen, Hermann Gunkel, Rolf Rendtorff, Gerhard von Rad, Erhard Blum; sources in the Hebrew scripture, e.g., documentary hypothesis, J, E, P, and D sources.

YEAR TWO

Read

Powell, Preface; Chapter 1, "The New Testament World"; and Chapter 2, "The New Testament Writings," pages 9–62

Focus

Identify and become familiar with pronunciation of: Essenes; Zealots; Mishnah; Talmud; Hellenism; apocalyptic thought; Septuagint; types of criticism; Dead Sea Scrolls

Terms to note: testament; apostolic; catholic; seven categories of New Testament writings; Justin Martyr's account of Christian worship; canon; stages in the transmission of the Gospel Tradition; Marcion; exegesis; hermeneutics

In the textbook chapter's section "Exegesis and Hermeneutics," Powell states, "All the exegetical methods and academic disciplines described above are used by people who operate with different hermeneutical assumptions and interests. The methods themselves are simply tools that are employed for very different purposes by people with different attitudes and goals."[10] When reading the New Testament or reading how someone else interprets a passage, it is best (if not essential) to know the purpose in reading the text or the commentary. As you read both the Bible and Powell's chapters, state for yourself your purpose in reading.

YEAR THREE

Read

MacCulloch, Acknowledgements; Introduction; and Chapter 1, "Greece and Rome," pages xxiii–46

Focus

Perspectives and concepts to notice: Christians of the Middle East; Latin-speaking Church; Orthodoxy; repentance and conversion; Bible as central text of Christianity; "Books are the storehouses for human ideas"; historical truth; conventions used throughout the book

Until recently, our church historians have primarily traced Christian history as the movement from Jerusalem, through the Roman Empire, and on to Europe, steadily moving westward to the New World. Such a focus of history is no longer practical.

MacCulloch's book has been chosen for Year Three study precisely because of his taking a more global approach. He presents Christian history by following three paths: the movement west of Jerusalem that became the Western-Latin expression of Christianity; the path into the Middle East and Far East; and the Eastern Orthodoxies of Byzantine empires.

Points to note: *Logos*; *Hellas*; *polis*; *ekklesia*; Plato's influence on Christianity; Hellenistic Greece; *res publica* (republic); Roman Republic; imperial monarchy

The Greek understanding of *polis* provides a way to flesh out a fuller understanding of living within a social and intellectual context (see pages 25 and 26). That understanding involves knowing the collective consciousness that greatly influences a person's identity. The *polis* greatly shapes how one behaves, thinks, and lives. MacCulloch writes extensively about the Greek and Roman worlds as the cultural contexts definitively impacting Christianity.

---

10. Mark Powell, *Introducing the New Testament* (Grand Rapids, MI: Baker Academic, 2009), 60.

YEAR FOUR

Read

Allen, Preface; Introduction, "What is Theology?," pages ix–xxiv

Focus

Identify the six motives Allen lists that draw people to Christianity. Reflect on which of the motives have been present in your being drawn to Christianity. How do those motives relate to your attraction to political groups, causes, or interests?

Allen notes that theological topics are sometimes organized under "rubrics." He includes such topics as creation, incarnation, Holy Spirit, etc. Compare Allen's "rubrics" to the theological perspective questions used in the exploration phase of the theological reflection process, such as creation (world view), sin, judgment, repentance, or redemption. Identify two or three different topics that Allen names. Use one of the Allen topics (rubrics) such as "providence" or "incarnation" to frame questions that could be used in theological reflection.

ALL YEARS: PREPARING FOR THE SEMINAR

Respond

What purposes, attitudes, and assumptions do you bring to your reading and study of the documents of Christianity, especially scripture and other valued documents?

How have your attitudes and assumptions been fashioned by the various cultures identified in your spiritual autobiography work? How have those attitudes and assumptions affected your reading of the New Testament, Christian history, and theology?

Use the notes or highlights you made during your assigned reading this week to reflect on the key contexts (concerns, interests, and issues) faced by the men and women of that time. What were some concerns for those who would live in faith?

Practice

For the next few weeks the seminar will center on reflecting on your reading and reflecting on spiritual autobiographies. When you share your autobiographical reflections, what do you need to do to communicate your thoughts? When you listen to others, what do you need to do to listen well? Which of Caine's "5 Pillars of Great Listening" directly support you in listening to others as they present their spiritual autobiographies?

Carefully defined concepts clarify complex and emotionally volatile situations. Diana Eck's work on the Pluralism Project at Harvard University uses several helpful definitions to sort out the complexities that arise from the interaction of diverse cultures. The plurality of religious traditions and cultures has come to characterize every part of the world today. Chief among the terms is pluralism. Consider these four points about pluralism to guide living faithfully in a multicultural world:

- First, pluralism is not diversity alone, but *the energetic engagement with diversity*. Diversity can and has meant the creation of religious ghettoes with little traffic between or among them. Today, religious diversity is a given, but pluralism is not a given; it is an achievement. Mere diversity without real encounter and relationship will yield increasing tensions in our societies.

- Second, pluralism is not just tolerance, but *the active seeking of understanding across lines of difference*. Tolerance is a necessary public virtue, but it does not require Christians and Muslims, Hindus, Jews, and ardent secularists to know anything about one another. Tolerance is too thin a foundation for a world of religious difference and proximity. It does nothing to remove our ignorance of one another, and leaves in place the stereotype, the half-truth, the fears that underlie old patterns of division and violence. In the world in which we live today, our ignorance of one another will be increasingly costly.

- Third, pluralism is not relativism, but *the encounter of commitments*. The new paradigm of pluralism does not require us to leave our identities and our commitments behind, for pluralism is the encounter of commitments. It means holding our deepest differences, even our religious differences, not in isolation, but in relationship to one another.

- Fourth, pluralism is *based on dialogue*. The language of pluralism is that of dialogue and encounter, give and take, criticism and self-criticism. Dialogue means both speaking and listening, and that process reveals both common understandings and real differences. Dialogue does not mean everyone at the "table" will agree with one another. Pluralism involves the commitment to being at the table—with one's commitments.[11]

Over the next several weeks, individual dimensions of pluralism will be presented to put into practice. Begin by identifying two or three feelings in response to how Eck shapes pluralism. What picture or image best envisions pluralism as she uses the term?

---

11. http://www.pluralism.org/pages/pluralism/what_is_pluralism

Week Four

YEAR ONE

Read

Genesis chapters 1–11
Collins, Chapter 3, "The Primeval History," pages 36–43

Focus

Terms to note: primeval; two creation stories; *'adam*, Atrahsis myth; Epic of Gilgamesh; Sons of God (Genesis 6); Enuma Elish

Stories delight and entertain. They come in various forms and styles. Myths, epics, legends, novellas, and fables each tell some tale that entertains as it instills values, guidance, and meaning. Often the values live implicitly within the hearers of the stories only to surface in moments of crisis that call for decisive action. Some myths come into being to explain why things are as they are; others prescribe "right" behavior; while others venture into offering explanations along with establishing meaning.

All people, to some degree or another, seek answers to fundamental questions. What is truth and can I know it? What endures? What is real? Is there purpose to my life? Where did we come from and where are we going? Stories in all their forms, one way or another, offer answers to basic concerns. Begin noticing how such questions play out in different cultures.

YEAR TWO

Read

Powell, Chapter 3, "Jesus"; Chapter 4, "The Gospels," pages 63–101

Focus

Points to note: The two doctrines of Jesus; kingdom of God; themes in Jesus' teaching; the historical Jesus

Terms to become familiar with: gospel as a literary genre; parables; miracle stories; pronouncement stories; passion and resurrection narratives; sayings of Jesus; the synoptic puzzle (*aka* problem); the Q source; Griesbach hypothesis; *Diatessaron*

Notice how Jesus is pictured in different ethnic groups.

YEAR THREE

Read

MacCulloch, Chapter 2, "Israel," pages 47–73

Focus

Terms to recognize: Maccabees; Tanakh; Apocrypha; the first and second exiles; Samaritans; the first and second temple; Septuagint; Hellenized Jews; creation out of nothingness; development of the notion of afterlife and individual soul; Hasmonean dynasty; Sadducees; Pharisees; Essenes; Zealots

Chapter 2 concludes Part I, "A Millennium of Beginnings" in which MacCulloch traces the social and intellectual "seeds" of Christianity. The two histories (Greco-Roman and Israeli) continually influence Christian life and thought.

MacCulloch notes that "even through their hardest and most wretched experiences of fighting with those they love most deeply, [Israel is] being given some glimpse of how they relate to God."[12] He connects this struggle with Jacob's formational struggle with the angel of the Lord, with God, at the River Jabok. This way of drawing meaning from experience allowed Israel to view history through the eyes of faith. History became the arena in which they could see God at work, bringing them into being as a people bound to God. Some consider this a re-writing of history only, merely a means of self-justification. There is plenty of room for that view. However, this is also a way of interpreting history, of seeing God at work in the life and experience of an individual and a group; this is salvation history—history that tells the story of God's work of redemption.

YEAR FOUR

Read

Allen, Chapter 1, "The Holy One of Israel," pages 3–18

Focus

Identify the following terms and concepts: henotheist; monotheist; transcendence; immanence; *mysterium tremendum et fascinans*; Otto; Anselm; intellectual repentance; holiness

Allen says that we know about God "because God makes God's self known or reveals God's self *in what God does.*"[13] Identify what God has done that reveals something about God.

---

12. Diarmaid MacCulloch, *Christianity: The First Three Thousand Years* (New York: Penguin Books, 2009), 50.

13. Diogenes Allen, *Theology for a Troubled Believer* (Louisville, KY: Westminster John Knox, 2010), 17.

ALL YEARS: PREPARING FOR THE SEMINAR

Respond

Use this ABCD schema to summarize learning from this week's study:[14]

A	B	C	D
What amazed you or gave you an "aha!" moment in this week's study?	What bothered you in this week's study?	What confused you?	What delighted you?

Tolerance moves along a spectrum from simply "putting up with someone" to actively showing respect to the other. What from your reading assignment informs how humanity moves along the tolerance spectrum?

Practice

PUTTING LISTENING INTO PRACTICE

Return to Geoffrey Caine's "5 Pillars of Listening." He identified them as:

1. We listen with our bodies as well as with our minds

2. We listen to both thoughts and feelings (even if we are unaware of it)

3. Listening is interactive

4. Listening is selective

5. We are always listening to life

Select one or two pillars from the list. Identify behaviors, barriers, and/or attitudes that block listening. For example, describe a behavior that impedes or even prevents the exercise of listening with both thoughts and feelings. Or consider how different kinds of stress prevent listening with one's body.

Become aware of how you or others you know impede listening. Especially attend to how the barrier to listening may be present when people of different cultures converse.

---

14. Offered by an Oklahoma mentor, Lauri Wilson, during mentor training in 2013 and refined by other mentors in an online conversation.

Week Five

YEAR ONE

Read

"The Priestly Creation Story" essay provided in Part II, pages 216–233

Focus

Identify and become familiar with pronunciation: covenant; Baals, cult; Sabbath, *ex nihilo*; Zoroastrianism; Manichaeism; dualism; Plato; Neo-Platonic; *via negativa*

The Priestly Creation Story, consisting of only ten verses in Genesis, poetically presents a full doctrine of creation. It also offers a doctrine of God. A guided study of the story draws out the meaning contained in this ancient poem. The story shows God as Wholly Other yet present to creation. God transcends all that is, thereby providing a corrective to all forms of dualism. Many theological difficulties get untangled by the implications in the story.

Identify creation stories from other cultures such as Native American or Australian Aborigine lore. What do you learn as you compare them with the Judeo-Christian creation story?

YEAR TWO

Read

The Gospel according to Matthew *(Try to set aside enough time to read this gospel in one or two sittings.)*

Focus

Note any terms or references you had to look up. Note anything that surprised you or that you don't remember hearing or noticing before.

The Gospel writers tell the story of the Good News of God in Christ. The Gospel in its entirety communicates the story. However, seldom do people hear the entire story, rather they either experience the scripture verse by verse or in short pieces heard within worship. Such reading is like watching a trailer of a film and believing you have seen the movie. Individual scenes make little or no sense without the context of the story. So too it is important to know the entire Gospel, to experience its drama unfolding. Once you have a sense of Matthew's story, you are positioned better to interpret individual scenes, teachings, and events.

How might people from very different cultures read Matthew's Gospel?

YEAR THREE

Read

MacCulloch, Chapter 3, "A Crucified Messiah," pages 77–111

Focus

Points to note: cluster of words (*evaggelion, evangelium,* Gospel); Julius Africanus; epiousios; parables; *abba*; *Kyrios*–"Jesus is Lord, the word for God"; Paul of Tarsus; *epistole*; Paul's use of the word church"; Johannine Christ; Jewish revolt and fall of Jerusalem

Change disrupts continuity. New ways of speaking and even newer ways of behaving create unrest. Yet without continuity, change evaporates into nothingness. Society's reordering of itself after chaotic change provides the stuff of history.

Change in the eastern region of the Roman Empire eventually upset the Roman Empire's social order. The history of Christianity began with seemingly insignificant events. The importance of those events became clear through the lenses of experience and hindsight.

In your reading of MacCulloch, reflect on how the clash of cultures shaped Christian beginnings.

YEAR FOUR

Read

Allen, Chapter 2, "Holiness for Today," pages 19–27

Focus

Compare Isaiah's vision of God with Moses's encounter with God. Identify Simone Weil; Jean Vanier; absolute value

State in your own words the justification of the claim that "human beings are significant, have dignity, and have absolute value."[15]

Describe how Allen's writing on holiness contributes to living faithfully in a multicultural world.

ALL YEARS: PREPARING FOR THE SEMINAR

Respond

Summarize your learning using the ABCD approach.

Diana Eck advocates developing the attitude and skill of dialogue to live creatively in a multicultural world. "Pluralism requires the nurturing

---

15. Allen, *Theology for a Troubled Believer,* 27.

of constructive dialogue to reveal both common understandings and real differences. Not everyone at the "table" will agree with one another; the process of public dialogue will inevitably reveal areas of disagreement as well . . ."[16] When, where, and how has dialogue been present in your experience?

Practice

Geographic regions within a country develop patterns of local culture, just as different parts of the world exhibit the distinctive patterns of their overall cultures. Pick one person this week and have a dialogue with him or her about the culture out of which that person came. Make some notes about the experience.

If you didn't have enough time before the seminar to accomplish the above practice, try to recall a conversation you may have had with someone that brought to light differences in your culture and theirs. Or recall what differences and similarities there were between the cultural upbringing you had and that of another person, such as a college roommate, a life-partner, or a co-worker.

---

16. Diana Eck, "From Diversity to Pluralism," http://pluralism.org/encounter/ challenges

Week Six

YEAR ONE

Read

Genesis 12–50
Collins, Chapter 4, "The Patriarchs," pages 44–55

Focus

Identify terms or references that you had to look up.

Reading the primary text is essential to understanding scripture. Your reading forms the basis for understanding what scholars and others say about the text. Dr. Robert Denton, professor of the Old Testament at General Theological Seminary, often reminded his students that they would be amazed by how much the text illuminates the commentary. Each person has unique experiences that shape how scripture is interpreted. While the work of biblical scholars is enormously valuable, only you can bring your distinctive experience to the learning process. Then, your experience with the text can be brought into dialogue with what scholars have written. It is within that dialogue that deeper learning occurs.

Identify, note, and define: Legends: etiological, ethnological, etymological, ceremonial; Hermon Gunkel; *Sitz im Lebem; bris*; Abraham Cycle; Jacob Cycle; Joseph Story

What sources do the "authors" of the stories of the patriarchs use to express the meaning of the story?

Notice what sources Collins uses in this chapter. (Possible candidates for the sources might be academic disciplines, Biblical references, cultural references, personal experience, or beliefs or conclusions he asserts.)

YEAR TWO

Read

Powell, Chapter 5, "Matthew," pages 103–123

Focus

Identify five speeches of Jesus.

Terms to note: Beatitudes; binding and loosing of the law; *oligopistoi; Eusebius; Ecclesiastical History*

YEAR THREE

Read

MacCulloch, Chapter 4, "Boundaries Defined," pages 112–154

Focus

Sprinkled throughout the chapter are references to primary sources. Many of them can be found in books such as Bettenson's, *Documents of the Christian Church.*[17] The Christian Classics Ethereal Library (www.ccel.org) provides numerous documents online, among them *The Teaching of the Twelve Apostles, Commonly Called the Didache.*[18] Find two or three of them to read, dipping in as you like.

Become familiar with pronunciation: *Hermas* (The Shepherd); *Didache*

Terms to learn: Letter to Philemon; *Didache*; gnosis, Gnosticism, Nag Hammadi; Docetism; key points of difference between gnostic and Jewish attitudes; Marcion; Diatessaron; *presbyteroi*; *diakonos*; *episkopoi*; the importance of Antioch and Jerusalem in the early church; Clement; Ignatius; Victor; Stephen of Rome

YEAR FOUR

Read

Allen, Chapter 3, "The Maker of Heaven and Earth"; Chapter 4, "Limits of Science," pages 28–43

Focus

Note the following terms: Von Rad; Israel's cosmology; Augustine's examination of time; contemporary cosmology; relationship of creation and salvation

State the difference between the biblical view of creation and the scientific view of the universe.

Draw a distinction between the origin of the universe and the purpose of creation.

ALL YEARS: PREPARING FOR THE SEMINAR

Respond

"From the historical perspective, the terms 'exclusion,' 'assimilation,' and 'pluralism' suggest three different ways in which Americans have approached this widening cultural and religious diversity."[19] Exclusion isolates the different groups, thereby reducing if not eliminating the difficulties of difference,

---

17. Henry Bettenson's *Documents of the Christian Church* (Oxford University Press) is available new and used in four editions. The newest contains more recent documents, but all editions include numerous documents from the early Christian periods.

18. http://www.ccel.org/ccel/richardson/fathers.viii.i.iii.html

19. Eck, http://pluralism.org/encounter/challenges

for segregation creates neighborhoods of separation. Assimilation seeks to eliminate separating differences by bringing all into a common "melting pot" where distinctions melt away into one another. The option of pluralism means honoring each other's differences through the demanding practice of dialogue. "Pluralism involves the commitment to being at the table–with one's beliefs."[20]

Dialogue requires knowing what one's core values and commitments are. As you have reviewed your life through the exercise of constructing your autobiography, what core values and commitments were uncovered?

Practice

Continue to utilize the ABCD means of summarizing your study for the week.

If you have enough time in your preparation, find some information about another culture with which you are unfamiliar and about which you are curious. Try to talk with someone who comes from that culture, if at all possible.

Find out what religious gathering places of other cultures are near you. Plan a time to visit one, if possible.

Amaze
Bother
Confund
Delighted

---

20. Eck, http://pluralism.org/encounter/challenges

Week Seven   *Oct 11*

YEAR ONE

Read

Exodus 1–15

Collins, Chapter 5, "The Exodus from Egypt," pages 55–63

Focus

Describe the meaning of the term "salvation history." Define any names, terms, or references that were unfamiliar to you in Exodus.

Name the images/metaphors for God that the writer of Exodus uses to tell the story of God's liberation of the children of Israel. Select two or three of the images for God and explore what qualities of God the image reveals.

Terms that address the historicity of the Exodus event: Manetho; Hyksos; Hecataeus; Rameses II; Habiru; *Yam Sup*; Passover

Terms that deal with the meaning of the past: "charter myth"; history; legend; folklore; founding myth

Words and phrases related to God: YHWH; Adonai (Lord); *HaShem*; *'ehyeh 'aser* (I AM WHO I AM); *'ehyeh; eimi ho on* (I am the one who is); absolute Being; YHWH is on the side of the weak

Themes to keep in mind: revelation of God; liberation of people

Review the first twelve chapters of Exodus looking for moments of God's self-disclosure and moments of liberation.

YEAR TWO

Read

The Gospel according to Mark

Powell, Chapter 6, "Mark," pages 125–145

Focus

Identify terms or references in Mark's Gospel that you had to look up.
    In Powell's text, note: John Mark; intercalation; major themes in Mark; messianic secret; *inclusio*
    Every discussion, written or spoken, draws on material (images, story, ideas) from different sources, which may include other writings, personal experiences, or beliefs held. Make note of the different sources that Powell uses throughout his chapter on Mark.

YEAR THREE

Read

MacCulloch, Chapter 5, "The Prince: Ally or Enemy?," pages 155–188

Focus

Terms and names to note and become familiar with pronunciation: *parousia*; *Apostolic Tradition*; Celus; *in catacumbas;* Origen; Plotinus; Mani; Manichee/Manichaean; Diocletian; Syriac Church; Osrhoene; Dura Europos; Armenia; Ephren; *Odes of Solomon*; Trdat (Tiridates)

Christianity not only survived but grew under the wave of persecutions from 100 to 300 CE. People willing to suffer and die for what they believe can provide powerful inspiration to others. When religious conviction is stronger than the fear of pain and death, people notice. It's as if the persecutor's sword sharpens one's beliefs into passionate convictions. Clarity comes whenever a person discovers relationships that matter more than death. The witness born from martyrdom has transformative power for both believers and non-believers.

YEAR FOUR

Read

Allen, Chapter 5, "What is Meant by 'God'," pages 44–53

Focus

Idea and images to note: universe as everything but God; hiddenness of God; cosmological argument for existence of God; faith as above reason

Having read the chapter, answer the question, "What is meant by God?"

ALL YEARS: PREPARING FOR THE SEMINAR

Respond

Diaspora, syncretism, xenophobia, and separatism emerge as refugees, conquerors, and immigrants enter new lands. How have any of these social interactions played in your readings? What experience have you had with such interactions?

Summarize your learning from the unit's study—what have you learned to do or do better during these weeks? What have you learned about listening? What stands out for you as a key learning in these first weeks of EfM?

Practice

Return to Week Three to review Caine's ideas about listening. Pick one of the areas he names to practice deeply this week. How does that activity represent Christian ministry?

pp 13-19

UNIT TWO

Theological Reflection as a Life Skill

Week Eight *Oct 18*

In this essay former Archbishop Rowan Williams reflects theologically on his experience in New York City on September 11, 2001. He was staying only a few blocks from the World Trade Center, preparing for a conference hosted by Trinity Church, Wall Street.

Read the essay from two standpoints. First, read it as a presentation intended to guide others in making sense of the horrific event. Second, read it as something that Williams writes to support his coming to terms personally with the experience in light of his theological convictions as a twenty-first-century person and a well-educated theologian.

ALL YEARS

Read

Last Words[21]

Last words. We have had the chance to read the messages sent by passengers on the planes to their spouses and families in the desperate last minutes; and we have seen the spiritual advice apparently given to the terrorists by one of their number, the thoughts that should be in their minds as they approach the death they have chosen (for themselves and for others). Something of the chill of September 11 lies in the contrast. The religious words are, in the cold light of day, the words that murderers are saying to themselves to make a martyr's drama out of a crime. The nonreligious words are testimony to what religious language is supposed to be about—the triumph of pointless, gratuitous love, the affirming of faithfulness even when there is nothing to be done or salvaged.

It should give us pause, especially if we think we are religious. You don't have to be Richard Dawkins to notice that there is a problem.

On the morning of September 11, I was getting ready to spend a day talking religious language with a group of clergy and spiritual directors. I am still thinking about what it meant to be interrupted like that; and to be presented with the record of a solemn and rich exhortation cast in evocative spiritual terms designed to make it easier for some people to kill others.

It isn't (say it now and get it over with) a problem about Muslims, about some kind of religiousness that is 'naturally' prone to violence. It's true that Islam seems to think differently about its language for God from the way

---

21. Rowan Williams, *Writing in the Dust: After September 11* (Grand Rapids, MI: Wm. B. Eerdmans, 2002), 3–12.

Christians and Jews do: Muslims will regard what we say as too ambiguous, too larded with irony or paradox, self-indulgent in comparison with the sober directness of the Qur'an. But Christians at least have used their irony and paradox often enough to slip out from under the demands of justice or compassion. They have found plenty of ways to be absent from what they say, to play with commitment. The Jewish-Christian Bible is not a very straightforward set of texts, after all. No wonder postmodernism blossoms on post-Christian soil.

We'd better acknowledge the sheer danger of religiousness. Yes, it *can* be a tool to reinforce diseased perceptions of reality. Muslim or not, it can be a way of teaching ourselves not to see the particular human agony in front of us; or worse, of teaching ourselves not to see ourselves, our violence, our actual guilt as opposed to our abstract 'religious' sinfulness. Our religious talking, seeing, knowing, needs a kind of cleansing.

Someone who is about to die in terrible anguish makes room in their mind for someone else; for the grief and terror of someone they love. They do what they can to take some atom of that pain away from the other by the inarticulate message on the mobile. That moment of 'making room' is what I as a religious person have to notice. It isn't 'pious', it isn't language about God; it's simply language that brings into the world something other than self-defensiveness. It's a breathing space in the asthmatic climate of self-concern and competition; a breathing space that religious language doesn't often manage to create by or for itself.

God always has to be rediscovered. Which means God always has to be heard or seen where there aren't yet words for him. Saying something for the sake of another in the presence of death must be one place of rediscovery. Mustn't it?

Careful. You can do this too quickly. It can sound as though you're gratefully borrowing someone else's terrible experience to make another pious point. And after all, not everyone dies with words of love. There will have been cursing and hysteria and frantic, deluded efforts to be safe at all costs when people knew what was going on in those planes. And would anyone want their private words of love butchered to make a sermon?

It proves nothing. But all I can say is that for someone who does believe, or tries to, the 'breathing space' is something that allows the words of religious faith for a moment not to be as formal or flat or self-serving as they usually are.

The morning after, very early, I was stopped in the street in New York by a youngish man who turned out to be an airline pilot and a Catholic. He wanted to know what the hell God was doing when the planes hit the towers. What do you say? The usual fumbling about how God doesn't intervene, which sounds like a lame apology for some kind of 'policy' on God's part, a policy exposed as heartless in the face of such suffering? Something about how God is there in the sacrificial work of the rescuers, in the risks they take? I tried saying bits of this, but there was no clearer answer than there ever is.

Any really outrageous human action tests to the limit our careful theological principles about God's refusal to interfere with created freedom. That God has made a world into which he doesn't casually step in to solve problems is fairly central to a lot of Christian faith. He has made the world so that evil choices can't just be frustrated or aborted (where would he stop, for goodness sake? he'd have to be intervening every instant of human history) but have to be confronted, suffered, taken forward, healed in the complex process of human history, always in collaboration with what we do and say and pray.

I do believe that; but I don't think you can *say* it with much conviction outside the context of people actually doing the action and the prayer. In the street that morning, all I had was words. I wasn't surprised that they didn't help. He was a lifelong Christian believer, but for the first time it came home to him that he might be committed to a God who could seem useless in a crisis.

Perhaps it's when we try to make God useful in crises, though, that we take the first steps towards the great lie of religion: the god who fits our agenda. There is a breathing space: then just breathe for a moment. Perhaps the words of faith will rise again slowly in that space (perhaps not). But don't try to tie it up quickly.

Breathing. A bit paradoxical to talk about that. When we finally escaped from our building, it was quite hard to breathe normally in the street: dense fumes, thick, thick dust, a sort of sandstorm or snowstorm of dust and debris, large flakes of soft grey burned stuff falling steadily. In the empty street, cars with windows blown in, a few dazed people, everything covered in this grey snow. It can't have been silent, there must have been (I know there were) shouts, sirens; a few minutes later, there was the indescribable long roar of the second tower collapsing. But I remember it as quiet; the very few words spoken to each other, the ghostliness of it all; surreal associations for Frost's lovely poem, 'Stopping by Woods on a Snowy Evening' ('The only other sound's the sweep / Of easy wind and downy flake'). Or a 'heart of the storm' feeling.

In that time, there is no possibility of thinking, of explanations, resolutions. I can't remember much sense of panic, much feeling about the agony going on a couple of hundred yards away, let alone much desire for justice or vengeance. It was an empty space. I don't want to forget that, as feeling returns in various ways. We don't know fully what goes on when, in the middle of terror or pain, this emptiness and anaesthesia set in (it happens in plenty of contexts). But somehow the emptiness 'resources' us. Not to run too fast to explore the feelings and recover the words seems important.

Simone Weil said that the danger of imagination was that it filled up the void when what we need is to learn how to live in the presence of the void. The more closely we bind God to our own purposes, use God to help ourselves avoid our own destructiveness, the more we fill up the void. It becomes very important to know how to use the language of belief; which is why the terrible simplicity of those last messages matters so intensely.

And why also we have to tread so carefully in not making some sort of religious capital out of them. Ultimately, the importance of these 'secular' words has to stand as a challenge to anything comfortably religious we might be tempted to say. This is what human beings *can* find to say in the face of death, religion or no religion. This is what truly makes breathing space for others.

Words like 'transcendent' hang around uneasily in the background of my mind. Careful again. But that moment of pointless loving communication is the best glimpse many of us will have of what the rather solemn and pompous word means. I have to *begin* with this. I know I shall be feeling my way towards making some verbal shape out of it all in terms of my Christian faith, but there is nowhere else to start except with that frightening contrast: the murderously spiritual and compassionately secular.

Focus

Rowan Williams's short essay on his experience of being in New York City on September 11, 2001 describes his theological reflection on his experience. Review the article and identify the various "voices" present in it. For example, he recalls knowing that people in the planes sent messages to their loved ones. Another voice would be his reference to Dawkins as a well-known atheist. Listen especially to the voices of culture and the Christian tradition.

Notice the voices from personal behavior and personal beliefs.

ALL YEARS: PREPARING FOR THE SEMINAR

Respond

The mix of cultures evidences a complex array of values, perspectives, practices, and social patterns that challenge, confuse, excite, and at times even frighten Christians formed within the western, English-speaking world. The challenge of living as a Christian within and among an ever-increasing diversity of cultures and faiths calls for the development of a strong identity that is fortified by an awareness and knowledge of the richness of the Christian heritage. A person can thrive within this environment by developing skill in the discipline of theological reflection.

The practice of theological reflection comprises an array of skills. Essentially, theological reflection is a way of thinking that joins personal experience and cultural realities in conversation with the knowledge and values of the Christian tradition. People "do theology" whenever they reflect on questions that lead to searching for ultimate meaning and significance. Theology, as practiced in EfM, is about increasing knowledge of God so that people grow more fully in knowing God.

The theme for our work this year, *Living Faithfully in a Multicultural World*, invites us to reflect theologically on the common good of contemporary humanity in relationship to the vision of God revealed and interpreted within the Christian tradition.

Theological reflection is a discipline that contributes to the formation of Christian ministry, with particular emphasis this year on how your own call to ministry is lived out in a multicultural context. Each person has an individual, unique identity. However, each person also has a corporate identity—a self that is "we." Our work in ministry formation this year will attend especially to the communal dimension of human identity—the self that is "we." The various approaches and disciplines, especially the discipline of theological reflection, emphasize the common humanity shared by all.

The communal heritage of a person influences the person's view of reality; the guiding values underlying how the person approaches life (that is, the canon of thought employed); and how truth is experienced, known, and expressed. Humankind is increasingly in need of a renewed sense of common humanity and an enlarged ecological perspective.

Theological reflection throughout this volume will engage the social identities a person experiences and how those identities have been fashioned and continue to be shaped by the interaction of the ethnic richness present in a multicultural environment. Inherited values impact daily decisions, often operating in an unconscious, tacit way. As people grow in their awareness of their inherited selves and listen deeply to other corporate identities, basic assumptions get uncovered. "Doesn't everybody do things this way?" is met with a resounding "No!" How authority and power are understood and trusted impact daily decisions. The confidence a person has is not only a product of individual experience, but is also the result of inherited, communal assumptions that color expectations. Distrust or trust of a particular ethnic group has been woven into the cultural inheritance that formed the person. For example, a person who grew up as a member of the majority race in a prosperous country generally views governmental authorities, such as police, as trusted servants of society. Another person who grew up as a member of a marginal ethnic group that for generations was oppressed by governmental authorities will be hard-pressed to trust any governmental authority, especially the police. Additionally, interaction among different cultures with differing assumptions can generate misunderstandings and miscommunication. Theological reflection provides a way to bring out cultural biases and clarify how miscommunication and conflict emerge in the interaction of cultural differences.

Theological reflection within a growing awareness of multicultural and global realities becomes an effective instrument to help realize the vision of God encountered in scripture and liturgy. The Episcopal Book of Common Prayer uses phrases that call for contributing to the common good as a way to reveal God's Realm. For example, the Prayers of the People, Form IV, in the Book of Common Prayer, prays, "Guide the people of this land, and of all the nations, in the ways of justice and peace; that we may honor one another and serve the common good."[22] Sprinkled throughout the prayer book one can find references to the call to act for the benefit of the entire human community.

As a person reflects theologically on experience and is encouraged to fold communal and ethnic understandings into the reflection, the importance of ethical implications easily arises. Identity moves from individualistic preoccupations into communal concerns—issues that involve all people. Global economic and political interactions encouraged, if not forced, by globalization, and environmental impacts on air and water demand attention.

What relationship do these global issues have to inclusive theological terms such as "heaven" or "the people of God"?

The EfM Four-source Model of Theological Reflection

Terms

Movement: primary steps of theological reflection—*identify* something that matters, *explore* the topic, *connect* to other areas of life and meaning (Sources, Voices), and *apply* learning to ministry.

Source/Category/Voice: interior and exterior areas of life from which a person draws when making sense out of something that has happened: *personal experience/action, faith tradition, culture/society (contemporary and/or traditional)*, and *personal beliefs/positions*. For instance, a person's belief forms in relationship to something that happened, something that was read, something that was learned. Each of those areas speaks with some kind of voice, contributing to how a person makes sense out of what has occurred. A belief about the sanctity of life can be explored to discover what formed that belief in a search for deeper awareness of God and of meaning.

Theological Perspective: questions asked in applying a theological lens to the reflection commonly use traditional terms developed in systematic theology (*creation, sin, judgment, repentance, redemption*); reframing or rephrasing them can bring out subtle differences in understanding. For example, in this volume you will be asked to consider the perspective questions in terms of *wholeness, brokenness, recognition, reorientation*, and *restoration*.

Every person uses images, ideas (concepts), feelings (intuitions), values, and behavior (action) as the substantive content for reflecting. Whenever one's thought process engages the heritage of the faith tradition in which one was raised, the reflection becomes theological in tone. While thoughts cannot be separated into discrete isolated units for consciousness, clarifying distinctions can be useful. The EfM program draws on or listens to four primary categories or sources/voices in theological reflection: **Faith Tradition; Culture/Society; Personal Experience/Action;** and **Personal Belief/ Position**. Each of these categories emerged from conversations in small

---

22. *The Book of Common Prayer* (New York: Church Hymnal Corporation, 1979), 388.

groups over the past several decades. The following statements summarize the categories.

"She has the Midas touch."–a voice of Culture via Greek mythology

"Don't we have Good Samaritan laws?"–a voice of Christian Tradition in scripture

"This is a strange place. I have a feeling we are not in Kansas anymore, Toto."–a voice of Culture via the movies to interpret experience

"I believe that all people are good to begin with."–a voice of Position or Personal Belief

"That's how I felt when I fell out of a tree and broke my arm."–a voice of Personal Experience

Each of these statements makes an assertion that states a belief, opinion, or a position. Yet, while the person making the statement expresses a belief, the way to communicate a fuller meaning is to use images or words that pull from other sources. Each statement "borrows" from some other story or experience to flesh out meaning centered on something that mattered.

Faith Tradition, Culture/Society, Personal Experience/Action, and Personal Belief/Position provide a common language for individuals and groups to use as they engage in theological reflection. The vocabulary might feel a bit like jargon; however, the words provide some definition that can guide and clarify the theological discussion, whether it is within a group conversation or an individual's internal conversation.

Faith Tradition: Whenever the language, concepts, terms, or images in a conversation come from the Bible or some other document or story that is part of the Christian lore, then one is drawing from the Christian Tradition source. Words like "creation" or "sin"; images like "Good Shepherd" or "walking on water" come from the Christian scriptural tradition. Concepts such as providence, eschatology, or incarnation make use of the terms used by theologians. In EfM's theological reflection model, the umbrella term "Tradition" more accurately refers to the Christian heritage and is the source that marks the reflective conversation as theological. However, someone *formed* in (not simply having a passing interest in) another faith tradition would hear the voices from *their* sacred writings or stories, their wisdom figures, or their leaders, and the contributions from such connections would enrich the reflection.

Culture/Society: This source of the four-source model refers to a very large body of material. Literature, music, paintings, and other artifacts are part of the Culture source. References from a movie or from a novel would be examples of something from the contemporary Culture source. The Culture source also includes traditional social or ethnic norms that might be referenced by "My grandmother used to say . . . ." The Culture source contains both written and oral content, and may have been handed down from one generation to another.

Notice that the Tradition and Culture sources have a common characteristic. They have an objective quality independent from an individual; that is, they are sources "from outside" a person. The material from these two sources resides in the "other." It may be contained in printed material or recorded in a way that can be referenced in much the same way as a footnote in a research paper. The oral content of the Culture source has a less impartial quality. What one's grandmother transmitted (Culture) often gets incorporated in the psyche of the person. Nevertheless, the content of the aphorism distinctly comes from outside the grandchild. Cultural and ethnic messages transmitted within a society are placed within the Culture source of the EfM model. These too have a quality of being embedded from the outside into the individual.

The other two sources in the theological reflection model have a more subjective nature. They can be modified with the pronoun "my" and refer to personal experience; drawing a distinction between them becomes somewhat awkward.

Personal Experience/Action: Behavior and activity define this source; what actually happened that can be communicated using neutral words. For example, a person draws from the Action source when she describes what happened such as, "One Halloween our family attended a city-wide celebration. I went as a pink bunny rabbit with a carrot in hand. I got separated from my siblings and followed the crowd as it left the stadium. My family found me walking along the side of the road. I was crying and felt alone. When they got me into the car, I was told that my rabbit ears had been tied together by someone." This is something that happened within a person's experience and which fostered some learning and viewpoints and attitudes that would continue long after the incident. The experience was formational to some extent and became a source/voice in that person's life.

Personal Belief/Position: Behavior centers on what is seen and heard. Any experience also contains the feelings and thoughts that shape the meaning attributed to the experience. Opinions, beliefs, viewpoints, and convictions held by a person constitute the position pole of the four-source model. A person's position arises out of the mix of behavior, images, feelings, and viewpoints. A person's history and the meaning attributed to the past contribute to the formation of beliefs. Positions rest, however tentatively, on the meaning attributed to behavior, learning, or life events.

The content of theological reflection comes from combining distinctive voices. Human consciousness employs reason, emotion, imagination, and praxis (the practical side of something, rather than its theory) to create meaning and value in life. Theological reflection, individually or with others, is a search for a glimpse of truth and meaning.

Reflection: What and How?

Reflection happens as the mind moves through the four steps of identifying a focus, exploring the focus, connecting to the sources/voices, and applying that focus to ministry. It begins as a topic is identified. Several skills help to arrive at a clear focus for conversation: recognizing that there is something that draws attention such as an experience, a painting, a piece of scripture, and so forth; focusing on the object of attention; discerning where the important consideration needs to center, that is, where the "heart-beat" is of the incident, movie, passage in scripture, painting, and so forth.

Once the topic for reflection is selected, it is possible to begin exploring its dimensions. As the various dynamics are considered, the mind naturally makes connections with other sources, as if each source has a voice that joins in the reflection. As the variety of voices converse, new awareness and insights emerge. Perhaps an individual or group experiences the sensation of being grasped by truth. New understanding leads to considering how insights might be applied. Identifying, exploring, connecting, and applying constitute the movements, phases, or steps of reflection.[23]

Practice

Theological reflection is a discipline that is learned best through practice. The goal of theological reflection is to help us more clearly hear God in the midst of our life; in the midst of moments or encounters that can draw us more deeply into awareness of God. Throughout the *Guide*, there are many opportunities to reflect. The four movements of identifying a focus, exploring the focus, connecting to other voices around and in us, and applying the learning are the elements that will be common to all of the reflection outlines. Reflecting so that doors are opened to those who have grown up in and been formed by differing cultures leads men and women into ministry with others. Multicultural experience begins to become intercultural experience, something more than just having a variety of cultures around us but rather, opportunity to awaken to the wonder of God's extravagant diversity in creation and to learn. This unit begins with the practice of reflecting theologically on a personal experience.

THEOLOGICAL REFLECTION BEGINNING WITH A PERSONAL EXPERIENCE

Identify a focus. Describe a short conversation that you recently had about something that mattered to you. Write it out or make some notes on what was said. Recall the tone, the points made, and the parts of the conversation that have stayed with you. What was it about? What does it mean to you

---

23. EfM's model of theological reflection follows these four movements as it considers the perspectives of the four sources in conversation with one another. In Part II you will find examples of the reflections used in the Reading and Reflection Guide series on pages 259–284. The only real difference between the examples is where each begins (i.e., from which source).

now? Starting from a conversation like this places you in the Action/Experience aspect of your life.

Name the central theme of the conversation (what it was about) and then try to come up with an image that captures that theme. If you could draw a picture of the theme, what would it be? Or, explore by naming the central issue in the conversation. Either image or issue will work as a focus for reflection.

Explore the issue or image focus by asking a question or two, such as:

How does that image or issue express facets that are creative and those that are destructive?

How would God be present in such a matter?

What values are present?

How would grace be represented?

Connect to other areas of your life. Listen for voices that speak from society or **Culture**, that is, from the world around you; from the Christian **Tradition**; and from your **Personal Beliefs**. Connect freely, without trying to do these in any order.

How and where do any of the questions stimulate response from you?

How do people or groups in your **Culture** deal with the image or issue?

How does the Christian **Tradition** (scripture, hymns, prayers, and so forth) speak to that matter?

What do you **Believe** or wrestle with about the theme upon which you are reflecting?

What other times have you had to deal with this matter (**Personal Experience**)?

What are you becoming aware of as you explore and connect to the issue or image? What do you see in a new way?

Apply

What difference, however great or small, does this reflection have for your daily life? What implications for ministry are there?

Further Practice for Reflecting Theologically

Playing with Images

Use any kind of image. The following are suggestions only.

- A shaker of salt
- A bowl of water
- A lit candle ~ *af meditation*
- An unlit candle

Pick any one or more of the above images and respond as follows:

- Draw the item depicted or find that item and set it before you.
- What are the characteristics and qualities of that item?
- Where do you find that image in the scriptures or hymns or prayers of your faith tradition?
- Where do you find that image represented in the world around you? What cultural issues, if any, are there relative to that image?
- When have you had an experience that was related to that item or image in some way?
- What do you believe about the matters that the image may be surfacing for you?

Match the questions above to the four movements of theological reflection: identifying a focus for reflection, exploring the focus, connecting the focus to other voices, and applying learning.

Match the four "voices" or sources to the last four questions in the exercise: Personal Experience; Position or Belief; Culture; Christian (or other faith) Tradition.

Feelings Have Roots

Use the following sets of thoughts and feelings to create images that capture those dynamics.

Feelings: angry, sad, tired	Thoughts: I can't do this anymore
Feelings: joyful, expectant	Thoughts: Is this real? I want to hold on forever.

Create one or more pictures that represent the sets of thoughts and feelings.

What does the image bring to mind for you?

Identify the source of your recalled connection—a personal experience, a piece of scripture, a piece of music, and so forth.

Where do you turn to make sense of such a connection? Think along these lines: If you recalled a personal experience based on the thoughts and feelings and image, what helps you interpret that experience? If you recalled a piece of scripture, what helps you draw meaning from that?

As your reflection deepens, what do you begin to understand, proclaim, question?

Write a brief prayer that relates to insights and implications that may surface from this reflection.

What ministry does your reflection suggest? Or how will your reflection contribute to ministry in your life and with a variety of cultures you may encounter?

Week Nine *QN 25*

YEAR ONE

Read

Exodus 16–40
Collins, Chapter 6, "Revelation at Sinai," pages 64–73

Focus

Identify: Mosaic/Sinai covenant; Hittite treaties; Assyrian treaties; vassal treaty; theophany; Baal; Asherah; Festival of Unleavened Bread; Sukkoth; Book of the Covenant
    Terms related to law: apodictic law; casuistic law; Yahwist Decalogue; ritual Decalogue; unwritten (oral) law

YEAR TWO

Read

The Gospel according to Luke

Focus

Define unfamiliar terms or references.

Make notes about what particularly interests you in Luke's Gospel.

What images for Jesus does Luke use?

Describe how Luke's images shade and color the Gospel he proclaims.

YEAR THREE

Read

MacCulloch, Chapter 6, "The Imperial Church," pages 189–228

Focus

Important names, places, and terms to note: Constantine; *Hagia Sophia;* Helena, Athanasius, Basil, Arius, Miaphysites, Nestorius; dates: 312, 325, 481; *homoousion, homoios, hypostasis, ousia, Theotokos;* monasticism; *The Acts of Thomas;* Councils; Chalcedonian Definition
    History presents a narrative that the author creates from primary or other secondary sources. What sources can you identify that MacCulloch used in this chapter?

YEAR FOUR

Read

Allen, Chapter 6, "Nature as Witness and Innocent Suffering," pages 57–67

Focus

Concepts, terms, and names to note: three elements of witness; nature's witness; "inner witness"; Testament; Job; *Vindicator;* William Temple

Allen presents theology, as do all theologians, by using content from other people as well as from his own thinking and experience. Identify sources he used as he presented his position in this chapter.

ALL YEARS: PREPARING FOR THE SEMINAR

Respond

The issues raised in each of the year's readings are real, ongoing, and perhaps difficult. Identify some of the issues faced by those considered in your reading this week. What has your experience taught you about one or more of those issues?

Practice

Use this week's assigned reading to reflect theologically.

Identify the focus of what you read.

Explore

Reflect on the views of the world, sin, judgment, repentance, and/or redemption that may have been expressed by people at the time of your reading; for example, in Year Four, someone could consider any or all of the following: views of human suffering in the reading (Creation); how suffering might draw someone away from faith in God (sin); how human suffering poses a crisis for either the one suffering or one exposed to another's suffering (judgment); what the crisis would be (judgment); how someone would recognize they can choose to change their response to the suffering (judgment); what choices there might be (judgment); what a new direction would look like or be (repentance); how someone would live creatively with the reality of suffering (redemption).

Connect

How does your identified reading focus get addressed in the **Culture** in which you live; i.e., are there political implications related to the focus you identified; is there a movie you have seen that dealt with the matter of your reading focus; are there social agencies that deal with the matter you focused on? How is God acting in today's world to respond to that focus?

How have the people of God in scripture or in the time of your reading assignment responded to that focus area? (**Tradition**)

Recall **Personal Experiences** related to the chapter's focus; in other words, when have you had something occur in your life that relates to the reading focus you identified?

Record your own **Beliefs/Positions** about the matter and make note of how those beliefs were formed. How is your belief affected by your theological reflection on the matter?

Apply

Given your reflection on the focus of your reading, what do you want to do or feel called to do? For example, does the reflection increase your interest in helping in a community project or agency? Are there areas you want to study more about? Is there someone in your life that you want to reach out to?

What implications are there for living faithfully in a multicultural world?

Find some way to discover how those in another culture relate and/or respond to the focus you used for your reflection.

If possible, make a commitment to one small action you could take in the near future as a result of your reflection and think about what you need to do or what would support you in order for you to take that action.

Week Ten

nov 1

YEAR ONE

Read

Leviticus
Numbers
Collins, Chapter 7, "The Priestly Theology: Exodus 25–40, Leviticus, and Numbers," pages 74–83

Focus

Terms and concepts to note: the Tabernacle; sacrificial system; Day of Atonement; stories of Nadab and Abihu and of Korah; impurity laws; Holiness Code; relationship of ethics and holiness; Cultic Calendar; Book of Numbers

YEAR TWO

Read

Powell, Chapter 7, "Luke," pages 147–167

Focus

Make a note of the following names, terms, and ideas: Theophilus; "the beloved physician"; Luke's Gospel in relationship to the "Acts of the Apostles"; the major themes in the Gospel of Luke; passages from Luke widely used in Christian liturgies

What interests or concerns you in Powell's presentation of Luke's Gospel?

Which of the major themes Powell identifies do you find interesting or even compelling?

What makes the Gospel of Luke sacred literature?

YEAR THREE

Read

MacCulloch, Chapter 7, "Defying Chalcedon (kal-**SEE**-don): Asia and Africa," pages 231–254

Focus

Learn the meaning of the following: *The Life of Balaam and Joasaph*; Tome of Leo; *Henotikon*; Jacob Baradeus; Syriac Orthodox Church; Armenian

Church; *Trisagion*; Dyophsite Christians; failure of the Marib Dam; School of the Persians in Edessa; "Mar Thoma" Church; Thomas Christians[24]

Identify the central opposition for one individual or group that defied Chalcedon.

YEAR FOUR

Read

Allen, Chapter 7, "Innocent Suffering and Life Beyond Death," pages 68–73

Focus

Concepts that provoke thoughtful reflection: transformation of suffering; sufferings as punishment for sin; prosperity as mark of righteousness; wrongdoing results in suffering; injustices of innocent suffering prompt affirmation of life beyond death; omnipotence (as can do anything); almighty (as having authority over all things); problem of natural evil

Which of the concepts listed above interested or challenged you the most?

ALL YEARS: PREPARING FOR THE SEMINAR

Respond

Consider how dynamics of multicultural interaction were present at the time of this week's study.

What tensions, if any, arose for those you read about? How were those dealt with?

Practice

THEOLOGICAL REFLECTION BEGINNING WITH SCRIPTURE

Identify

The following passages involve the people of Samaria, a group that fostered strong feelings among the Jews. Carefully read the passages and identify two or three topics common to both.

---

24. An eBook English translation of *The Life of Balaam and Joasaph* can be found at http://omacl.org/Barlaam/

When the days drew near for him to be taken up, he set his face to go to Jerusalem. And he sent messengers ahead of him. On their way they entered a village of the Samaritans to make ready for him; but they did not receive him, because his face was set toward Jerusalem. When his disciples James and John saw it, they said, "Lord, do you want us to command fire to come down from heaven and consume them?" But he turned and rebuked them. Then they went on to another village.

Luke 9:51–56

But wanting to justify himself, he asked Jesus, "And who is my neighbor?" Jesus replied, "A man was going down from Jerusalem to Jericho, and fell into the hands of robbers, who stripped him, beat him, and went away, leaving him half dead. Now by chance a priest was going down that road; and when he saw him, he passed by on the other side. So likewise a Levite, when he came to the place and saw him, passed by on the other side. But a Samaritan while traveling came near him; and when he saw him, he was moved with pity. He went to him and bandaged his wounds, having poured oil and wine on them. Then he put him on his own animal, brought him to an inn, and took care of him. The next day he took out two denarii, gave them to the innkeeper, and said, 'Take care of him; and when I come back, I will repay you whatever more you spend.' Which of these three, do you think, was a neighbor to the man who fell into the hands of the robbers?" He said, "The one who showed him mercy." Jesus said to him, "Go and do likewise."

Luke 10:29–37

Note: Though the above scripture passages are quoted from the NRSV translation, reading the passages in a variety of translations may increase the sense of meaning.

Focus the passages by considering where the key energy/heart of the passage is, what the passages seem to be about.

Develop an image in words or a drawing that brings the point of the passages into focus.

Explore the image or central idea of the passages, using questions from the theological themes of Creation, Sin, Judgment, Repentance, or Redemption, such as:

What kind of community the image-world/theme suggests (Creation).

Or, What might get in the way of relationships in that image-world/theme (Sin).

Or, What could make those in that world realize there's something wrong, or what choices there are (Judgment).

Or, What would represent a change of direction (Repentance).

Or, What a new, life-giving creation might look like (Redemption).

Connect

Connecting happens best if some freedom is allowed. Listen to each of the "voices" or "sources" below and let your responses emerge in any order. You may not make a connection in one area; that is okay. That may occur at a later time, or not at all. Mainly, allow your inner life to speak, connecting you to these areas of potential meaning and revelation.

Personal Experience–When has something happened in your life that is like the world of the image/metaphor? For instance, if the image created for the passages is "extending a party invitation," when have you given or sent such an invitation?

   Compare your experience with the preceding theological exploration. How do your experience and the image relate to one another?

Culture/Society–Who or what has taught you something that is helpful when life is like the image? In our world, how is there opposition to that image? How is there support for it? Where is God extending party invitations in the world in which you live?

Christian Tradition–What other scripture passages or church history events remind you of the image or central point of the passages from Luke?

Beliefs/Positions–What key issues do the metaphor and personal experience and contemporary culture raise? State your Beliefs and Positions relative to those issues.

Apply meaning and purpose to the reflection by identifying learning and clarifying questions.

How do the beliefs and insights of the exploration support you in ministry?

Notice where you might want to make some changes in action or viewpoint about the matter covered in the reflection.

Write a prayer in response to the discoveries in this reflection.

Week Eleven *Nov 15*

YEAR ONE

Read

Deuteronomy
Collins, Chapter 8, "Deuteronomy," pages 84–93

Focus

As you read Deuteronomy, define the Mosaic covenant and notice how the covenant underwent renewal and reinterpretation.

YEAR TWO

Read

The Gospel of John

Focus

Make note of anything you had to look up and any surprising ideas or images that you found in reading John's Gospel. Especially note how John's Gospel presents the message of Jesus. Compare John's proclamation (*kerygma*) with the other Gospels' proclamations.

YEAR THREE

Read

MacCulloch, Chapter 8, "Islam: the Great Realignment," pages 255–285

Focus

Note the following terms and concepts:

Rise of Islam: *Qur'an*; three possible "borrowings" of Islam from Christianity, *al-ilah* (Allah), identify how Christian *divisions* contributed to Muslim conquests, Mosques of Umar (Dome of the Rock), Islam's impact on Christians in East: John of Damascus, Timothy I. Church in China: Ta Qin monastery, Bishop Alopen's writing. Christianity among Mongols: Khan of the Keratis' vision of St. Sergius, Kublai Khan and Dyophysite Christianity, Christians of Baghdad.

Islam and African Churches: North African Church, Coptic patriarchs, Ethiopian Christianity, *The Miracles of Mary*, Prester John myth.

YEAR FOUR

Read

Allen, Chapter 8, "Suffering from Nature and Extreme Human Cruelty," pages 74–84

Focus

Key concepts to consider: David Hume's view of the natural world in relation to humanity's well-being; the Stoic Epictetus' view of humankind in relation to nature; Julia de Beausobre and her experience with suffering at the hand of human cruelty; God's love in the midst of suffering; two possible responses to the Holocaust

ALL YEARS: PREPARING FOR THE SEMINAR

Respond

What challenges and opportunities of multi-cultural interaction occurred during the time period you read about and thought about this week?

Identify the cultural diversity you encounter today and compare that to what things were like as you grew up. What have been or are the challenges and opportunities of cultural diversity you have experienced, or currently experience?

Name one culture different from your own that you would like to learn more about.

Practice

Identify the focus or primary point of your EfM reading (Christian **Tradition**) this week.

Explore the focus by identifying the views of the world, sin, judgment, repentance, and/or redemption reflected in the focus.

Connect

Continue to connect as described in the note in Week Ten.

Identify a specific example of where that reading focus shows up in other areas of Christian **Tradition**; i.e., name a particular scripture passage or story, a hymn, a prayer, or so forth, that relates to the identified focus.

Identify how the focus you selected is present in today's world (**Culture**).

Compare and contrast the connections to the world around you and the connections of Christian tradition. What issues or concerns do you become aware of?

What **Personal Experiences** have you had that relate to this reflection area?

Identify your personal **Beliefs** that come up in thinking about this focus and its relationship to the world and life you know. How did those beliefs form? When has it been difficult for you to act on those beliefs?

Apply

If you could do just one thing about the concerns that surfaced in this reflection, what would that be?

What do you want to say to God about the matters that have come up in your reflection?

Week Twelve  *Nov 22*

YEAR ONE

Read

Joshua
Judges

Focus

As you read the Book of Joshua, note the concerns of the people. Especially think about the nature of God that the narrative presented and how that understanding of God shaped their understanding of their world and themselves.

YEAR TWO

Read

Powell, Chapter 8, "John," pages 169–189

Focus

Terms, ideas, and images: Book of Signs; Book of Glory; Logos; beloved disciple; abundant life; Paraclete; Sacred Heart piety; Raising of Lazarus; Washing the Feet; *Christ of Saint John of the Cross*
   Major themes in John's Gospel: true revelation of God; Jesus as God; Glorification of Jesus in his death; world and Jews; loving one another

YEAR THREE

Read

MacCulloch, Chapter 9, "The Making of Latin Christianity," pages 289–318

Focus

Make note of the following terms and ideas:
   The Rome of the Popes: *Papa*, catholic, Latin Rite, St. Lawrence, Bascilica of St. Peter, Damascus, Jerome, Vulgate. A Religion Fit for Gentlemen: Faltonia Betitia Proba, Prudentius, Ambrose. Augustine, Shaper of the Western Church: *Confessions*, Monica, Manichaeism, "*tolle lege*," Donatists, *City of God*, Pelagius, 410 CE, Augustine's analogy of Trinity, double processions of the Holy Spirit. Early Monasticism in the West: Martin, Sulpicius Severus, *capellae*, Cassian, Benedict, Rule of St. Benedict.

YEAR FOUR

Read

Allen, Chapter 9, "The Sacrifice in Creation," pages 87–95
William Porcher Dubose's essay "The Trinity," found in Part II of the *Guide*, pages 234–241

By the time that Dubose had written his essay on the Trinity, he was near retirement from a long, productive, and challenging career as a professor and dean of the School of Theology of the University of the South. Before he arrived at the university he served as a soldier and then as chaplain in the Confederate Army. Wounded several times and confined as a prisoner of war, Dubose knew the dark side of humanity. Upon his release as a POW, he even had the experience of reading his own obituary, having been reported as killed in action.

His brilliance, apparent throughout his writing, resulted in an international reputation as one of, if not the, most original and creative among American theologians. Dogma and experience, which DuBose understood as part of the meaning of incarnation, were in constant dialogue in all his writings.

Focus

Concepts to note: Power of God; creator's self-renunciation; connection between God's creative self-sacrificing and human moral action; *de facto* person and moral person; doctrine of Trinity in relation to doctrine of creation

Identifications to make with reference to the sacrifice in creation: Dorothy Sayers; Iris Murdoch; W. H. Auden; Dante; Bonaventure

Terms and phrases to note from the essay: *logos; telos;* grace of the Son; *gratia gratiata; gratia gratians;* love is grace *potential;* grace is love *actu;* three constituents of the gospel; *ex pare Dei; salvation salvans; ex parte hominis*

ALL YEARS: PREPARING FOR THE SEMINAR

Respond

One of the ideas offered by the writer of the Gospel according to John is "abundant life." What does that term mean to you personally? What might the term mean in a larger societal context?

Practice

THEOLOGICAL REFLECTION BEGINNING WITH A SOCIAL CONCERN

Philosophical anthropology studies the nature of humankind. Questions of identity, both individual and communal, comprise the field of study. Theological anthropology addresses human nature in relation to God. Both philosophical and theological anthropology address related questions: What is the end (*telos*) of human beings? What does human flourishing involve? What is "the common good"—the actions, values and policies that allow people to flourish? In theological terminology, what is God's vision for all people? Such questions involve thinking about the meaning of terms such as the Kingdom of God, heaven, and the *eschaton* (end-time).

The following theological reflection outline provides a way to consider philosophical and theological anthropological matters.

Identify a focus.

Develop a list of social concerns that are presently being deliberated in your Culture/society. The items on the list might come from politics, news media, documentaries, current cinema, or advertisements.

For example:

- Environmental concerns

- Universal health care

- National security

- Distribution of wealth

- Economic well-being

Select one topic from the list you create and reflect theologically on that voice from the Culture source. You will have a chance to make additional connections to the voice of Culture when you add the Connect movement to your reflection.

Explore some dimensions of your selected social concern. For example:

- Notice what is revealed about human nature in the identified concern, both individually and corporately. What human values seem to be operating around the social concern? Describe what the identified social concern seems to assert about "the common good"; that is, if the concern you are working with is "economic well-being," how does that concern relate to the common good?

- What characteristics of God are present or absent in that concern? Possibly, a social concern around national security could reflect God's characteristic of protector. What about God's self-emptying?

- Identify the deep hopes that are present or implied in the nature of the social concern.

Connect

Describe various ways the identified social concern gets manifested at the present time. For example, if universal health care is the identified concern under reflection, then identify the ways in which that concern has come to the foreground in the culture/society where you live, such as:

- U.S. news report on congressional action

- Canadian experience of universal health care

- English experience of universal health care

Where do you hear God's voice in your social structure, or your culture?

Learn something new. Find a way to hear the voice of Cultures/societies other than your own, such as how other countries handle the same or similar concern. How do varying cultural groups handle such a matter, perhaps even within the same country? Please resist the temptation to "talk off the cuff" about another place or people; rather, try to talk to someone from that culture or look up information that you could consider authoritative and reliable.

Personal Experience: Name concrete ways in which the issue has intersected your life. For example:

- Retirement brought change in how medical insurance was obtained

- Got ill and had to receive medical attention over an extended period of time

- Health of a friend's parent deteriorated and he/she required extended health care

- Visit to emergency room of hospital and noticing who was there and why

- Change in a person's life that required addressing the need for medical insurance

When have you had personal experience related to that concern or issue? What emotions have you experienced as that concern has intersected your life: fear, frustration, sorrow mixed with gratitude? Name your thoughts and feelings in relation to the focus you have selected.

Personal Belief/Position: What seems to be at stake in the reflection as you have explored and connected to the identified concern? What statements of conviction are you willing to make? What is alive for you in this matter?

- State what you value and hold important that is touched by the identified social concern.

- State your best vision or hope for the world. For creation.

Tradition: Listen to the voice of Christian tradition, especially the way Christian tradition speaks to the questions of God, common good (reign of God), or human nature.

What specific stories from the Christian tradition speak to the concern?
Note what scripture stories, perhaps ones you remember from your childhood, give shape to the concern.

As you access the various voices in Personal Experience, Christian Tradition, Culture(s), Personal Beliefs, what rings true for you or seems new to you? Express, as best you can, any intuitive sense of what "should" be, "ought" to be, could be, or "must" be done relative to the social concern. In other words, what matters to you about this?

Describe actions that you could take that might contribute to the reign of God, the common good, in the matter of the social concern on which you reflected.

Apply

Apply the insight and new awareness from the reflection within the context of the social concern you named above.

How do the dimensions of the social concern point to the common good?

In what way does participation in the social concern/issue contribute to a vision of God's reign?

How does human flourishing revealed through the reflective theological conversation point toward action and behavior and practices?

In other words, what are you going to do (ministry) with what you have considered?

What would support you? Where/how will you reach out for that support?

Week Thirteen

YEAR ONE

Read

Collins, Chapter 9, "Joshua," and Chapter 10, "Judges," pages 94–115

Focus

Judges in the Hebrew Bible are more aptly described as warlords than magistrates. Collins writes that the selection criterion for a judge was might. As you step back into the time of Judges, why would these stories be recorded and valued? State how you think the people would have understood God to be present.

YEAR TWO

Read

The Acts of the Apostles
Powell, Chapter 9, "Acts," pages 191–213

Focus

Note: the differences in goals between Paul and Peter; the role of the Church in Jerusalem; Stephen; the relationship between Paul and the Roman Empire
    Make note of what surprises you in reading Acts; what you had to look up; and the events, images, or ideas that interest you.

YEAR THREE

Read

MacCulloch, Chapter 10, "Latin Christendom: New Frontiers," pages 319–362

Focus

MacCulloch organizes five hundred years of Latin Christianity history around several areas:

• Changing Allegiances: Rome, Byzantium, and Others

• Mission in Northern Europe (500–600)

• Obedient Anglo-Saxons and Other Converts (600–800)

• Charlemagne, Carolingians, and a New Roman Empire (800–1000)

Identify the key persons and events related to each section, especially noticing how MacCulloch's presentation sheds light on the "human capacity for relationship."

YEAR FOUR

Read

Allen, Chapter 10, "The Incarnation as Sacrifice," pages 96–106

Focus

Key concepts to identify: God's self-limitation; incarnation as sacrifice; "dwelling place of God"; Kierkegaard's allegory in *Philosophical Fragments*; concept from geometry to point to Jesus' divinity and humanity; miracles ("signs of wonder"; "deeds of power"; "mighty works") and natural science

ALL YEARS: PREPARING FOR THE SEMINAR

Respond

What multicultural issues arose in the lives of people you read about in the material you studied this week? What resources were available for interaction among the people in the variety of cultures?

Practice

In some way, visit another **Culture** this week.

- Perhaps there are places of worship in your community, town, and city representing faith traditions with which you are unfamiliar. Go there if possible. Talk to people there.

- Are there movies you could watch about another culture?

- Are there family members you could talk to?

- What about books or friends?

THEOLOGICAL REFLECTION BEGINNING WITH THE CULTURE SOURCE

Identify

Once you have explored another culture in some way, identify a focus, then create an image or metaphor of your limited understanding of that culture, if possible.

Explore the focus from some theological perspectives, such as:

- What beliefs about creation are reflected in the image?

- What is considered sin in the world of your image?

- How does one find forgiveness in that image world?

- What constitutes ultimate fulfillment as that culture understands it?

- What do you regard as the meaning of life for that culture?

- What is the meaning of death?

Connect by listening to other voices. (Reminder: You can do the following in any order.)

Christian Tradition—What passages in scripture or church history come to mind as you explore the image above? Read the passages or material you recall.

Compare and contrast the world you found in the scripture or church history passage with the world you explored with the theological questions.

Personal Experience—What has occurred in your life that provides answers to some of those theological questions?

Compare and contrast your personal experience with the experiences of those in the culture you explored briefly. What differences and similarities are there? What begins to matter to you as you make the comparisons?

Contemporary Culture/Society—How does your culture/society view that of the one you explored? What are the challenges and possibilities?

Personal Beliefs—What beliefs of yours are challenged by those of the other culture? How could that challenge create road blocks? How could it create opportunity? What would you have to give up in order to change your beliefs? What might someone from the culture you explored have to give up?

Apply the reflection by noting your insights and how those insights might make a difference in ministry in your life.

FIRST INTERLUDE UNIT

Developing a Multicultural Community

Week Fourteen

ALL YEARS

Read

Law, *The Bush Was Blazing but Not Consumed*, Preface and Chapters 1–8, pages ix–73

Focus

Note how Law uses these terms: multicultural community; community; dialogue; culture; interracial dialogue; intercultural dialogue; divine judgment; unholy fire; win/lose dichotomy; ethnocentrism; ethnorelativism; sympathy, empathy, and interpathy; cultural pluralism; contextual evaluation; power analysis; creative marginality

Note how Law draws his central images from the Bible: holy fire/the burning bush; the tower of Babel; the golden calf; "Choose life!"

ALL YEARS: PREPARING FOR THE SEMINAR

Respond

In *The Bush Was Blazing but Not Consumed*, Law refers to a number of tools for working in multicultural groups introduced in his previous book, *The Wolf Shall Dwell with the Lamb*. One of these is power analysis, which he names as an essential skill for leadership.

Power, defined in society's terms as the ability to manipulate the environment and others, is often contextual. A person may have power in some contexts but not in others. It is also perceived. A person may believe herself to be powerless when others in the group see her as powerful. A culturally competent leader must be able to use power analysis to understand the group's context.

In his work, Law often divides a group into smaller affinity groups, groups that have some aspect in common, to facilitate conversation. In a multicultural setting in the United States a group might be divided into two, one containing those who identify as white (representing the dominant culture in the United States) and one containing persons of color. If these two groups are asked which group has more power, both almost always will agree that those in the white group are more powerful. If the larger group is divided instead by gender, the smaller groups will say that men have more power. But if the larger group is divided by economic status, both smaller groups will include white men. Although they were perceived in the first two instances as being the most powerful, in this case the white men with lesser income will be perceived as having less power. Other possibilities for dividing groups to illustrate differences in power and perceived power include educational level and physical ability. What other societal categories that denote power or powerlessness can you think of? In what aspects of your life are you among the powerful? In what aspects are you among the powerless? How does your own sense of power or powerlessness govern your behavior?

Practice

Identify a time when you felt powerful or a time when you felt powerless.

Explore that time. What was the situation? What role were you playing? Who was with you? How did you know you had power (or were powerless)? Consider the situation using all or some of the following:

- What indicated wholeness or goodness in that situation?

- What indicated brokenness or undermined wholeness?

- What brought you to recognition that the situation could/should be different?

- What would/did offer an opportunity for reorientation?

- What would restore the brokenness to wholeness?

Connect to other sources. Consider the Christian tradition. Name a powerful or powerless (according to the example you chose above) person Jesus encounters in his ministry. What is the situation? What role does that person play in society? Who is with him/her? What are the signs that this person is either powerful or powerless? What does Jesus say to that person, or what does he do to that person? What constitutes wholeness, brokenness, recognition, reorientation, and/or restoration in this story?

What does your culture/society say to those who are powerful/powerless? What does it say about them?

What are your own beliefs about having power (or no power) and who does or should have it? What position(s) do you hold about how the powerful interact with the powerless? How does your position compare to the tradition source above? To what you have said about the culture source?

Apply to your ministry. What have you learned or what implications do you find in this reflection for how you are called to respond to others when you have power (or no power)?

What might prevent you from responding in this way?

How might you find opportunities to practice responding as one who is powerful or powerless?

Dec 13

Week Fifteen

ALL YEARS

Read

Law, *The Bush Was Blazing but Not Consumed*, Chapters 9–13, pages 61–126

Focus

How does Law use his holy fire image to describe the three steps in intercultural dialogue?

Review the communication ground rules and respectful communication guidelines

Notice how Law uses these terms and concepts: high-context culture; low-context culture; high-context and low-context communication styles; person-centered leadership; form-centered leadership; dialogue as liturgy; dialogue as ritual; liturgy as multicultural dialogue

ALL YEARS: PREPARING FOR THE SEMINAR

Respond

Law's Cycle of Gospel Living

The difference in attitude toward the powerful and the powerless was very clear throughout the ministry of Jesus. Jesus never told the poor and powerless to sell all they own and give to the poor. That would obviously be an absurd thing to say. Jesus healed them, loved them, ate with them, touched them, comforted them, blessed them, served them, encouraged them, taught them, and liberated them by his own suffering, death, and resurrection. Finally, Jesus breathed on them to infuse them with the power of the Holy Spirit—the power to teach, heal, and forgive in the name of God. On the other hand, Jesus never told the rich and powerful that they are blessed. Instead, Jesus warned them and challenged them to serve and to humble themselves. He reminded them of what the law and the prophets had said.

The Gospel invites the powerful to take up their cross and follow Jesus. Salvation for the powerful comes from the decision to give up power and take up the cross. The Gospel, however, never asks the powerless to choose the cross because the powerless, by the condition of their powerlessness, are already on the cross. There is no need for them to choose it, just as there is no need for the poor to give up what they have and give to the poor because they are already poor. Because the powerless are already on the cross, salvation comes from endurance and faithfulness in the hope of God's deliverance through the resurrection.

Choosing the cross and the resurrection of Jesus are part of the same Gospel story. But we interact with the different parts of the story differently depending on our place of power in a particular situation. As a Chinese American working in the Episcopal Church, I often find myself in situations where I am set up to be powerless. For example I am sometimes invited to be the token Asian in a meeting. When I am in this kind of situation, I actually spend some time before I enter the meeting to get in touch with the empty tomb, the resurrection side of the Gospel. I tell myself that I am blessed and a child of God no matter what happens. I ask God to breathe the Holy Spirit through me to give me strength to endure and power to speak and challenge the system I am about to enter.

On the other hand, as a trainer and consultant I also find myself in situations where I am given power and authority to influence others. In my preparation for each training session, I spend time reflecting on what it means to choose the cross. I tell myself that I am a servant to the participants. I tell myself that even though I may be treated as an expert, I must be humble. I tell myself that my job is to work myself out of my job by giving my knowledge, skills, and power away freely, so that at the end of the session the participants will know what I know and my services are no longer needed.

It is crucial to determine in a given situation which side of the cross we are on if we are to experience the wholeness of the Gospel. No one can stay on one side of the cross all the time. That would be neglecting the wholeness of the Gospel. Living the Gospel involves moving through the cycle of death and resurrection, the cross and the empty tomb, again and again. The moment I am resurrected into a new life of empowerment, I must begin to think about serving and giving away my power and take up the cross again, or I stand the chance of abusing my power. The moment I take up the cross and become powerless, I must begin to think about faithfulness and endurance and look toward empowerment through the empty tomb. It is in this dynamic of death and resurrection, cross and empty tomb, Lent and Easter, that the Gospel comes to life in each one of us.[25]

25. Eric H. F. Law, *The Wolf Shall Dwell with the Lamb: A Spirituality for Leadership in a Multicultural Community* (St. Louis: Chalice Press, 1993), 41–43.

Law uses this diagram to illustrate his Cycle of Gospel Living.

Cycle of Gospel Living

Mutual Invitation is a tool Law uses to facilitate communication in multicultural groups. Your EfM group may already be using this process from time to time. If you are not familiar with Mutual Invitation, directions for its use are on page 287 in Part II of this Guide.

Consider how Mutual Invitation follows the Gospel cycle in group dynamics. When is a person empowered in a conversation using Mutual Invitation? When does that person take up the cross? Where is wholeness in this process?

Practice

Think about where you might find opportunities for introducing Mutual Invitation to a group you belong to.

How would you explain the process to a parish or church-connected group? How would you use Law's Gospel cycle schema with this group?

How would you explain Mutual Invitation at work or to a non-religious community group? Would you incorporate the Gospel cycle in your explanation? If so, how would you describe it?

Do you find you would address these groups differently? What implications do you see for how you minister in different contexts?

UNIT THREE

Developing a Sustaining Spirituality

The Purpose of Unit Three is to deepen personal spiritual practices through disciplines of study, prayer, and worship in order to live more faithfully in a multicultural world.

GOALS:

- Examine and explore the significance of living within a postmodernity context

- Experience EfM study as a spiritual discipline

- Develop a discipline of prayer as listening and responding to God within multicultural experiences

- Reflect on how worship through liturgical practices forms humanity's heart and loves

- Attend to how poetry and music contribute to a sustaining spirituality, especially within the context of diverse cultures

- Respond to an invitation to practice a rule of life tailored for living in a multicultural world

Introduction

He often sits alone in the coffee shop for his morning coffee. The surroundings are familiar and comfortable. This particular morning across from him are two women with young children, one an infant, enjoying one another's company, chatting over the noise of their small children. Clearly they were not of his "world," for their dress, language, and parenting were foreign to him. Their conversation was energetic and one that they seemingly enjoyed. Yet, he could not understand a single word. He felt he was in a different country, yet it was the city in which he grew up. He felt the way he did when he worked in a foreign country and experienced what his mentors described as culture shock. The major difference now was that he was home and in his own culture. His thoughts and feelings were in turmoil.

What happens to people whose familiar environment changes and they no longer feel at home?

Now imagine listening in on the women's conversation. Perhaps they were enjoying one another because they had found in their outing a kind of momentary break from their loneliness of living in a strange land in which dress, language, and customs were alien to them. The hour or two they were able to spend outside their homes served as a kind of oasis, bringing some relief from the culture shock they felt as strangers in a foreign land.

Whether a person lives in a minority group within a dominant culture, or as a member of the cultural majority in a changing society, each experiences inner disturbances that transition brings. How someone responds or adjusts to cultural upheaval is directly related to an unconscious knowing, what contemporary French philosophical anthropologists have called *habitus*.

People navigate through their world drawing on commonly accepted practices and attitudes. Many daily activities are conducted by a kind of knowing that is a "complex of inclinations and dispositions that make us lean into the world with a habituated momentum in certain directions."[26] People navigate through their world drawing on "habituated inclinations that spawn meaningful action." The view of human nature expressed by this philosophical anthropology leads to an increased awareness and appreciation of how often actions are not based on articulated propositions and beliefs, but on cultural practices that arise out of a non-rational ethos. Often as assumed communal practices are challenged through the interaction of significantly different cultures, people act and react out of bias and prejudice. The actions seldom result from a deliberated decision. They are the consequence of a cultural *habitus* thrown into disequilibrium. Such disturbances are best addressed through the resources of spirituality, particularly prayer and liturgies.

James K. A. Smith builds a case for the importance and power of liturgy, which begins with a fresh articulation of human nature.

> We are what we love, and our love is shaped, primed, and aimed by liturgical practices that take hold of our gut and aim our heart to certain ends. So we are not primarily *homo rationale* or *homo faber* or *homo economicus*; we are not even generically *homo religiosis*. We are more concretely *homo liturgicus*; humans are those animals that are religious animals not because we are primarily believing animals but because we are liturgical animals—embodied, practicing creatures whose love/desire is aimed at something ultimate.[27]

Because spirituality intertwines with ethics, economics, and politics, Christians seeking to live faithfully in a multicultural world need a sustaining and maturing spiritual discipline. It must be capable of responding to the refugees and immigrants created by regional wars, economic deprivation, natural disasters, and climate change.

---

26. James K. A. Smith, *Imagining the Kingdom (Cultural Liturgies): How Worship Works*, Kindle edition (Grand Rapids, MI: Baker Publishing Group, 2013), Kindle location 1814–1821.

27. James K. A. Smith, *Desiring the Kingdom (Cultural Liturgies): Worship, Worldview, and Cultural Formation* (Grand Rapids, MI: Baker Publishing Group, 2009), 40.

Week Sixteen

ALL YEARS

Read

Each person faces the challenges of adjusting to the rapid cultural changes present in society. Episcopal Bishop Steven Charleston sketches the social and intellectual climate that sets the stage upon which contemporary western Christianity lives as players in God's drama.

The Rt. Rev. Steven Charleston is a citizen of the Choctaw Nation of Oklahoma. He comes from a family with a long history of service in the Native American community. His great-grandfather and grandfather were both ordained pastors who preached in their native language in rural communities throughout the state. Following in their footsteps, Steven was ordained at Wakpala, South Dakota, on the Standing Rock Sioux Reservation.

Steven was the national director for Native American ministries in the Episcopal Church, a tenured professor of systematic theology at Luther Seminary, the bishop of Alaska, and the president and dean of the Episcopal Divinity School in Cambridge, Massachusetts. Currently he teaches at the Saint Paul School of Theology at Oklahoma City University.[28]

A Graph of Spirituality: Understanding Where We Are Going By Knowing Where We Have Been[29]

AMHERST—Contemplating an agenda for the future, University of Massachusetts at Amherst Chancellor David K. Scott envisions bringing religion back into higher education. He is not talking about a department here or there devoted to the teaching of a particular faith. He wants to infuse spirituality into every part of academic life.

—Boston Globe, October 3, 1999

The article in the *Boston Globe* was a surprise. While I had become accustomed to hearing about the influence of "spirituality" in the church, even in business and science, this was the first time I had encountered it so clearly identified in higher education. The *Globe* article described how Dr. Scott, a physicist, believes that we are entering an age of integration, a time when people will need to use spirituality to process the flood of data they receive

---

28. http://redmoonpublications.com/meet-steve-charleston.html

29. Norvene Vest, ed., *Still Listening: New Horizons in Spiritual Direction* (New York: Church Publishing, 2000), 183–198.

on a daily basis. Therefore, spirituality will return to the curriculum of major universities, not as a single subject to be taught on its own, but rather as a new way of thinking which underlies and integrates all knowledge.

What struck me about Dr. Scott's bold hope for the future of academic life in America was its location. Our culture has operated under the assumption that segregation must exist between the state university and the denominational church. We have prided ourselves on keeping this boundary clear. Far from the medieval image of the academy as only an extension of the church, we have compartmentalized learning to the point where religion has been relegated to the periphery. We have done so for what we believe are good reasons.

As with the separation of "church and state," we have believed that mixing intellectual formation and spiritual formation is a volatile combination within a democratic society. Fearing the intolerance and demands for religious conformity of the past, a history from which we believed we had escaped, we have maintained careful distance between spiritual viewpoints and the free classroom. In the process, of course, many critics assume that we have so sanitized the university from faith that we have created a value-less learning environment. That the chancellor of a major university would publicly question this assumption makes front-page news. It calls into question one of the fundamental principles of American higher education and raises the issue of denominational influence in education. It challenges us to consider again what we mean by "spirituality" and the role it plays in our postmodern culture.

I cannot predict the outcome of Dr. Scott's vision, but I can take it as a starting point to analyze how pervasive the subject of spirituality has become. If a renewal of interest in spirituality has brought scientists like Dr. Scott to call for a reevaluation of spiritual practice in the formative centers of American learning, then it seems to me that the tide of spirituality has reached a new level in our national consciousness. The concern is no longer for the religious few, but for the spiritual many. In other words, spirituality as a subtext at the start of the twenty-first century has filtered out into so many areas of our awareness that it has begun to erode the bedrock of our traditional assumptions as a culture—the foundation of the European Enlightenment. The assumptions of the Enlightenment, with science at the center and politics enclosed in a "faith-free zone," have gradually been undercut by forces that have brought spirituality back to a place of primacy.

I propose to sketch those forces as they have emerged in recent history and as they will carry us into a new history. I offer a rough graph to delineate how spirituality has come to occupy such an important place in our consciousness. Admittedly, the graph will be drawn only in broad strokes. I do not pretend to be a sociologist of spirituality: the statements in the Boston Globe caught my attention as an academic and a practicing Christian. Consequently, I am a stakeholder in the outcome of the history I observe. I am not a neutral party, but a person with both practical experience in the field of the spiritual and with a vested interest in its future. What I share is a practitioner's model. It is not exhaustive or extensive, but a working model for spiritual directors.[30]

There are three simple lines on my rough chart. They begin in the late 1960s and move to the turn of the century. They aim beyond the year 2000, suggesting directions we will follow as spirituality continues to shape the agenda of history. But before I draw them out, I need to say something about background. I need to look at the graph paper itself, the much deeper history of North American religious life from which the three lines emerge.

The Enlightenment as Paradigm (The Graph Paper)

If any area of scholarship could be described as having burgeoned in the last thirty years, it would be cultural studies. Beginning with such seminal figures as Stuart Hall in Great Britain and radiating into a global network of new researchers, cultural studies has radically changed our intellectual worldview. While this boomtown mentality of excitement makes defining cultural studies precarious, there are some definitive threads. Cultural studies as a discipline questions the colonial assumptions that have dominated world history; the gender bias that has been a hidden subtext within that history; and, ultimately, the paradigm of the Enlightenment as the matrix of human thought. Ironically, the spread of spirituality into the academic community has been paralleled by the spread of cultural studies into theological education. The secular and the religious are twin streams of education, both eroding the cultural premise on which they have been built.

If we are to understand the future of spirituality, we must understand its past in terms of the Enlightenment, the era in intellectual European history that has cast such a long shadow. The Enlightenment as global mindset was transported to North America with the colonists. Just as it had altered both social and religious development in the mother countries of Europe, so it altered the new cultures planted in the Americas. Its assumptions about science and government organization were especially important in North America. American spirituality was a European design modified to fit a more democratic body politic.

Looking at American history as a piece of imaginary paper, its texture and color have clearly been imprinted by the Eurocentric vision of the Enlightenment. The institutions we created, the schools we founded, the principles of our governance, the methods behind our technologies, even the social fabric of our attitudes toward race, gender, and class—all derive from our understanding of European philosophy as expressed in the Enlightenment. Our paper is white, etched with the graphic lines of scientific and social theory that we thought normative for all times and places.

---

30. The article's primary audience is the spiritual director; however, what Bishop Charleston writes here applies equally well to the spiritual practices of the practicing Christian.

This is precisely why people like Dr. Scott catch us off guard. They surprise us with fundamental questions about our background. They question the paper itself even before new lines can be drawn. While to some it may still seem almost sacrilegious to wonder about principles we have been taught to cherish—for example, that science knows best—the rolling back of the Enlightenment, a fixed model for reality, has been the countercurrent to colonialism in creating what we now call the postmodern world.

In describing this complex history through the metaphor of the paper itself, I suggest that if we are serious about spirituality, we need to be aware that its points of origin are deeply influenced by the acceptance of the Enlightenment as the foundation for our cultures. The Enlightenment is the historical reality on which I will trace a few lines of spirituality. Those lines will only make sense if we remember that they are not drawn in thin air, but that there is a philosophical context to what we describe as "spirituality." Spirituality is never culture-neutral, nor does it exist outside the history from which it arises. Any study of contemporary American spirituality is grounded in the colonial experience of the Enlightenment. That's where we begin.

The Proliferation of Spirituality (The First Line)

The first line on our graph represents what I call the proliferation of spirituality. The line in some ways begins at the very edge, because the American experience is of a proliferation of spiritualities. It is axiomatic to say that American colonial history was the playing out of European religious history on the shores of North America. Competing denominations found a safe, if temporary, haven in what with casual arrogance they described as a "New World." Religious pluralism has been integral to American spirituality for generations.

However, if we fast-forward to the mid-1960s, we encounter a very noticeable "blip" in the chart. Something spikes in the 1960s. In a climate of drugs and free love, the definition of spirituality gets hazy. What the veterans of World War II had taken for granted in the late 1940s and throughout the prosperous 1950s—a solid Christian spirituality firmly rooted in the comfortable pieties of the institutional church—suddenly starts to unravel when entrusted to their children.

For the postwar generation, spirituality was no longer institutionally based, no longer confined to the church or synagogue. These institutions that had always been assumed to be the home of spirituality (neatly compartmentalized by the Enlightenment into the appropriate places for the exercise of religion) were directly challenged as being sterile museums of an outdated religion. Looking for spirituality, a large segment of the population walked out of church and into the streets.

They discovered a supermarket of spiritual possibilities. In the late 1960s and early 1970s, spirituality became like a medieval fair. People could stroll through the carnival, browse esoteric wares, and stop for any guru who cast a spell of hope and wisdom. Some of these encounters, of course, were harmless and diverting; others were disastrous, even terminal.

One element causing the "blip" in this line was connected with the rediscovery of "Eastern" thought. The dialogue among Christianity and Judaism—the "Western" religions—and Buddhism and Hinduism, their "Eastern" neighbors, began a mixed conversation in which spiritual images and practices wove together like strands of religious DNA, producing abundant hybrids and mutations. Native American traditions became popular. The traditional teachings of authentic indigenous leaders were widely circulated and absorbed into the fertile spiritual soil. More dubious claimants to the title of "medicine man" or "shaman" also appeared, adding to the exotic nature of spirituality that was constantly shifting, but endlessly appealing. Finally, a vast area we have often encompassed with the term "New Age" created too many variations to list.

At this time the old models of Enlightenment religion ruptured, and new spiritualities proliferated. This rupture created a new assumption: that religion was no longer institutional. The twin definitions of what constituted religion and spirituality blurred. Religion was often seen as monolithic, reactionary, and enclosed. Spirituality in the popular consciousness became fluid, progressive, and inclusive. Even as the hinge year of 1968 dampened the fervor for change, the belief in a pluralism of religious expression remained. The "hippie" influence of the period might have been shed in the aftermath of assassinations and riots, but spiritual proliferation continued into the following decades and, as I will suggest, beyond.

One other point should be made. What I have sketched as spiritual proliferation includes not only variety, but content. It is important to remember that the proliferation was not just a matter of choice, but of choice that mattered. The political context of spirituality was fundamental and deeply affected American religious life. The civil rights movement was of definitive importance to this historic transition. Liberation theology offered a powerful political and spiritual counterpoint to the gurus of the 1960s. The radicalization of spirituality from the American Black, Latino, Asian, and Native communities provided a charged critique of power and brought new consciousness of the connection between the religious and the political. The Vietnam War and the national struggle over its justification infused American spirituality with a rejection of the status quo. If some Americans partied through the 1960s and early 1970s, many others grew up and were changed forever.

In the end, a major dynamic behind the proliferation of spirituality, whether ephemeral or substantive, has been a trajectory of the alternative. In the late 1960s and early 1970s, two discoveries were made: (a) that religion offers many spiritual alternatives, and, (b) that spirituality itself can become its own alternative. What had congealed in national religious life—the church on the corner where religion was business as usual—exploded into a question of the alternative. It became possible to envision an authentic religious life outside the church, to discover hybrid forms of that expression in a wide array of spiritualities. It became possible also to self-identify spirituality as an alternative lifestyle, a personal embodiment of religion that centered reality outside the parameters of the old Enlightenment models and within the individual as the final arbiter of his or her own salvation.

The Privatization of Spirituality (The Second Line)

If the countercultural movements of the 1960s and early 1970s saw institutional religion as suspect, by implication, they saw community religion as suspect. The older models of Christian and Jewish worship—the Norman Rockwell image of religion in America—were always community-based. They were grounded firmly in the traditional liturgies of parish and synagogue. By breaking down the walls of the institution, the counterculture also broke down boundaries that had held individuals within a worshiping community. Religion became more of an individual choice. Spirituality became privatized.

It is not surprising that the group following the Woodstock generation was the much more bland, though still deeply self-indulgent, "me" generation. Scholars have shown how the apparent failures of the countercultural dream (social, political, and spiritual) drove many Americans to reject faith in shared ideals, and to begin an inner search for either pleasure or meaning or both.

The late 1970s and 1980s, as marked by a line on the spirituality graph, show a deep valley of introspection. The personal need for fulfillment replaced the more traditional need for community. In fact, the definitions of community began to fall apart as, in the light of Watergate, people retreated from blind patriotism into cynicism about political institutions in general. The hope of the civil rights movement faded, and the realities of race, class, and gender intensified. Rapid changes in the church (e.g., in liturgy and the ordination of women) rocked many denominations and splintered them into factions. In family life, people claimed a variety of new relationships as constitutive of family. The unifying limits that had always served to define community began to be breached. In reaction, people turned within, seeking validation for the self, which became the true measure of spirituality.

The rise of self-help groups is symbolic of the movement of this line on the graph. The rapid expansion of personal growth industries reflects the movement inward during this period. In the most positive forms, these self-focused strategies improved personal health, increased self-awareness, and opened doors for marginalized persons to claim a sense of dignity. In more negative forms, the strategies were personality cults, phony therapies, and diversions from reality.

The underlying issue, however, is the way in which spirituality became a more private affair. The mega-theories of faith, the calls to a universal consciousness or to institutional solidarity, had to struggle against spiritual privatization, in which individuals could accept or reject any aspect of religion and still claim to be valid practitioners. Those who remained within institutions found themselves in turmoil as splinter groups clamored for power.

The 1980s brought political ferment to every branch of the Christian faith in the United States. Coming out of Vatican II and decisions to ordain women, once-solid institutional veneers cracked into shifting configurations of believers, each claiming some hold on the banner of tradition.

Confidence in the group eroded as reliance on the self increased. Institutional responses to this privatization of spirituality sought to recapture the believer's attention. Among Christian "fundamentalists," for example, the emergence of televangelists provided a subtle twist to the privatization of spirituality. Beneath the anything-but-subtle techniques of many televised ministries was a consistently "private" message: individual healing, individual happiness, individual prosperity, individual salvation. The emphasis is on the word individual, because televised ministries implied that these benefits of faith are guaranteed for the person alone. The spiritual message pointed toward what the viewer could get from religion, not on what he or she might give. The aim was to recruit the individual believer by appealing to what he or she wanted, needed, or expected. An entitlement focus runs within this kind of privatization: a feeling that a person deserves these benefits.

It is not accidental that this spiritual entitlement mirrored an increase in litigation. In a society characterized as whining and litigious, the clamor of "what's in it for me" found an echo in the popularity of religious messages that were self-help oriented. Religious television's promise to meet individual needs illustrates the trajectory of this line away from community and toward privatization.

Focusing on Christian fundamentalism allows us to see the privatization of spirituality in places we might otherwise overlook. It is perhaps easier to spotlight New Age philosophies or "therapy spiritualities," which presented spirituality as magic, intended unashamedly for self-benefit, or therapeutic science, in which attention is fixed on the person as client or patient. Individualism seeped both into the spas and trailer parks with a spirituality tuned into the electronic hope for health, prosperity, and success.

In the 1980s, the roller coaster of technological change also began. As the institutions of community either collapsed or were shaken, information flooded the home through the personal computer. The information brought a paradox: people felt more isolated just as they became more connected. The phenomenon of privatized spirituality rides this crest of isolation. The individual, who is not physically isolated but spiritually isolated, increasingly is thrown into an interior reality. Human contact is reduced. The privatization of spirituality, therefore, is aided and abetted by isolation.

The irony is that spiritual isolation accompanies entry into a global community. The person in the spa is part of an elite international network that transcends, even supersedes, national frontiers. The person in the trailer park is only a push of a button away from contact with the world. As spirituality in this nation continues to be challenged by privatization, it will also be challenged by globalization.

The Globalization of Spirituality (The Third Line)

Through the 1990s, spirituality has continued to move upward into the international context. In an increasingly permeable global network the boundaries of spirituality have opened: spirituality has been franchised. It is now possible to speak of spirituality from a variety of sources and in a variety of locations.

Developments at the University of Massachusetts are only one example. In the academic, scientific, political, and corporate worlds, we are growing accustomed to spiritual talk. A new language of spirituality speaks in accents unfamiliar to those accustomed to faith in the context of religion. For example, major companies influenced in their business conduct by ecological or social issues use a form of spiritual expression; the practice might be termed "ethical commerce." While the motivation may be either altruistic or promotional, this corporate language helps create an international spiritual vocabulary. As business has become multinational, it has also become multispiritual. Cultural influences, international political realities, and the need to speak to universal values have brought corporations to this point. Spirituality may seem a strange partner in the corporate boardroom, but it has earned a place for its ability to communicate across global frontiers. While the authority of spirituality to change policy within these networks may still be marginal, that more businesses are using spiritual or quasi-spiritual images means that this generic spirituality is expanding globally along with capitalism.

The content of this spirituality is the question. Corporations may assume publicly ethical postures, but is this genuine spirituality? Universities and scientific communities may announce their spiritual connections, but what kind of spirituality are they describing? The globalization of spirituality is evident in the way that the word spirituality is being co-opted, integrated into networks that are not only national or denominational, but also global and pan-religious. International business, education, and science are all new conduits for carrying the message of spirituality around the planet. The term is being redefined as it is being disseminated to new audiences. Different amalgamations are forming as local spiritualities, so to speak, are mixed, creating transnational mutations.

Taoism, a form of magical spirituality within traditional Chinese culture, provides one example. The Tao was by no means a household word in the spiritual lexicon. At the beginning of the twenty-first century, however, that is no longer true. Through its new connections to science (the Tao of physics), business (the Tao of management), education (the Tao of teaching), and commercialized lifestyles (the Tao of Pooh), this once esoteric spirituality has become a brand name. Its traditional content, of course, has mutated into forms that the Chinese sage Lao-tzu would never have recognized, much less approved. But the fact remains that the spiritual veneer of Taoism has been overlaid on a wide range of institutions and cultures. Whether we perceive this as cheap commercialization or provocative insight, the "Tao" is a new shorthand linguistic symbol recognizable from Taiwan to Tanzania.

Nor is the Tao alone in representing the globalization of spirituality. The crosscurrents of international exchange mean that Western spirituality enters Asian wedding liturgies; that Asian spirituality enters the West through holistic medicine; that African spirituality travels through a global music market; that the Gregorian chant of a Christian monastic order becomes an international hit as Hollywood celebrities embrace Tibetan Buddhism.

The sources of spirituality have been franchised. Religion is no longer the lone source of spirituality, which has become a free agent, available on the Internet, used to sell fashion and make movies, to instruct corporate retreatants, and to realign education departments. Spirituality is sound bite and logo.

Consequently, the "it" in spirituality, the defining quality, has been submerged. In the 1990s, the United States became used to encountering spirituality in almost every cultural locale. Substance was not always important. Simply the perception of the spiritual was sufficient. Spiritual association was enough to communicate reassurance. In whatever form, generic spirituality offered a positive link to the emerging global awareness. Our culture in particular began to be satisfied with the perception that something was spiritual without fussing about the details. Is the Tao a true form of spirituality or a label? What does the Tao mean? With the globalization of spirituality, the answer is: it doesn't matter. It is enough to perceive that the "Tao," a mystical integrating principle linking us to a benign universal reality, is an end in itself. Confronted with multiple choices, we seek comforting images vaguely reminiscent of an older spiritual form, while still acceptable to the new global agenda.

The globalization of spirituality represents the deconstruction of spirituality. Spirituality has infused postmodern life in an instantaneous translation that puts religious, ethical, and moral information into easily transmitted shorthand. Which is not to say that spirituality of this kind is value-less. Only that it is root-less.

At the change in the millennium raw materials are emerging for a new transnational, even transreligious, spirituality. While orthodox centers of religion wage relentless action against such syncretism, the forces of globalization continue to produce new strains of spirituality that both embody and express international culture. Fundamentalism is a powerful opponent, but the populist, hybrid spirituality endures precisely because it is popular. The new missionary movement of world religions rides the Internet. Spirituality bypasses orthodoxy by hitchhiking on the information superhighway.

The question is one of perception versus substance. While many entering the twenty-first century may long for the substance of religious faith that provides a genuinely spiritual life, many more embrace a popular spirituality that keeps them free from commitments. Even more important, given the general loss of grounding in what organized religions would call the "basics," the expanding number of spirituality shoppers is searching more for designer labels than for discipleship. The name will do. What this bodes for both spirituality and religion in the twenty-first century is open to debate, but I believe that the three trends of proliferation, privatization, and globalization are predictive of the future.

The Integration of Spirituality

What will spirituality be like in the years to come? What should spiritual directors expect? I believe that Dr. Scott, whose surprising announcement opened this essay, offers some answers: in the decades to come spirituality will be an integrative force in religious as well as secular life.

Integrating spirituality into life is the work of future spiritual directors. Trends over the last three or four decades will play themselves out, continuing to weave spirituality into the fabric of American society. The threads of spirituality will appear in all areas. Dr. Scott is right in assuming that higher education will continue to explore spiritual values as a process for collating the intellectual data of higher education. Spirituality will continue to play a role in the debates over ethics in science, medicine, and law. Issues such as euthanasia, capital punishment, genetic research, environmental protection, social engineering, global debt, and political morality will open doors for spiritual talk. International business and communications will globalize (as well as trivialize) spirituality, synthesizing its content in world cultures and reducing it to sound bites to sell ideas and products. Hybrid forms of spirituality will multiply. The gnostic-style spirituality of life management through magic will offer solutions to many persons bewildered by change. The orthodox spirituality of religious fundamentalism will grow as millions from all faiths seek certainty and conformity as answers to their need for security in the faith. The media and the arts will turn increasingly to spiritual subjects. Spiritually based countercultural youth movements will attract a new generation of young men and women wishing to "discover" an alternative to traditional religion. Ultimately, the combination of these many strands will mark the next decades as an era of religious reformation, spiritual renewal, and cultural upheaval. While I do not pretend to predict the future, I do believe that these several trajectories offer spiritual practitioners some helpful clues.

1. We must be aware that the spiritual ground will continue to shift. The reality check for future spirituality is anxiety. As the familiar paradigm of the European Enlightenment gradually deconstructs, spiritual seekers will be looking for safe ground. In this time of transition, foundations of culture and social institutions will realign like tectonic plates. The changes may be subtle (e.g., the choice of diet); negotiated (e.g., remaining in organized religion but practicing a hybrid spirituality); dramatic (e.g., conversion to faith as the source of integration); or reactionary (e.g., practicing religious fundamentalism over against change perceived as negative). Moreover, spiritual directors will need to be aware that many people who come to them for counsel will be persons seeking redress from spiritual stress. Whether these men and women embrace or reject the transitions in

their social environment, the common denominator will be the struggle for balance as old assumptions are replaced. The European Enlightenment will be exchanged for a different paradigm, whose shape we can only now glimpse in outline. Future generations, of course, will inherit the outcome and consider it normative, but those of us living through the birth will be marked by both trauma and liberation.

2. Practitioners will need to be flexible in understanding religion as just one alternative in the spiritual search. Persons will not seek one spiritual path to fulfillment as much as a road map of alternatives. Combinations of spiritual influences will be common. The spiritual director who relies on a formula for guidance may quickly be bypassed by seekers wary of dogma. The challenge will be to chart new directions in spirituality without losing the integrity of the search itself. The concept that "the journey is the destination" will continue to be popular, but the danger will be that the journey is going nowhere. Finding ultimate value will be tricky in a culture that will tend to relativize faith. Like a pharmacist mixing ingredients, the spiritual practitioner will need to understand the core qualities of the alternatives of twenty-first-century spirituality. Some mixtures will be harmful, while others can reinvigorate spiritual health. Like theological education, spiritual direction will become more multicultural. With the backdrop of the Enlightenment removed, the task of spirituality will be to help in constructing a rational worldview with ethical value.

Eventually, the proliferation of spiritualities will begin to narrow into more definable patterns. Integration will occur and, already, connections are being made. What we thought of as exotic "Eastern" spirituality in the late 1960s is emerging as a solid presence in the United States and Canada. This is especially true of Buddhism. "New Age" spiritualities are forming around media and workshop outlets that are becoming part of the commercial landscape. Conservative spirituality has entered the political process and will be a factor in coming elections. As these forms of spirituality merge into stronger definitions, they will affect the organizational church by accelerating institutional change. Issues such as the ordination of homosexuals and the blessing of same-sex unions will move toward resolution under pressure from the consolidating spiritualities, often embodied within denominations in special-interest lobbies, changing the internal nature of the churches themselves. As with the ordination of women, these changes will divide denominations into factions. Ultimately, the internalizing pressure exerted by spirituality will cause some mainline denominations to split, creating synergy for the Second Reformation.

The outcome will be watershed reform of Christianity toward the end of the twenty-first century. Spirituality, the underground river of emotion running beneath the crust of organized denominations, will flow out into the global community with enough force to splinter the church into new denominational configurations. In both Protestantism and Roman Catholicism, this reform will divide persons into the "progressive" and "traditionalist" factions, which will merge into a Christianity in which "Protestant" and

"Catholic" have new meanings. As a consequence, the coming Reformation will be a much more important event in the global history of Christianity than the regional shifts of the sixteenth century.

3. The privatization of spirituality will confront spiritual directors with the difficult dilemma of the lonely person. As global communications erases physical isolation, it will create vast areas of emotional isolation. Those seeking the refuge of spirituality will be coming in from the cold, cut off from the warmth of emotional interaction they describe as transcendent and intimate. The longing for this intimacy will drive many out of isolation and into spiritual journeys. Many will find a home after living as strangers, but many will not.

What defines community, therefore, will be a central question. The loss of community through the breakdown of traditional "family" and the fragmentation of religious institutions will create a vacuum, which will be filled by social spirituality. Spirituality will be seen as a catalyst for community. Groups of individuals, to escape the isolation of a highly technological world or the culture shock of being thrust into such a world, will come together as new communities, whose charter will be a shared spirituality.

For example, the next century will see the return of two older forms of community: the monastic tradition and the utopian adventure. While celibacy will be dropped as a requirement for ordination, the attraction of a monastic vocation will increase. Men and women who have felt deep alienation will seek the antidote of intense community experience. The growth of religious orders may be one of the small but significant spikes on the graph of the mid-2000s. Some orders will follow the ancient patterns of a life dedicated to poverty, obedience, and chastity, but others will develop gender-inclusive patterns open to married or even same-sex couples. In a similar way, utopian projects will increase as part of this experimentation in meaningful spiritual community. These New Zions will not just be agrarian cousins to the communes of the nineteenth or twentieth centuries, but new efforts at colonizing urban areas. Cooperative ventures among like-minded spiritual people will create clusters of mini-communities in urban centers. The gentrification of spirituality will occur as suburban spirituality reclaims the city center as a new frontier.

Privatization will also offer spiritual directors increasingly close connection to related sciences and pseudosciences. Spirituality will be interpreted as physicality and more directly associated with issues of health and body image. In coming decades, the grounding of spiritual discipline in exercise, diet, therapy, and lifestyle will become foundational. Future spiritual directors will likely be proponents of a lifestyle rather than a theology. Spirituality will relate less to the "head" than to the "body." Consequently, the *practice* of spirituality will become primary. Meditation, fasting, physical exercise, and group therapies will be seen as integral to a true spiritual life. Nutrition in general and vegetarianism in particular will be rapidly expanding areas of spirituality. Physical programs such as tai chi or yoga will be much more common, especially as Buddhism in North America continues to grow.

Future spiritual directors will not be contemplative "couch potatoes" but active men and women who can keep pace with the personal investment people make in their own spiritual well-being. *Wellness* and *wholeness* will cease to be catchphrases, but will describe a profound shift in spirituality from the mind to the body.

4. Finally, the globalization of spirituality will become the immediate concern of spiritual directors as they combat the trivialization of the sacred. On the future's darker fringes, a negative antimatter will develop to spirituality. The counterforce will run parallel to positive spiritual growth, diminishing the spiritual as purely commercial. If the spiritual is everywhere, it may also be nowhere. The suspicion of spirituality as an escape from reality will grow among those raised with conflicting images of the divine, which have caused them to lose respect for anything holy. As they watch older forms of religion crumble or retreat into rigidity, they will feel the sacred has lost its meaning. The supermarket of spiritual alternatives will not appeal to such persons if they have been convinced that these are shallow options for a bankrupt religion.

Consequently, the field of spiritual practice will be heavily contested by an entertainment industry that globalizes escapism. Imagining Disneyland in China may be a stretch at present, but it will be a natural extension for the generation to come. The worldwide media will become more sophisticated at standardizing images of the good life. The generic expectation of wealth, beauty, and self-indulgence will become a counterpoint to the rise of global spirituality. As more people expect to find fun, rather than purpose, in life, the values of spirituality will be watered down. A kind of cheapening effect of spirituality will occur, allowing people to substitute entertainment for enlightenment.

Even more ominous will be the rise of rage, which will bubble into the next century like magma. The loss of a spiritual value to life, the stress of competing, hostile religious beliefs, the pressure of fundamentalism across all religious frontiers, and the redress to violence by those who feel cheated of the media promise of the good life will result in a backlash against spirituality. Spiritual directors will not just be safe practitioners of fluffy religion, but will be on the front lines of a spiritual struggle. As capitalism divides humanity into winners and losers, as racism intensifies, and as intolerance grows, future spiritual directors may be religious medics on global battlefields.

The ethnic wars of the 1990s will, tragically, play out again and again. This same crisis in the human spirit will begin to erupt within cosmopolitan areas. Nations like the United States, which have been relatively peaceful over the last few decades, will see the resumption of racially fueled urban riots and ethnic clashes. The endemic quality of violence will take on spiritual trappings in the next century as cults flourish. A spiritual community's responses will be severely tested as it seeks to offer reconciliation and hope. Consequently, spirituality will not be the softer reality that it is today, but a hard reaction to an even harder disruption of human life.

In the end, the integration that spirituality offers will be critical, not only for individual well-being, but for the struggle to produce community in the next century. How spiritual practitioners succeed in bringing that integration will affect not only schools like Dr. Scott's, but populations yet unborn. The peaceful transition from the old Enlightenment to the new millennium will fall under the stewardship of religiously minded people who see spirituality as a force for good, not just as a tool for personal salvation. The great-great-grandchildren of those from the 1960s, 1970s, 1980s, and 1990s will inherit a spirituality that is diverse, multicultural, intimate, and tough. In the community centers that will be the churches of their time, they will practice a physical spirituality. In an America that will speak Spanish as often as it speaks English, and that will be heavily Asian, spirituality will serve as a bridge to a global network made possible by a technology that allows face-to-face conversation from any point on the globe. Urban missionaries will plant monastic orders in cities with triple-digit populations. The regreening of the earth will be the debate of the moment. In this brave new world, spiritual directors will not graph their vocation on paper of one color—paper will be an artifact—but on multicolored holograms that reflect the light of a deeply integrated faith.

Focus

Define the term "postmodern."

Explore critical thinking: Critical thinking is not simply about registering positive or negative judgments on something. Critical thinking involves a process of analysis and honest reflection before asserting one's opinion. Use the following questions to clarify your understanding of Charleston's essay.

What are Bishop Charleston's assertions?

What is the supporting evidence for his assertions?

What are his underlying assumptions?

What is the quality/critical value of the assertions; that is in what way has he made his case?

ALL YEARS: PREPARING FOR THE SEMINAR

Respond

Bishop Charleston discusses spirituality and its future in terms of the following.

The Enlightenment as Paradigm (The Graph Paper)

The Proliferation of Spirituality (The First Line)

The Privatization of Spirituality (The Second Line)

The Globalization of Spirituality (The Third Line)

Attempt to create an image according to Bishop Charleston's metaphor of the paper and lines. Add the time frames and key aspects represented in each line.

What changes would you make in the metaphor?

As you review Charleston's predictions for the future, how does what he projects square with what you anticipate? State your position concerning the development of spiritual disciplines in the world you sense is emerging.

Practice

Reflect on the idea of a sustaining spirituality, using a statement from the Charleston essay.

THEOLOGICAL REFLECTION BEGINNING WITH A TEXT

Identify a statement in the essay that seems especially strong to you. What kind of a picture could represent the position represented by that statement?

For example, Bishop Charleston's statement, "The great-great-grandchildren of those from the 1960s, 1970s, 1980s, and 1990s will inherit a spirituality that is diverse, multicultural, intimate, and tough," might be pictured using an image of an individual of mixed ethnic features and dress holding hands with someone who looks very different, both of them facing a storm with resolve and hope.

His statement that "The outcome will be watershed reform of Christianity toward the end of the twenty-first century," might produce a picture of a cross (or a person holding a cross) rushing over a waterfall fed by a variety of religious and cultural "streams."

Find an essay statement or idea that you want to reflect on and create an image to capture something of that statement.

What seems to be the essence of the statement and/or the image you developed?

Note: The Explore movement precedes the Connect movement in order to allow the reflection to take on a larger and deeper perspective before making additional connections to the other Source voices. Connections often begin to emerge on their own in the midst of exploring. Trust what emerges and allow it to develop.

Explore the image from one or more theological perspectives based on terms used by Bishop Desmond Tutu: Wholeness/goodness (Creation), Brokenness/separation from God (Sin), Recognition (Judgment), Reorientation (Repentance), and/or Restoration to wholeness (Redemption). Choose any one or more of the following questions to pose to your picture.

What wholeness or goodness does the image or statement reflect?

What demonstrates brokenness in the image/statement?

What represents recognition of the brokenness in the image/statement?

What reorientation is possible in the image/statement?

How would restoration come about for those in the image or statement?

What seems to be at the heart of the consideration at this point?

Connect

Bishop Charleston's essay presents his personal position about the future of spirituality, drawn from his personal experience.

What do you believe about the central matter of the image or statement you chose to explore?

Compare and contrast Bishop Charleston's position with your own. What seems to be "at stake" in the comparing and contrasting?

How does your personal experience connect with the image or statement you are exploring?

What spiritual practices does your faith tradition/background teach that support and sustain your spiritual life?

What do you see or understand in a new way?

Apply

What does your new (or reaffirmed) understanding suggest for your ongoing life in Christ?

In light of the reflection, name some implications for ministry in your life. Think especially of how this reflection contributes to living faithfully in a multicultural world.

Week Seventeen

YEAR ONE

Read

The Book of Psalms

Do not feel you must read every psalm closely, rather feel free to skim through at first, then read with greater attention individual psalms that catch your attention. You also may find it helpful to read an introduction to the Psalms in any good study Bible or on the Oxford Biblical Studies Online website. Next week, you will read Collins's consideration of Psalms and the Song of Songs.

Focus

Notice how the Psalms are grouped and reflect on the purpose of that arrangement. Notice any patterns in form, repeating verses, or themes.

What stands out for you in the psalms?

Identify one psalm that illustrates each of the following categories:

- complaints

- hymns of praise

- royal psalms

- thanksgivings

YEAR TWO

Read

Powell, Chapter 10, "New Testament Letters" and Chapter 11, "Paul,"
pages 215–253
Hyperlinks 10.1–10.4 at www.IntroducingNT.com

Focus

Identify the following terms, people, and ideas: Pastoral Epistles; Prison Letters; Catholic Epistles; *cuneiform; ostraca; papyrus; amanuensis;* structure of epistles; *chiasm;* authenticity: pseudepigraphy; Muratorian fragment

Using the material in Powell's eleventh chapter, construct a first-person spiritual autobiography of Paul's life. For example, identify ten to twelve events that cover his entire life: "I was born and raised as a member of the people of Israel within the tribe of Benjamin"; "I lived as a Pharisee observing the Jewish law"; "I studied at the feet of Gamaliel." Read through the events of Paul's life to get a sense of his life as a whole.

Note the different experiences Paul had that shaped his spirituality—how he prayed and worshiped; revelations and/or visions he reported; encounters with other cultures; encounters within his own faith tradition; and other experiences that formed his relationship with God.

Key theological ideas: gospel (*euangelion*); Jesus' death, resurrection, and ascension; life after death; being made right with God (justification); new age of God; nature of Jesus

YEAR THREE

Read

MacCulloch, Chapter 11, "The West: Universal Emperor or Universal Pope?," pages 363–395

Focus

Identify the following terms, people, and ideas:

Recounting waves of renewal
Monastic revival in England; Cluny Abby's legacy, especially noting the agrarian economy, pilgrimage piety, origin of purgatory, and the Peace of God movement

Power and authority
universal monarchy; marriage as sacrament; rise of the papacy—from Vicar of Peter to Vicar of Christ; clerical celibacy; dividing lay and clergy

YEAR FOUR

Read

Allen, Chapter 11, "The Temptation in the Wilderness," pages 107–116

Focus

Note these theological concepts and their significance:

Biblical use of the number 40; Jesus' three temptations for ministry in daily life; misguided theology that faith in God means being protected from harm; Matthew 5:45b; felicity and joy in God's presence; self-limitation of Jesus; hiddenness of God

ALL YEARS: PREPARING FOR THE SEMINAR

Respond

Gustavo Gutierrez was born and raised in Peru. His academic work helped create the twentieth-century theological movement known as liberation theology. His theological writings emerged out of living in the midst of slum poverty in Rimac, Peru. The following excerpt from *We Drink from Our Own Wells* helps clarify the relationship between theological reflection and spirituality.

A spirituality is a walking in freedom according to the Spirit of love and life. This walking has its point of departure in an encounter with the Lord. Such an encounter is a spiritual experience that produces and gives meaning to the freedom of which I have been speaking. The encounter itself springs from the Lord's initiative. The scriptures state this repeatedly: "This is why I told you that no one can come to me unless it is granted him by the Father" (John 6: 65). "You did not choose me, but I chose you" (John 15: 16). A spiritual experience, then, stands at the beginning of a spiritual journey.[31] That experience becomes the subject of later reflection and is proposed to the entire ecclesial community as a way of being disciples of Christ. The spirituality in question is therefore not, as is sometimes said, an application of a particular theology. Let me begin by clarifying this point.

Spirituality and Theology

The adoption of a spiritual perspective is followed by a reflection on faith (therefore, a theology) as lived in that perspective. This sequence is clear from the historical course followed in all the great spiritualties.[32]

I Believe in Order to Understand

Spiritual experience is the terrain in which theological reflection strikes root. Intellectual comprehension makes it possible to carry the experience of faith to a deeper level, but the experience always comes first and is the source. St. Anselm (1033–1109) reminds us of this in a well-known passage:

---

31. The theme of an experiential Christology in Mark has been deepened by the recent work of Edward Schillebeeckx.

32. Many years ago, in a well-known book that was much misunderstood at the time, M. D. Chenu wrote as follows about doing theology: "The fact is that in the final analysis theological systems are simply the expressions of a spirituality. It is this that gives them their interest and grandeur. If we are surprised by the theological divergences found within the unity of dogma, then we must also be surprised at seeing one and the same faith give rise to such varied spiritualities. The grandeur and truth of Bonaventuran and Scotist Augustinianism is entirely derived from the spiritual experience of St. Francis, which inspired his sons; the grandeur and truth of Molinism derives from the spiritual experience of the Exercises of St. Ignatius. One does not get to the heart of a system via the logical coherence of its structure or the plausibility of its conclusions. One gets to that heart by grasping it in its origins via that fundamental intuition that serves to guide a spiritual life and provides the intellectual regimen proper to that life" (Le Saulchoir: Una scuola di teologia [Casale Monferrato: Marietti, 1982], 59; the French original dates from 1937).

Lord, I do not attempt to comprehend Your sublimity, because my intellect is not at all equal to such a task. But I yearn to understand some measure of Your truth, which my heart believes and loves. For I do not seek to understand in order to believe but I believe in order to understand. For I believe even this: that I shall not understand unless I believe.[33]

I believe in order to understand. The level of the experience of faith supports a particular level of the understanding of faith. For theology is in fact a reflection that, even in its rational aspect, moves entirely within the confines of faith and direct testimony. "This is the disciple who is bearing witness to these things, and who has written these things; and we know that his testimony is true" (John 21: 24).[34]

Study can become a spiritual discipline when learning arises out of an integration of experience and reading content. Theological reflection becomes a spiritual discipline whenever it allows a person "to carry the experience of faith to a deeper level." Reflection provides substance for spiritual growth whenever a person connects the wisdom of the past to the realities of present experience.

Often if a person is asked to identify times when they have encountered God, they go blank. The God-encounters that Gutierrez points to are those that result from reflecting on things that matter to a person. Experiences that have existential import to the individual hold the potential for finding the work of "the Spirit of love and life." Too often "spiritual experiences" are confined to dramatic on-the-road-to-Damascus occurrences. As people give their studied attention through the discipline of theological reflection to incidents that matter, they can discover the "encounters with the Lord" as God's dwelling among humanity in most daily circumstances.

Develop the practice of noticing what matters to you; things that interest you; things that excite or disturb you; that you want to know more about. List three or four of such experiences. These can be beginning points for theological reflection either in a group or individually.

Practice

Reflect theologically on the spirituality of a psalm.

Identify

Choose one of the following psalms for reflection, or any psalm especially meaningful to you: Psalm 1, 23, 42, 51, 63, 108, 124, 139, 150, or one of your choice

Focus the psalm by identifying the overall tone of the psalm.

---

33. Proslogion 1, Anselm of Canterbury (New York: Edwin Mellon Press, 1974), vol. l, 3.

34. Gustavo Gutierrez, *We Drink from Our Own Wells* (Maryknoll, NY: Orbis Books, 1985), 35–36.

Find what experience of God the psalmist expressed or recalled. What state of the psalmist's mind or body seems to be evident?

What verse especially stands out for you?

What does the psalm seem to be about?

Explore

Create an image or write a phrase that captures the central energy of the psalm. For instance, a psalm may express deep reliance on and joy in God. An image reflecting that sense might be a person nestled deep in the arms of a loved one; or someone dancing with delight in the middle of a field of flowers.

What do you most want to try to depict about the psalm in an image or phrase?

Once you have an image you want to explore, ask one or more of the following theological perspective questions. (Note, it is not necessary and may be counter-productive to ask every question.) Choose the ones that seem most important to you right now:

Wholeness/goodness—What does the image reveal about the wholeness or goodness of creation?

Brokenness/separation from God—What might threaten the goodness of the image?

Recognition—How would the person in the image recognize the threat to goodness?

Reorientation—Where might the person in the image turn in order to move back into wholeness? What would help that to happen?

Restoration to wholeness—How would the person in the image recognize that restoration to wholeness was occurring?

Connect

The psalm is a representative of the "voice" of Tradition. Connect your own life (Personal Experience/Action) to the image or phrase you created. When has life been like the image you developed?

Compare and contrast the Christian Tradition (the selected psalm) and the Personal Experience/Action (your personal experience) sources. How do they illuminate, reflect, challenge, and/or support one another?

What seems to be important to you about the relationship between your personal experience and the psalm?

Continue connecting to the sources of Personal Position/Belief and to the Culture/Social Environment you inhabit.

As you compare and contrast the psalm and your own experience, what personal beliefs are evident for you?

What has someone or something in our social environment experienced that relates to the image or phrase you created?

Describe how you personally and how the social messages around you relate to the image or phrase you have focused on.

Apply

Where in your life or in the world around you does your image or phrase most need to be presented? Why?

What would keep that from happening?

What do you want to talk over with God about the image or phrase you chose as a focus?

Note: Next week, please allow enough time between your study and your seminar gathering to write briefly about what you encounter during your study.

Week Eighteen

YEAR ONE

Read

Song of Songs
Collins, Chapter 23, "Psalms and Song of Songs," pages 236–247

Focus

Given the fact that the Song of Songs does not mention God, in what ways might it convey a theology? Make a case for why or why not the book conveys a theology.

Psalms tell of the kingship of God, the human situation, and the character of God. Name two or three features of the theology found in the Psalms.

YEAR TWO

Read

The Letter to the Romans

Focus

The Letter to the Romans likely contains familiar quotations. Be sure to place any you notice in the context of the letter. Note how the letter is structured and how Paul builds his case.

YEAR THREE

Read

MacCulloch, Chapter 12, "A Church for All People?," pages 396–423

Focus

Identify the following terms, events, and people: Waldensians; *scholae* educational method; Peter Abelard's *Theologia Christiana*; Dominic and Dominicans (Blackfriars); Francis, Franciscans, and Francis' *Testament*; Carmelites; Fourth Lateran Council; transubstantiation (Real Presence); Thomas Aquinas; *Summa Theologiae* (Sum Total of Theology); Anselm, Abelard, Hildegard of Bingen; *The Cloud of Unknowing*; Meister Eckhart; Bridget of Sweden; Catherine of Siena

Make a note of persons or events of interest to you that MacCulloch writes about in this week's reading assignment.

YEAR FOUR

Read

Allen, Chapter 12, "The Sacrifice of the Cross," pages 117–127

Focus

The chapter discusses teachings on atonement—the only doctrine that has no established consensus. Note:

Different atonement theories: ransom; satisfaction/substitutionary

Key figures who expressed different theories: Paul; Anselm; Abelard

Images/metaphors: distance; Suffering Servant

Concepts: self-limitation of God; ancient meaning of passion; sin as life apart from God; biblical view of God's power, wisdom, and goodness; atonement as the restoration of the human capacity to know, love, and obey God

ALL YEARS: PREPARING FOR THE SEMINAR

Respond

Philip Sheldrake, in a 2009 article, links the practice of contemplative prayer to public action:

> A number of recent writers also suggest that contemplative spirituality is vital to the public realm. The Spanish theologian Gaspar Martinez notes that modern Catholic theologies engaged with public or political life also focus sharply on spirituality. He cites in particular Johannes Baptist Metz, Gustavo Gutierrez, and David Tracy—inspired in different ways by the Jesuit Karl Rahner.[35] Rahner himself defined prayer fundamentally in terms of relationship rather than merely as practices and went on to say that: "All positive religious acts which are directly and explicitly related, both knowingly and willingly, to God may be called prayer."[36] So, it is possible to think of our committed Christian lives as prayer and formal moments of meditation or common liturgy as explicit articulations of our larger business of living for God.[37]

---

35. Gaspar Martinez, *Confronting the Mystery of God: Political, Liberation and Public Theologies* (New York: Continuum, 2001).

36. Karl Rahner, "Prayer," *Encyclopedia of Theology* (London: Burns & Oates, 1975), 1275.

37. Philip F. Sheldrake, "Spirituality and Social Change: Rebuilding the Human City," *Spiritus: A Journal of Christian Spirituality*, vol. 9, no. 2 (Fall 2009), 139.

Identify several experiences that you have witnessed or lived that might be considered "positive religious acts which are directly and explicitly related, both knowingly and willingly, to God . . ."

Additionally, how might you understand the spiritual disciplines of study, prayer, and worship as part of "our larger business of living for God."

Practice

Identify a focus.

Select something that caught your attention from your study this week. This can be a piece of scripture or something you read in your textbook that may have produced responses in you either of affirmation or disagreement or confusion.

Review the selected passage carefully.

Write three paragraphs about your response to that passage. Summarize/focus your work with a statement or image of what you believe is the central idea of your response.

Explore your response.

Read through your paragraphs again, looking for any of the following:

Wholeness/goodness—What does your writing reveal about wholeness or goodness of creation?

Brokenness/separation from God—What does your writing recognize as threats to wholeness or goodness or as brokenness or separation from God?

Recognition—How does your writing show that there is a threat to goodness or to a relationship to God? How would you recognize such a threat?

Reorientation—How is a reorientation to relationship with God discussed in what you wrote? How would you discuss that if you see no evidence of that reorientation in your writing? What would such a reorientation cost? What would it promise?

Restoration to wholeness—How does your writing express a possibility of restoration to wholeness?

Connect with the voices of our other three sources of wisdom (Culture, Position, and Experience).

Again, drawing on your writing, mark places where you referred to personal experience or to something you have come across in the world around you, such as a reference to an author, a news story, or a television/movie presentation.

Your summary statement represents a personal position, something you believe. In what ways has the reflection affected that statement?

Apply this exercise to your life.

Write a prayer or litany, drawing from your reflections above.

To whom do you pray?

What do you offer?

What do you ask?

For whom do you pray?

How do you close your prayer?

Be prepared to offer what you are comfortable sharing at your seminar meeting.

Week Nineteen

YEAR ONE

Read

Proverbs
Collins, Chapter 24, "Proverbs," pages 248–255

Focus

Cite four or five passages from Proverbs that appeal to you and note those that do not.

What significance does Proverbs 8 have for faith today?

The Psalms contain five smaller books with different kinds of psalms. As poetry, they are best read aloud or sung. They also give voice to the human experience. The Song of Songs is also largely composed of poetry. Proverbs mainly consists of ancient aphorisms.

Scan the Psalms, Song of Songs, and Proverbs and select four or five passages. Read the selections aloud, noticing what stirs in you. Reflect on how the passages you selected reveal something of your deeper self: your hopes, your concerns, your experience.

YEAR TWO

Read

Powell, Chapter 12, "Romans," pages 255–271

Focus

For Western Christianity, the Pauline teaching on justification is highly influential and formative. Powell presents on page 263 "Models for Understanding Justification." Which model or combination of models best clarify the "justification issue" for you? Define your understanding of the term "justification."

YEAR THREE

Read

MacCulloch, Chapter 13, "Faith in a New Rome," pages 427–465

Focus

Consider the following terms:

Hagia Sophia (pronunciation = **EYE**-yah so-**FEE**-yah)–sacred space shaping Eastern Orthodox Christianity:
  Describe three or four characteristics of Orthodoxy.

Byzantine Spirituality:
  Name distinctive qualities of Byzantine spirituality.

Iconoclastic controversy:
  What concerns motivated both sides of the iconoclastic controversy? Name one or two reasons why understanding the controversy is important to you as you live in today's world.

Orthodox Missions to the West:
  In a nutshell, describe Photios's missionary strategy and the significance for Christianity in the twenty-first century.

YEAR FOUR

Read

Allen, Chapter 13, "The Resurrection of Jesus and Eternal Life," pages 131–146

Focus

Everlasting life or eternal life issues turn on the understanding one holds of life. *Bios* and *zoe* distinctions frame thinking about the nature and purpose of life. Think about how those distinctions affect your theology of ministry.
  Allen used a painting analogy to support understanding the Good News found in the Gospels. Which of the resurrection "pictures" painted in the Gospels appeal to you?
  All in all, what difference might a person's view of life after death have on daily ministry?

ALL YEARS: PREPARING FOR THE SEMINAR

Respond

James K. A. Smith, a philosophy professor at Calvin College in Grand Rapids, Michigan, writes as a Christian who is at home in the Reformed tradition. He has begun a trilogy on the power of liturgy, especially practices that he calls cultural liturgies.

If historic Christian worship and ancient spiritual disciplines carry the Story that seeps into our social imaginary, this is in no small part because liturgical practices are also intentionally aesthetic and tap into our imaginative core. It is no accident that the poetry of the psalms has long constituted the church's prayerbook, nor is it mere coincidence that the worship of the people of God has always been marked by singing. In these and countless other ways, the inherited treasury of formative disciplines has been characterized by an allusivity and metaphoricity that means more than we can say. There is a reason to our rhymes—a logic carried in the meter of our hymns and the shape of our gestures. Worship innovations that are inattentive to this may end up adopting forms that forfeit precisely those aspects of worship that sanctify perception by forming the imagination.[38] Hence wise worship planning and leadership is not only discerning about content—the lyrics of songs, the content of a pastoral prayer, the message of a sermon—but also discerning about the kin/aesthetic meaning of the form of our worship. We will be concerned not only with the what but also with the how, because Christian faith is not only a knowing-that but also a kind of know-how, a "practical sense" or *praktognosia* that is absorbed in the "between" of our incarnate significance. Because meter and tune each *means* in its own irreducible way, for example, the form of our songs is as important as the content. It is in this sense that to sing is to pray twice.[39, 40]

Summarize Smith's thoughts in a sentence or two.

How do Smith's thoughts relate to the material you studied this week?

What do Smith's thoughts contribute to the work of building a sustaining spirituality in the context of living faithfully in a multicultural world?

---

38. This is not to say that there is no room for innovation or improvisation in Christian worship or that affirming the formative wisdom of historic Christian worship requires merely repeating status quo forms. The point is rather that improvisations and innovations of worship form need to be attentive to the narrative arc of the form and the unique "incarnate significance" of worship practices. Innovations that are "faithful" will preserve the plot of that narrative arc and deepen the imaginative impact of worship. Unfaithful and unhelpful innovations will be developments that are detrimental to the imaginative coherence of worship. [309].

39. See Brian Wren's unpacking of this famous epigram in *Praying Twice: The Music and Words of Congregational Song* (Louisville, KY: Westminster John Knox, 2000), particularly his discussion of how hymns "work" as "poems of faith," 253–294. My thanks to Kevin Twit for pointing me to this resource.

40. James K. A. Smith, *Imagining the Kingdom (Cultural Liturgies): How Worship Works* (Grand Rapids, MI: Baker Publishing Group), 174.

Practice

THEOLOGICAL REFLECTION BEGINNING WITH A PERSONAL POSITION

Identify a focus.

Begin with a focus on the value of music and poetry in worship and prayer.

Explore the focus.

Make a statement or image that reflects a connection between music and poetry and prayer or worship. For instance, someone might express that he only likes a certain type of music in worship because another kind destroys the sense of peace and beauty. Or another person might create an image that depicts people singing or playing instruments and the music notes floating outward towards God and the world.

Explore your statement or image theologically, using a few of the questions provided, or create your own questions for the image:

How does the overall statement or image reflect wholeness or goodness?

What view of the world is contained in your statement or image?

What view of the relationship between God and creation exists in your statement/image?

How would someone experience God in that statement/image?

What might disrupt someone's relationship with God and others in that focus?

What view of restoration to wholeness is contained in the focus?

Connect to other sources.

State your personal belief that undergirds your initial image or statement.

How do your personal belief and the exploration above coincide and how do they conflict?

What troubles you about the comparison? What comforts you about the comparison?

Find one or two scripture references to the place of music and poetry in liturgy and worship. Or, select one or two hymns to connect to. How do those hymns relate to your focusing image or statement and to your position? How do they relate to the exploration?

What view of the world around you is contained in your personal belief statement, in the image, in the hymns you chose?

Apply what is learned to daily life.

Once a person takes a stance or affirms a position, implications for ministry begin to emerge.

What do you see for your ministry as you live day to day?

Close by composing a prayer adapting the structure of Jewish prayers:

Blessed are you, O Lord God, _____
(description of God),

for you _____

and make us _____

through _____. _Amen._

Week Twenty

YEAR ONE

Read

Job
Ecclesiastes (Qoheleth)
Collins, Chapter 25, "Job and Qoheleth," pages 256–267

Focus

Job and Qoheleth (Ecclesiastes) provide literary classics from the world of the Hebrew Bible. They expose humanity's agony and glory. The giftedness of the main characters lay hidden amid the dramatic rubble of their lives.

YEAR TWO

Read

Hebrews
Powell, Chapter 23, "Hebrews," pages 427–443

Focus

Powell notes that "persistent Christians have found real substance in this [Hebrews] letter teaching not only who Christ is but also discloses who they are (and can be) in relation to him." What significance does knowing who Christ is and who people are in relation to him have for sustaining one's spirituality? Notice especially the role faith plays in fostering spirituality.

YEAR THREE

Read

MacCulloch, Chapter 14, "Orthodoxy: More Than an Empire," pages 466–502

Focus

MacCulloch used a sweep of eight centuries of history to show how Orthodoxy became more than an empire's religion. Describe the profile of Orthodoxy that comes through to you from the chapter. What key figures, ideas, and events contributed to what Orthodoxy became?

YEAR FOUR

Read

Allen, Chapter 14, "Jesus as Lord and Jesus as Servant," pages 147–168

Focus

Allen outlines a theology of Jesus as Servant–Lord that defines a Christian's relationship with God and with one another. Describe the essence of the doctrine of discipleship asserted by Allen and the importance for ministry in daily life.

ALL YEARS: PREPARING FOR THE SEMINAR

Respond

Review the following quote from James K. A. Smith, first introduced and annotated in the Unit Three Introduction.

> We are what we love, and our love is shaped, primed, and aimed by liturgical practices that take hold of our gut and aim our heart to certain ends. So we are not primarily *homo rationale* or *homo faber* or *homo economicus*; we are not even generically *homo religiosis*. We are more concretely *homo liturgicus*; humans are those animals that are religious animals not because we are primarily believing animals but because we are liturgical animals—embodied, practicing creatures whose love/desire is aimed at something ultimate.

Describe liturgy among the people you have been studying. State the value and meaning of those practices. Show how the practices supported the faith community's relationship to God and how they interfered.

Practice

Try reflecting using the following form provided by Professor Patricia Bleicher (an EfM mentor of long experience). It has been slightly modified to include the movements of Identify, Explore, Connect, and Apply.

Theological Reflection Beginning with a Provocative Word

do at home – the prayer

Identify

Select a word that has impact. For the purpose of this reflection and the practice, try the word "DESIRING."

What revelations on the meaning of the word do you have? Anything it denotes or connotes?

Explore

Next, ask the six "journalist's questions" about the feeling the word conveys:

WHO was involved when you were feeling _____?
(Action . . . tell the stories from your life)

WHAT image comes to mind about the feeling(s) _____?
(Image . . . explore the metaphor—its reflection of wholeness, brokenness, recognition, reorientation, and/or restoration)

Connect

Go to the other sources we use to help explore meaning.

WHERE does this feeling come from and WHERE is it found in society?
(Source/Culture)

WHEN does this feeling come up in the Bible, lives of saints, hymns, and so forth?
(Source/Tradition . . . explore the world of tradition)

WHY is this feeling manifest in our lives?
(Source/Position)

HOW might God redeem any negatives in this?
(Hope in Christ)

Consider insights and implications.

WHAT have you learned for the next time you feel _____?

Apply

Write a collect using the outline:

Dear God . . .	**(naming of God's aspects)**
You . . .	**(connect situation of the image to that aspect)**
We pray that . . .	**(petition of our hearts)**
So that . . .	**(result we desire)**
Amen.	

Week Twenty-one

YEAR ONE

Read

Ruth
Jonah
Esther
Collins, Chapter 26, "The Hebrew Short Story," pages 268–277

Focus

Imagine Ruth, Jonah, and Esther were three stories in a volume of fictional short stories. Now consider them as nonfiction stories that are to be taken as literally and historically true.

Notice what happens to the stories when read as fictional prose or as history. What contribution does each reading bring to developing one's spirituality?

In what way is each of these a story of intercultural encounter?

YEAR TWO

Read
1 Peter, 2 Peter
Powell, Chapter 25, "1 Peter" and Chapter 26, "2 Peter," pages 463–491

Focus

As you read 1 Peter and 2 Peter and what Powell has to say about them, notice what each contributes to developing one's spirituality.

YEAR THREE

Read

MacCulloch, Chapter 15, "Russia: The Third Rome," pages 503–547

Focus

Indicate how MacCulloch's discourse on the advent of Christianity to Russia contributes to your understanding of his perspective on the view of God, society, and human nature reflected in the time period of the assigned chapter.

YEAR FOUR

Read

Allen, Chapter 15, "Revelation and Faith," pages 155–168

Focus

Allen uses the metaphor of a flashlight to point to how theology functions to illuminate our view of important questions and issues. How does the theology that Allen presents shed light on understanding humanity, the world, and God?

ALL YEARS: PREPARING FOR THE SEMINAR

Respond

Contemporary society is replete with challenges and opportunities, difficulties and delights, fear-fed violence and astonishing compassion–all set within the complexities of living in a multicultural world. Disciplines of study, prayer, and worship along with others lead Christians into a sustaining spirituality that supports and encourages ministry in daily life. Consider the following collect and its implications for ministry in a multicultural environment.

> O God, who created all peoples in your image, we thank you for the wonderful diversity of races and cultures in this world. Enrich our lives by ever-widening circles of fellowship, and show us your presence in those who differ most from us, until our knowledge of your love is made perfect in our love for all your children; through Jesus Christ our Lord. Amen.[41]

Practice

Create a Rule of Life: Collaboration between Washington National Cathedral and the Friends of St. Benedict resulted in a Community of Reconciliation to provide an "ecumenical network of individuals seeking radical balance in life and a deepening commitment to reconciliation in the world."[42] This EfM *Guide* will draw from the booklet produced by the Community that provides guidance in creating a Rule of Life, a guide toward the journey of the reconciling life.

For the EfM community, a Rule of Life could be a balance of prayer, study, action, and reflection. Key elements in developing a Rule of Life are first listening–listen to what your life has revealed to you; listen to what

---

41. Collect "For the Diversity of Races and Culture," *The Book of Common Prayer* (New York: Church Hymnal Corporation, 1979), 840.

42. *Creating a Rule of Life*, Washington National Cathedral and the Friends of St. Benedict, 2009. [Washington, DC]

voices of your family, friends, church, and society have revealed to you; listen to the still, small voice within your soul that reveals, prods, calls you. Second, commitment—be willing to open this gift for yourself and then to accept it. Third, time—make the time to create the beginning of the Rule, knowing that it is a lifelong activity. Fourth, reflection—take time to reflect on experience and to make a renewed commitment to the Rule. Fifth, hospitality—be open to God, to others, and above all to self, our humanness with all the glory and strength and weakness that encompasses.

Keep in mind that the term "Rule" used in this manner is a synonym for teaching, training, education, coaching. A Rule of Life serves as a guide to help an individual or group learn to attend to their relationship with God and others.

Creating a Rule of Life

The following will help to prepare the soil of your life for the activity of strengthening your spiritual muscle through a Rule of Life.

Listen

Review your spiritual autobiography. Be aware of when you "heard" God in your journey. Note what you have learned from others in your life that has been of significance to you regarding your spiritual growth. Consider what the world around you has been making known to you.

Commit

Make yourself available to God's Holy Spirit. Decide how you will do that. Express your availability to God.

Time

Decide on how much time you are willing to give to focused spiritual practice of prayer, study, action, and reflection. What will you need to do to set time aside for creating a Rule?

Hospitality

Identify what you are going to have to "befriend" in yourself, to make room for, as you move into a more conscious life of prayer, study, reflection, and action. How will you make room for hospitality inside yourself? Think about what you will need to welcome from others.

Reflection

This may mean keeping a journal so that you can review aspects of your life as you encounter others and the circumstances of daily living and study and prayer. Taking time to reflect helps to deepen an understanding of how God is moving in a life and of how any of us might be allowing other distractions to pull us away. Reflection will include reviewing these five preparations regularly.

Create the Rule

Keep this simple to start. When you are ready (or at least willing), begin by writing, "With God's help I will . . . " and continue by making statements regarding the practices of:

Prayer

Study

Action

Reflection

Attending to the Gaps— Integrating Belief, Behavior, and Doctrine in a Multicultural World

Week Twenty-two

ALL YEARS

    Read

Attending to the Gaps: Integrating Belief, Behavior, and Doctrine in a Multicultural World

EfM provides resources and processes that are intended to support a person in living authentically as a Christian. Authenticity involves coherence, wholeness, integrity, and honesty. Something is incoherent whenever a dissonance occurs between thought and actions or even between two incongruent ideas. For example, a person receiving the benefits of twenty-first-century technology, whether received through medicine, transportation, or communication, may well hold beliefs that contradict or even deny the science that gave rise to the technological innovations. In addition, a person can easily fall into judging others by a double standard, by instituting a restrictive policy that is to be universally applied—that is, except for good friends. Beliefs (positions) and behaviors (actions) easily can become fragmented and separated from one another.

Integration brings the fragments of a person's life into conversation with one another so that the person moves toward wholeness in a process of continual growth that brings disparate fragments together. What does it mean to flourish in relationship with God as a human being, both as an individual and as a member of the human community? In traditional theological language, integration includes the theological process known by various terms: sanctification, deification, *theosis*, and participation in God. The integrative process at its deepest level is none other than the movement into communion with God. A. M. Allchin, in *Participation in God: A Forgotten Strand in Anglican Tradition*, concluded his introduction with:

> To become fully human, to realise our human potential, we need to enter into communion with our Creator. . . . There is nothing static about this communion. It is the beginning of a process which will lead us through death into life, life in this world and life in the world beyond this one, "an eternal process into the inexhaustible riches of the divine life."[43]

---

43. A. M. Allchin, *Participation in God: A Forgotten Strand in Anglican Tradition* (Wilton, CT: Morehouse–Barlow, 1988), 6. The end of the quotation includes a phrase from John Meyendorff's *Byzantine Theology* (New York: Fordham University Press, 1974), 225–226.

This unit in modest ways begins the process by focusing on gaps that exist between:

- beliefs and behavior;
- Christian teaching (doctrine) and personal beliefs;
- and behavior and doctrines.

As a person becomes aware of multicultural forces that shape the world, the gaps take on different nuances. In a homogeneous community, the belief and behavior gaps grow out of familiar tensions. In a multicultural world the tensions grow out of the soil of unfamiliarity and ignorance.

The tension between behavior and beliefs has a long history in Christianity. The technical theological terms that have developed are "orthodoxy" and "orthopraxis." Both, in their purest expressions, seek wholeness. Right belief (orthodoxy) is to bring wholeness and health. That same is to be said of right action (orthopraxis). However, history is replete with examples of how orthodox positions, separated from concerns about orthopraxis, wrought destruction and death.

The next several weeks call EfM participants into the work of integration. Integrating requires awareness, attention, and intention: awareness of one's beliefs, attention to one's actions, and a commitment to acting in ways that reflect core beliefs as much as human frailty and faithfulness allow. Such integration, congruency, and consistency are desirable in any context, multicultural or otherwise. Clarifying one's beliefs helps a person take action but also permits that person to adjust those beliefs in light of God's revelation through personal experience. However, clarity alone, without the humility to leave room for God's ongoing revelation through the Holy Spirit, can foster rigidity and lifelessness; there is no breath. Education for Ministry encourages ongoing examination of beliefs and behavior, and openness to revelation through study, reflection, group interaction, and prayer.

A diverse, multicultural world has long been a given. Encounters between differing cultures and their consequent differences in beliefs and practices are the "stuff" of history books. Conflict has frequently emerged in those encounters. The current reality of travel over highways both real and virtual makes the truth of our multicultural context even more evident and imminent. How can one know the truth? How can personal beliefs that differ permit peaceful coexistence and humble openness? How can "the holy" be worshipped? How can integration and wholeness be achieved?

The following excerpt from Diana Butler Bass's *Christianity after Religion: The End of Church and the Birth of a New Spiritual Awakening* provides a careful examination of what "believing" means. Her essay supports integration by increasing awareness of the dimensions of belief, both individual and doctrinal.

Believing[44]

The gym was packed for the baccalaureate service, not only with people, but also with anticipation, because a respected Christian scholar would be preaching on this happy academic occasion. Like everyone else, I looked forward to hearing his words of wisdom. Glancing through the program, I read the scripture passage chosen for the occasion:

> **Let the same mind be in you that was in Christ Jesus,**
> **who, though he was in the form of God,**
> > **did not regard equality with God**
> > **as something to be exploited,**
> **but emptied himself,**
> > **taking the form of a slave,**
> > **being born of human likeness,**
> **And being found in human form,**
> > **he humbled himself**
> > **and became obedient to the point of death—**
> > **even death on a cross.**
> **Therefore God also highly exalted him**
> > **and gave him the name**
> > **that is above every name,**
> **so that at the name of Jesus**
> > **every knee should bend,**
> > **in heaven and on earth and under the earth,**
> **and every tongue should confess**
> > **that Jesus Christ is Lord,**
> > **to the glory of God the Father.**

The sermon text is from the New Testament book of Philippians, ascribed to the apostle Paul (2:5–11). The unusual arrangement of the words indicates that the author is quoting a hymn, one most likely used in early Christian worship. It is an ancient and beautiful text.

It is also a rich theological passage. These words form the basis of the doctrine of kenosis, or the "emptying" of Christ. Jesus surrendered aspects of divinity in order to become human. Although there are many theological complexities regarding this idea, the spiritual intent of the passage moves from the humility of God toward a triumphant Jesus lifted up in glory.

The preacher mounted the pulpit dressed in the scarlet regalia conferred upon him by a prestigious university, thus reminding the audience of his authority to interpret the Bible's deeper meanings. As expected, he spoke of kenosis and humility. But then his tone changed. He told us that the

---

44. Diana Butler Bass, *Christianity After Religion: The End of Church and the Birth of a New Spiritual Awakening* (New York: HarperOne, 2012), 103–136.

word "Lord" used in the passage was the same word used for Caesar in the Roman Empire. Hence, "Jesus Christ is Lord" was to say "Jesus Christ is Caesar." This, of course, is true. He, however, proclaimed that one day Jesus—like Caesar of old—would exert his imperial will across the world and "force every living thing to its knees" to confess his name. At the end of time, God would make everyone worship him, just as everyone subject to Caesar had to pay homage to the Roman emperor—crawling backward to the imperial throne.

He continued likening Jesus to an imperialist warlord whose triumph over recalcitrant sinners, doubters, discontents, and rebels was assured. Emphasizing Jesus's regal glorification, he turned God into a vengeful king out to get those who had killed his son. Oddly enough, his tone was not that of a hellfire-and-brimstone evangelist. Instead, the entire lecture was delivered with stern intellectual certainty and detached professorial authority. "You will confess Jesus is Lord someday," he stated coolly. "Believe and confess this now."

I wanted to run out of the gym. Instead, I quietly slipped from my seat and stood shaking outside on the balcony. A friend, who was equally as distraught, joined me.

"How could he do that?" I exclaimed. "He turned Jesus into Caesar, a hierarchical and tyrannical monster!"

My friend draped her arm around my shoulder and said, "I think that's what he honestly believes. That's what many people believe."

I looked at her and replied hopelessly, "How could I believe that Jesus is like Caesar? That's not my God, and if that's what Christianity is, I don't want any part of it."

The Belief Gap

That sermon marked the moment in which I fell into the belief gap. I may have been walking near the edge for some time, but this sermon pushed me over. What once made sense no longer did. It was not a case of rejecting everything; rather, it was more like seeing from some angle you never imagined. Like slipping off a wet rock and finding yourself in the river rather than above it. There are lots of questions when you slip. Will I stop falling? Will I regain my footing? Will I reach solid ground? Where will the current take me?

That baccalaureate service was twenty years ago. I admit that through the haze of middle-age memory, I cannot recall the preacher's words verbatim. But I remember the increasing alarm I felt as he preached, and I wondered, "Is this what Christians really believe?" At an earlier time in my own life, I would have approved of the professor's sermon. On that evening, however, I heard Jesus presented in a deeply discomforting way, a way that made me understand why others might not like Jesus, embrace Christianity, or want to go to church. Up until then, I could not fathom the hurtful side of Christian faith. It was the first (but it would not be the last) time that I felt horrified by a presentation of Christian doctrine. A gap of belief opened before me. I knew that Christians believed as the professor did, but I just could not believe it anymore myself.

A few months later, I was preaching in a small, rural Lutheran church. The church was charming and old-fashioned, mostly older people with only a few young families; their weekly bulletin announced a quilting bee and plans for members to pave the parking lot the next Saturday. About seventy people gathered for church in a cozy sanctuary where we listened to the Bible being read and sang hymns together. After my sermon, we all shared a potluck lunch. A young woman sat next to me and shared her story of being in the belief gap.

She was a student at the nearby university, one of the only young and single members of the church. "I love this congregation," she said. "The people have become my family." She paused, and her voice dropped to a confessional whisper. "But I don't know what to say to my classmates when they ask me what I believe. Whenever I say 'I believe in Christianity,' they look at me as if I'm crazy. Besides, I don't even know if I believe 'in' Christianity or Lutheran doctrine or anything like that. I just experience how to love God and how God loves me through these people, by learning how to quilt and singing these hymns. I don't know what to call it, but it is less about believing and more about living. Does that still count as being Christian?"

Her confession remained with me, because it was one of the first gap stories that anyone shared with me. In the two decades since, the gap has widened, and the confessional whisper is gone. The gap is everywhere, and people are not afraid to share the news. On November 9, 2010, I was sitting at O'Hare airport and opened *USA Today*. A large advertisement trumpeted the gap:

> What some believe: "A woman should learn in quietness and full submission. I do not permit a woman to teach or to have authority over a man; she must be silent" (1 Timothy 2). What humanists think: "The rights of men and women should be equal and sacred" (Robert Ingersoll).

It was an ad for an atheist group. Between the time of the student's confession and that November day, hundreds of people have trusted me with their stories of not believing—not believing that wives must submit to their husbands, not believing in the virgin birth, not believing in an inerrant Bible, not believing in hell, not believing that Jesus is the only way to salvation, not believing that only one religion is true, not believing that the institutional church is important, not believing in Jesus, not believing in the resurrection, not believing that God cares or heals or loves, not believing that God exists. They don't believe in Christianity anymore. When many people slip from believing into not believing, they find it difficult to regain their footing. Maybe because they are trying to climb back on the same rock. Or maybe because they know they cannot go back to the path that landed them in the drink in the first place.

Despite the differences of detail in testimonies, almost all of them share an important assumption about belief. "Belief" is the intellectual content of faith. Typically, belief entails some sort of list—a rehearsal of ideas about God, Jesus, salvation, and the church. What to believe? If I am slipping, do I hold on tighter or let go? If I no longer believe, am I still a Christian? Am I spiritual, but not religious? An agnostic? An atheist?

Belief, especially Christian belief, has entered a critical stage in Western society. Masses of people now reject belief. For many centuries, Christians have equated faith with belief. Being faithful meant that one accepted certain ideas about God and Jesus, especially as articulated in creedal statements. Denominations specified what adherents must believe about the sacraments, salvation, and authority. Confirmation in faith entailed memorization and recitation of doctrine or facts about the Bible. Some groups even insisted that true Christians must further believe particular ideas about drinking, women, science, the end times, or politics. Layers of beliefs, stacked through the centuries from the apostles to our own times. Alongside this weighty pile of beliefs, it often seems as if Christians actually live their beliefs less—beliefs like "God is love" or "Blessed are the peacemakers" or "Love your neighbor as yourself"—thus leading to often heard charges of hypocrisy.

With this accretion of beliefs, a corresponding incredulity spread through Western culture, leading to doctrinal boredom, skepticism, agnosticism, and atheism. As science, history, and psychology offered ever more sophisticated understandings of the universe and human experience, some Christians became increasingly hostile to secular knowledge, building museums to creationism, proclaiming that America is a Christian nation, and excommunicating those who would question the existence of hell. Put simply, as they reacted to unbelief, certain Christians asked for more belief about increasingly unbelievable things.

Meanwhile, other Christians began to wonder if belief was even the point. At the college where the professor who delivered the baccalaureate sermon taught, for example, the majority of younger faculty signed the institution's doctrinal statement with crossed fingers and a knowing wink to their friends, telling sympathetic souls that they "agreed in spirit" with the statement, even if the exact words rang hollow. Eventually, they revised their statement of faith to be more open and inclusive. It is not only the case that the Western world has grown weary of doctrine, but that Christianity itself is changing—shifting away from being a belief-centered religion toward an experiential faith.

Many philosophers, scholars, and theologians have explored the shift in Western culture away from beliefs toward experience, a move from rationalism toward practice. Harvey Cox proposed that Christianity reflects this broader transformation regarding human knowledge and experience by dividing church history into three ages: the Age of Faith, the Age of Belief, and the Age of the Spirit. During the first period, roughly from the time of Jesus to 400 CE, Christianity was understood as a way of life based upon faith (i.e., trust) in Jesus. Or, as Cox states, "To be a Christian meant to live in his Spirit, embrace his hope, and to follow him in the work that he had begun." Between 300 and 400, however, this dynamic sense of living in Jesus was displaced by an increasing emphasis on creeds and beliefs, leading Professor Cox to claim that this tendency increased until nascent beliefs "thickened into catechisms, replacing faith *in* Jesus with tenets *about* him. . . . From an energetic movement of faith [Christianity] coagulated into a phalanx of required beliefs."[45] Cox argues that the Age of Belief lasted some fifteen centuries and began to give way around 1900, its demise increasing in speed and urgency through the twentieth century. We have now entered into a new phase of Christian history, which he calls the Age of the Spirit.

If the Age of Faith was a time of "faith *in* Jesus" and the Age of Belief a period of "belief *about* Christ," the Age of the Spirit is best understood as a Christianity based in an "experience *of* Jesus." The Age of the Spirit is nondogmatic, noninstitutional, and nonhierarchical Christianity, based on a person's connection to the "volatile expression" of God's Spirit through mystery, wonder, and awe. "Faith is resurgent," Cox claims, "while dogma is dying. The spiritual, communal, and justice-seeking dimensions of Christianity are now its leading edge. . . . A religion based on subscribing to mandatory beliefs is no longer viable."[46] When questioned by an interviewer about his thesis, Cox further explained:

> What I see, and what a lot of others see too, is that people frequently want to refer to themselves now as not really "religious," but "spiritual." I used to be very suspicious of that. But I began asking questions and finding out what the dimensions of the term are. . . . What I think it really means is that people want to have access to the sacred without going through institutional and doctrinal scaffolding. They want a more direct experience of God and Spirit. And I don't think it's really going to go away. This is an increasing tendency across the board.[47]

Accordingly, Christianity is moving from being a religion about God to being an experience of God. In a real sense, both the baccalaureate speaker and the student questioning her faith at the Lutheran church I preached at were right. The professor's world of "belief about" God was eroding, leading him to reassert ideas he believed necessary to faith; and the student's intuition regarding an experiential future has been coming to pass, leading her to question the older definitions of "Christian." Although I have no idea what happened to the young woman, the professor has called for a new fundamentalism, writing books that few people read, arguing that what is old is better, and defending narrow understandings of belief and piety, something

---

45. Harvey Cox, *The Future of Faith: The Rise and Fall of Beliefs and the Coming Age of the Spirit* (San Francisco: HarperOne, 2009), 5–6.

46. Ibid., 213, 221.

47. Nathan Schneider, "Age of Spirit: An Interview with Harvey Cox," October 30, 2009, blogs.ssrc.org/tif/2009/10/30/age-of-spirit-an-interview-with-harvey-cox

clearly evident in his sermon two decades ago. If one believes that Christianity is about belief, taking refuge in fundamentalism is logical. On the face of things, it sometimes seems as if fundamentalism may be the only vibrant form of faith. As Harvey Cox argues, however, "Fundamentalisms, with their insistence on obligatory belief systems, their nostalgia for a mythical uncorrupted past, their claims to an exclusive grasp on truth . . . are turning out to be rearguard attempts to stem a more sweeping tidal change."[48] The professor's "Jesus/Caesar" was like Romulus Augustus, the last ruler of a collapsing Roman Empire.

The Religious Question: What Do I Believe?

Despite such obvious changes, most religious institutions act as if the gap does not exist and that the questions have not substantially changed in recent decades. Conservative or liberal, evangelical or mainline, Protestant or Catholic, denominations and churches still provide answers to questions *about* God. Most assume that dogma and doctrine are the right approach to holy matters, differing only on the details of their preferred answers. Religion answers *what* questions: What should one believe? What do Christians believe?

This is bad news for Christianity. The *what* questions are the very questions causing people to slip into the gap. Doctrine is seen as not only divisive, but as contrary to the message Jesus himself taught. Many people stumble on the creeds, thinking them to be a sort of doctrinal test for church membership, and are unable to recite them in full or even part. As a pastor asked me, "Can we stop reciting the creed now? I'm tired of it driving people away from church." Theologian Dwight Friesen puts it bluntly—and speaks for many—when he says that Jesus had no interest in orthodoxy, but rather offered his followers "a full and flourishing human life."[49] At an event I was leading recently, an Episcopal priest inquired, with a sense of hopeful anticipation, "Isn't it true that belief-oriented faith is disappearing?" His colleague chimed in, "My generation doesn't really care about doctrine; that's just not the way we think." Indeed, even among Christians, there is a sense of mild relief, maybe even quiet jubilation, that the Age of Belief is giving way to something else.

The erosion of belief has occasioned many a new jeremiad from those who, like the professor, feel threatened by the current situation. The college faculty who fudge the truth about the doctrinal statement or the clergy who wish they could get rid of creeds are, both in my experience and as surveys seem to point out, fairly typical. Yet they fear someone finding out—that they might lose their jobs in religious institutions that continue to mark

---

48. Cox, *Future of Faith*, 2.

49. Dwight Friesen, "Orthoparadoxy: Emerging Hope for Embracing Difference," in Doug Pagitt and Tony Jones, eds., *An Emergent Manifesto of Hope* (Grand Rapids, MI: Baker, 2007), 204.

their boundaries with such beliefs *about* God. It is not only loss of employment or community that they fear, but the cultural ridicule that comes upon people pondering such questions. The media scorn them as "cafeteria Christians" and "spiritual consumers" who pick and choose what they like about faith, while conservative pastors accuse them of vacuity and spiritual shallowness and use them as scapegoats for all that is wrong in religion.

It may be easy to dismiss anxiety about belief as anti-intellectualism or as a theological problem associated with Western religious decline. But something else is at work. On the face of it, *what* questions should be benign. After all, *what* is a fairly objective question, a request that seeks information. "What time is it?" "What color is the sky?" "What day does school start?" "What would you like for dinner tonight?" Even more philosophical questions, like "What is art?" or "What do you want to do with your life?" assume a well-formed opinion, if not a conclusive answer.

During the last few centuries, to ask "What do you believe?" in the religious realm was to demand intellectual answers about things that cannot be comprehended entirely by the mind. Thus masked as objective truth, religion increasingly became a matter of opinion, personal taste, individual interpretation, and wishful thinking. People became quite militant about the answers they liked the best. The *what* questions often divided families and neighbors into rival churches, started theological quarrels, initiated inquisitions, fueled political and social conflict, and led, on occasion, to one losing one's head.

It's time to face up to the truth: an increasingly large number of people are experiencing the *what* questions in profoundly negative ways. In the minds of many, dogma deserves to die.

SPIRITUAL QUESTION I:
How Do I Believe?

"You're a Christian?" quizzed my acquaintance. "How do you believe in that? I don't know how I could ever believe that."

Belief is not going to disappear, and it will not become a relic of the religious past. Rather, as religion gives way to spirituality, the question of belief shifts from *what* to *how*. People generally assume that they know the *what* of religion. For example, they may know that Christians believe that Jesus died and was raised, that Jews believe that Moses freed the slaves from Egypt, or that Buddhists believe that the Buddha achieved Enlightenment. Indeed, in many years of discussing faith in public, few have ever asked me, "What do Christians believe?" *What* is not the issue—the world of religion is a world full of *what*. Instead, they have asked *how*. Belief questions have become, "How do you believe?" "How could I ever believe?" "How does this make sense?" "How would believing this make my life different?" or "How would this change the world?"

How differs from *what*. "How do I get to your house?" "How would that move change my family's life?" "How do I love?" *How* is the interrogator of direction, of doing, of curiosity, of process, of learning, of living. When we ask *how*, we are not asking for a fact, conclusion, or opinion. Rather, we are seeking a hands-on deeper knowledge of the thing–a neighborhood or city, a craft or recipe, an open possibility, an idea, a sense of ourselves or of a relationship. *How* moves us around in the question. Instead of being above the information, giving an expert opinion about something, *how* weaves our lives with the information as we receive, review, reflect, and act upon what we sought. *How* provides actionable information; we can choose to act upon the answer or not, and we choose the extent of our action. *How* is a question of meaning and purpose that pushes people into a deeper engagement in the world, rather than memorizing facts. Parker Palmer refers to the shift from *what* to *how* as part of the "inner search" that enables individuals to develop the "habits of the heart" necessary to forming both a grounded moral life and a caring community. He asserts that inner-life questions are the sort of questions Americans ask most regularly, and the *how* questions are the ones our schools and churches often fail to address. Institutions cannot "dictate" answers to *how* questions. Instead, spiritual communities must open space to engage the inner search: "*How can I connect with something larger than my own ego?*" This, Palmer insists, involves going "beyond teaching the *what* of things into the labor-intensive process of teaching the *how* of things."[50]

From *what* to *how* is a shift from information *about* to experience *of*. *What* is a conventional religious question, one of dogma and doctrine; how is an emerging spiritual question, one of experience and connection. We have lived through many generations of *what* and have nearly exhausted ourselves by doing so. But *how* opens the question of belief anew: How do I believe? How do we believe? How does belief make a difference? How is the world transformed by believing? Belief will not entirely go away. Rather, "believing *about*" appears to be going away. Belief itself is being enfolded into a new spiritual awareness as belief questions morph from *what* to *how*, from seeking information about God to nurturing experience of the divine.

SPIRITUAL QUESTION 2:
Who Do I Believe?

Several years ago, I asked students in a seminary class a question: "To whom do you turn when you have an ethical or spiritual concern?" One quickly said, "I ask my friends." Another laughed, saying, "I ask Google." For the next few minutes, they came up with a variety of answers, mostly those involving personal relationships, the media, or the Internet. Interestingly enough, none of these future pastors said that they asked a bishop, priest, or seminary professor about their religious questions, much less read a book of canon law or turned to a creed.

---

50. This paragraph follows the argument laid out by Parker J. Palmer, *Healing the Heart of Democracy: The Courage to Create a Politics Worthy of the Human Spirit* (San Francisco: Jossey-Bass, 2011), 119–150.

The question is, of course, a question of religious authority. Who provides trustworthy answers to difficult questions? Once upon a time, Americans would have deferred to the clergy, a teacher, or a parent on issues of belief. When it comes to questions of meaning and purpose, however, it no longer seems adequate to say, "The church teaches," "Christians have always believed," or "the Bible said it, so I believe it." External authorities do not carry the weight they once did. Thus, questions of belief have not only morphed from *what* to *how*, but they necessarily include the secondary dimension of *who*. My seminary students did not look to conventional institutional authorities for answers. Instead, they looked to relationships and online sources and social networks. Who is trustworthy in the search for meaning?

As the question of *how* is experiential, so is the question of *who*. In the early twenty-first century, trustworthiness is not simply a matter of an expert who holds a degree or a certain role in an institution. Rather, authority springs from two sources: one, relationship, and two, authenticity. People trust those with whom they are friends or feel they could be friends—thus the presidential election question, "With which candidate would you rather have a beer?" Authority comes through connection, personal investment, and communal accountability, rather than submission to systems or structures of expertise. Related closely to friendship is the test of authenticity. Something is true and trustworthy because it springs from good motives and praiseworthy intentions, with results that prove to increase happiness and make peoples' lives better. Practicing what one preaches is a mark of spiritual truth, and humanity and humility foster trust. Although certain people will always hanker for authoritarian or charismatic leaders, there is a much broader longing for authentic leaders in these times—those whose message and actions validate their deepest beliefs. In the emerging spiritual culture, *what* matters much less than who is sharing the news, and the messenger has become the message.

This is a very interesting development in terms of faith. After all, Christians, Jews, and Muslims consider God to be personal and truthful, the Messenger of Good News to humankind. Thus, religious organizations, ordained leaders, and conventional creeds recede in importance as mediators in favor of direct friendship with God through prayer and discernment as means to spiritual understanding. Friendship with God can be mystical and individual, but it is also communal and corporate—every major faith asserts that friendship with God is strengthened through friendship with our neighbor. Ultimately, spiritual authority rests in the voice of God, the voices of community, and in our own voices. It is a harder path to hear answers than to ask someone to give us an answer, but it is the path that many people have embarked upon.

Spiritual Insight: Belief as Experience

As demonstrated in the polling data, about 9 percent of Americans understand themselves as "religious" only. They are probably still greatly concerned with the *what* of faith. About a third of Americans describe themselves as "spiritual" only. They have embarked on a quest of *how* to relate to transcendent things. But half of all Americans claim to be "spiritual and religious." For them, *what* is not necessarily being replaced by *how*; the *what* of religion is being redefined by the *how*. When belief springs from and is rewoven with experience, we arrive at the territory of being spiritual and religious: experiential belief.

Understanding belief-as-experience is not a new concept. Actually, it is much closer to the original definition of believing than the popular definitions we have inherited from more recent centuries. In his essay "Believing: An Historical Perspective" (first published in 1977), Wilfred Cantwell Smith argues for a distinction between "faith" and "belief" based upon the etymologies of the terms. Although the words overlapped at one time, he says, the "English word 'believe' has, in usage, connotation, and denotation, undergone an arresting transformation" in recent centuries—one that has had an unprecedented negative impact on Western religious life.[51]

"To believe" in Latin (the shaping language for much of Western theological thought) is *opinor, opinari*, meaning "opinion," which was not typically a religious word. Instead, Latin used *credo*, "I set my heart upon" or "I give my loyalty to," as the word to describe religious "believing," that is, "faith." In medieval English, the concept of *credo* was translated as "believe," meaning roughly the same thing as its German cousin *belieben*, "to prize, treasure, or hold dear," which comes from the root word *Liebe*, "love."[52] Thus, in early English, to "believe" was to "belove" something or someone as an act of trust or loyalty. Belief was not an intellectual opinion. As Smith says:

> The affirmation "I believe in God" used to mean: "Given the reality of God as a fact of the universe, I hereby pledge to Him my heart and soul. I committedly opt to live in loyalty to Him.". . . Today the statement may be taken by some as meaning: "Given the uncertainty as to whether there be a God or not, as a fact of modern life, I announce that my opinion is 'yes.' I judge God to be existent."[53]

In previous centuries, belief had nothing to do with one's weighing of evidence or intellectual choice. Belief was not a doctrinal test. Instead, belief

---

51. Wilfred Cantwell Smith, *Believing: An Historical Perspective* (Oxford: One World, 1998), 40. First published as *Belief and History* (Charlottsville: Univ. of Virginia Press, 1977), Marcus Borg has written about the shift of the language of belief. See his *The Heart of Christianity: Rediscovering a Life of Faith* (San Francisco: HarperOne, 2003), chapter 2, 26–42; and *Speaking Christian*, chapter 10.

52. Ibid., 41.

53. Ibid., 44

was more like a marriage vow—"I do" as a pledge of faithfulness and loving service to and with the other. Indeed, in early English usage, you could not hold, claim, or possess a belief about God, but you could cherish, love, trust in, or devote yourself to God.

From a historical perspective, the misidentification of faith-as-experience and belief-as-opinion also involved the translation of the Bible from Greek (the other theology-shaping language of Christian thought) into English. In Greek, there is a verb for the experience of beloving God: "to faith" (i.e., *pist*-). In English, however, "faith" is a noun and not a verb. With no equivalent active word, English translators rendered the Greek verb "to faith" in English as "to believe." The verb "to believe" (meaning "to belove, prize, or treasure," as explained above) appears frequently in the English Bible. It typically occurs without a direct object, in the forms "I believe" or "I believe you" (or "him," "her," or "God"). This reinforces its original meaning of "belove" as a general confession of trust or a specific disposition of trusting someone—it is a personal and relational action initiated by love. In only 12 percent of scriptural cases does "to believe" appear as "I believe that. . . ," an impersonal affirmation about something.

To read the Bible with this understanding orients our attention away from cognitive speculation about God toward the state and direction of our hearts. For example, John 3: 16 might be the most well-known Bible verse across North America as a result of signs held up by evangelistically minded Christians at sporting events: "For God so loved the world that he gave his only Son, so that everyone who believes in him won't perish, but will have eternal life" (CEB). If we think that "believe" means doctrinal truth, then the verse means "everyone who agrees that Jesus is the Son of God won't perish" or "everyone who thinks that Jesus is the Second Person of the Trinity won't perish." According to its more ancient rendering, however, the verse would better read, "everyone who trusts in Jesus" or "everyone who directs his or her heart toward Jesus" will not perish. You may or not may want to trust in or incline your love toward Jesus, but it is an entirely different, and more spiritually compelling, invitation than an offer of debate about Jesus. And it is a fresh way of understanding a widely misused text.

Smith demonstrates how belief shifted away from "trusting the beloved" toward being a word that is "increasingly technocratic and thing-oriented," outside the realm of personal relationships.[54] The shift occurred gradually in the eighteenth century, mostly through the work of the influential philosopher David Hume. When people use the word "believe" today, it is often for factually erroneous opinions, disconnected from any aspect of interpersonal trust or love: "I believe that dinosaurs walked the earth at the same time as human beings," or "I don't believe in global warming." No wonder people can no longer "believe" in Christianity. For masses of contemporary people, to believe in Christianity is like believing in aliens or that President Obama

---

54. Ibid., 58.

was born in Kenya, since "the word [belief] denotes doubt, and connotes falsehood."[55] Thus, Smith claims, "The idea that believing is religiously important turns out to be a modern idea. . . . [A] great modern heresy of the Church is the heresy of believing. Not of believing this or that, but of believing as such."[56] Christianity was never intended to be a system or structure of belief in the modern sense; it originated as a disposition of the heart.

From an ancient perspective—whether of Latin or Greek, of the creeds or the Christian scriptures—the words "belief" and "believing" implicitly carried within them relational and lived dimensions.

Accordingly, you cannot "believe" distinct from trust, loyalty, and love. Wilfred Cantwell Smith, analyzing this history some forty years ago, had a dim view of the future of belief. He writes:

> The English "belief," which used to be the verbal sign designating allegiance, loyalty, integrity, love, commitment, trust, and entrusting, and the capacity to perceive and to respond to transcendent qualities in oneself and one's environment—in short, faith; the Christian form of God's most momentous gift to each person—has come to be the term by which we designate rather a series of dubious, or at best problematic, propositions.[57]

Smith clearly wished this were not the case, but held little hope that it might change.

A surprising thing has happened, however. In those same forty years, in some quarters at least, there has been a return to the older understanding of belief-as-trust. Half of the American population now claims to have had "a mystical experience," a statistic that suggests we are in the process of returning to the idea of faith as an encounter with God. As religion in the modern sense fails, we appear to be busily restitching the ancient fabric of belief. It seems we may have entered a new (or perhaps very old) theological door, the way of experiential belief.

Spiritual and Religious: Experiential Belief

The Priority of Experience. I spend most of my work time with mainline, liberal, and progressive Protestants, religious groups with high educational attainments and little patience for faith without reason. They are doubters and skeptics (that is, indeed, their spiritual gift) and downright skittish regarding experience. Despite the fact that many of them share the cultural anxiety about the creeds (worrying that the creeds are not factually true), they are not entirely comfortable with the shift toward experiential faith either. Put the words "experiential" and "belief" in the same sentence, and you are asking for trouble.

---

55. Ibid., 65.
56. Ibid., v.
57. Ibid., 69.

At a United Church of Christ clergy education day, I explained Harvey Cox's chronology, saying: "Professor Cox argues that the 'Age of the Spirit' began around the turn of the twentieth century with the modern Pentecostalism movement. That was the first expression of the turn toward experience." Silence filled the room.

Then one pastor said, "You mean we're all going to become Pentecostals? My congregation would rather die first! Faith isn't about feelings. It has to have intellectual content."

Her reaction is not unique. When Americans think about religious experience, the first thing that often comes to mind is some form of religious enthusiasm—a fulminating revivalist, a frenzied faith healer, or a fainting congregant. A significant tension in American religious identity is shaped by two enduring images—one, the orderly parish church, and the other, the exuberant tent meeting. Since the First Great Awakening, Americans have often felt forced to choose: the pew or the anxious bench, the prayer book or the praise chorus, restraint or revival, mind or heart? Or, as one of my Facebook correspondents bemoaned, "Why is it that the choice among churches always seems to be the choice between intelligence on ice and ignorance on fire?"

Religious experience and the Spirit are often associated with Pentecostalism, the global form of Christianity that emphasizes the work of the Holy Spirit in and through religious ecstasy, miraculous gifts, and healing. In the 1880s and 1890s, an intense and radical form of evangelical religion took hold in the form of healing revivals and holiness meetings emphasizing the power of the "Holy Ghost baptism." On January 1, 1901, Agnes Ozman, a Topeka Bible school student, prayed to receive the gift of the Holy Spirit. After her friends laid hands on her to pray, she began to speak in tongues—thus began the modern Pentecostal movement.

An African-American evangelist named William Seymour heard Agnes's story and embraced the new teaching. He moved in 1906 from the American heartland to Los Angeles, where his preaching sparked the Azusa Street revival and thence spread around the world.[58] For Pentecostals, the experience of speaking in tongues validated and confirmed true faith and empowered believers to do God's will. For them, faith, feeling, action, and experience were a tightly woven cloth of Christian life, the threads of which could not be pulled apart. This experiential rendering of faith made sense to the poor, the deprived, working-class people, and rising middle-class folks, many of whom felt marginalized by liberal elites and their restrained religion. In Pentecostalism, many outsiders discovered a new sense of self and God and a sort of spiritual land of opportunity. By the end of the century, Pentecostalism had given birth to scores of new denominations, claiming hundreds of millions of adherents in nearly every country on earth.

Pentecostalism developed, however, within a larger historical context—one increasingly fascinated with the territory of human and divine experience.

---

58. Grant Wacker, *Heaven Below: Early Pentecostals and American Culture* (Cambridge, MA: Harvard Univ. Press 2001), 4.

Grant Wacker, a leading expert on Pentecostal history, points out the similarities between Pentecostalism, Protestant liberalism, and Roman Catholicism at the turn of the twentieth century. Despite the "vast gulf" between Pentecostals and liberals, Wacker suggests that both traditions emphasize "the nearness and salvific power of God's Spirit in history," while Roman Catholics "evince unprecedented interest in the Holy Spirit's sanctifying presence."[59] As the "Age of the Spirit" dawned, radical evangelicals, liberal Protestants, and Roman Catholics alike were caught up in a quest for transforming religious experience–they wanted to know how God's Spirit made a difference in their lives and the world around them.

This was certainly fostered by a more general, and even secular, impulse toward understanding the nature of human behavior–how experiences molded human personality, thought, and action and how personality, thought, and action were shaped by experience. As the Pentecostal movement began in the early years of the twentieth century, Sigmund Freud published the first of his books exploring the connection between conscious and unconscious experience and its relationship to human development.

With enthusiastic Pentecostals on one side and secular Freud on the other, liberal Protestants also opened up issues of religious experience as a way to protest spiritual ennui in organized religion. The most influential of these was American Transcendentalism, a movement that appeared some fifty years before Pentecostalism and Freud, replete with its rejection of church in favor of nature mysticism, poetry, and spiritual solitude. Although not every Protestant embraced Transcendentalism, the movement created a yeasty spiritual environment in which experiential religion could eventually grow. By the time Protestant liberalism emerged in the late 1800s, its most thoughtful proponents argued that experience was central to vital faith.

The insight regarding experience was partly the result of the American religious environment and partly the result of the theological influence of the first liberal Protestant theologian, Friedrich Schleiermacher, who wrote:

> Religion is the outcome neither of the fear of death, nor of the fear of God. It answers a deep need in man. It is neither a metaphysic, nor a morality, but above all and essentially an intuition and a feeling. . . . Dogmas are not, properly speaking, part of religion: rather it is that they are derived from it. Religion is the miracle of direct relationship with the infinite; and dogmas are the reflection of this miracle.[60]

There are many ways to criticize Schleiermacher, but if you read these words simply and directly, you intuit that there is something to them. Religion is not its accretions of dogma; rather, faith is a divine encounter. Experience needed to be the starting place to engage a skeptical,

---

59. Wacker, *Heaven Below*, 4.

60. Friedrich Schleiermacher, *Addresses on Religious Experience* (1799), quoted in Kedourie, Elie, *Nationalism* Praeger University Series, 1961, 26.

dogma-weary world. Belief is "derived" from a "direct relationship with the infinite." Beliefs gain credibility insofar as they spring from rightly directed human experience.

William James wrote of this impulse in his *Varieties of Religious Experience* in 1902, an essay on the "feelings, acts, and experiences of individual men in their solitude, so far as they apprehend themselves to stand in relation to whatever they may consider the divine."[61] James discussed saints and mysticism and philosophy. In the end, James concluded that religious experience is useful even if not provable. Experiences connect human beings with an "altogether other dimension of existence" and enable people to live more meaningful lives.[62]

Thus, at the beginning of the twentieth century, Pentecostalism and liberal Protestantism—as well as various streams of mystical Catholicism—came together in a quest for an experience of God. The Age of the Spirit dawned not only with Pentecostal fervor, but experiential faith also arrived with the reflections of William James at Harvard and in the candle-lit prayer of Roman Catholics to their saints. And it was not only Christians exploring the realm of the Spirit—restless seekers appeared across the landscape with new spiritual practices and formed new communities.[63] These groups competed with each other, to be sure, and often did not think the adherents of other ways would find salvation. But they all shared the traits of experiential belief—a practical spirituality that transformed beliefs about God into a living relationship with the divine. The impulse toward experience grew, developed, and deepened throughout the twentieth century, leading to increasing awareness that the nature of Christianity itself was changing. Mysticism and religious experience were no longer limited to a spiritual elite in a monastery or a forest cabin. As once predicted by the ancient Hebrew prophet Joel, the Spirit was poured out on all flesh (2:28).

The Need for Reason. "But anyone can have a religious experience," protested a minister during a question-and-answer discussion. "The members of the Taliban have religious experiences; Hitler might have had mystical experiences. Experience can't be the basis for religion, because you can't say what counts as a valid experience. Creeds and doctrine have to be the test."

Experiential religion is not a new phenomenon; it is an ancient one. And the question as to the validity of religious experience is about as ancient as the experiences themselves. Although many people in a tribe may have had spiritual experiences, only one arose as the shaman or wise woman. Thus, even primitive people recognized that some religious experiences were more profound than others and set up authorities to help others achieve certain kinds of experiences. People adjudicated between experiences, discerning

---

61. William James, *Varieties of Religious Experience* (London, New York, and Bombay: Longmans, Green, 1911), 31.

62. James, *Varieties of Religious Experience*, 515.

63. Leigh Schmidt, *Restless Souls: The Making of American Spirituality* (San Francisco: Harper San Francisco, 2005), 170–171.

which ones nurtured the tribe and which ones might not foster group prosperity. Meaningful religious experiences were shared through story and ritual in an attempt to enable other people to participate in a sense of the divine. Occasionally, an independent mystic would challenge the authority of established religious leaders or rituals by claiming a new experience, leading the tribe to either accept the new insights or reject the messenger. History is rife with accounts of experiential religious figures facing the wrath of institutional doubters—Jesus, Joan of Arc, and Oscar Romero, to name only a very few.

Although Western Christianity turned toward the rational and away from the mystical in the seventeenth and eighteenth centuries, the question of religious experience actually remained important. In the 1740s, a group of religious protesters called "evangelicals" argued against established Christians by claiming that an experience of being "born again" was necessary to faith. Their experiential religion wreaked havoc in English and colonial churches, where revivalists interrupted worship services, led people to psychological breakdowns, and undermined the social order. Women preachers and unlettered male evangelists roamed the land and stirred up the religious rabble, inciting everyone to believe that their experiences of God were equal to any theological insight proclaimed by the educated clergy. In the midst of revival fervor, Jonathan Edwards, a philosopher and pastor deeply shaped by an experience of God, tried to discern true religious affections from delusion.

Edwards condemned both intellectualism and emotionalism in religion, arguing instead that "true religion, in great part, consists in holy affections." Although some of his learned colleagues said that "affections" were "inferior animal passions," Edwards oriented true religion toward what he called "the heart," a unitary faculty of will and love. "The Holy Scriptures do everywhere place religion very much in the affections," he wrote, "such as fear, hope, love, hatred, desire, joy, sorrow, gratitude, compassion and zeal."[64] Affections were not only emotions, however. Affections were the capacity of the heart willing and acting upon that which was good or generous or lovely. How is one's will directed toward beauty? Edwards insisted that true religious experience emanated from a divine source that opened human beings to sensing the unity of God's love and beauty in all things. Put simply, human beings apprehend the spiritual dimension of the universe from beyond themselves through a transformative experience of what Edwards called "a divine and supernatural light."

The experience of divine light reshaped men and women in the virtues of humility, mercy, and justice. An experience of the divine leads people toward greater "tenderness of spirit. . . and a readiness to esteem others better than themselves."[65] True religious experience manifested itself in "beautiful symmetry and proportion" in one's character. Edwards argued that this

---

64. George Marsden, *Jonathan Edwards: A Life* (New Haven, CT: Yale Univ. Press, 2003), 285.
65. Ibid., 284.

culminated in a well-ordered and disciplined life: "Gracious and holy affections have their exercise and fruit in Christian practice."[66]

Of his own argument, Edwards claimed, "As that is called experimental philosophy, which brings opinion and notions to the test of fact; so is that properly called experimental religion, which bring religious affections and intentions to like test."[67] Edwards may sound like a rationalist here, as if he needed a scientific experiment to prove the goodness of religious experience. What counted as evidence for Edwards? The quality of one's life. Quite simply, truthful religious experience started with the affections and deepened one's character, one's love of God, and service to neighbor; it unified and balanced head and heart. In turn, the movement toward love served as the test for valid religious experience. Spiritual experience initiates the well-lived life; the well-lived life confirms the nature of one's spiritual experience.

Jonathan Edwards was both a mystic and a philosopher. At the time he lived, it was fashionable to speak of the "beauty of reason." For vast numbers of Christians, reason was an experience, and it was a powerful, life-changing one at that. Although difficult to remember now, *reason* had not yet hardened into *rationalism*. Reason was a capacity of deep understanding, not a set of opinions; it was a journey, a practice, and an inner adventure of soul, not a finished philosophical or theological product.

European Christianity was just moving out of a time when religious passion had resulted in schism, excommunications, exile, witch hunts, inquisitions, and wars of religion. Critical thought provided welcome relief from religious excess; reason, thankfully, muted the fervor of theological hubris and wild spiritual speculations. Reason was the gift of individuals to think for themselves, the ability to judge rightly, to make good choices. Reason sowed seeds of freedom and human rights. It was the philosophical twin of political democracy and the economic engine of an emerging middle class.

Reason did not oppose religion or religious experience. Rather, reason softened religion's sharp edges by providing balance, harmony, and order in a supernatural world too often ruled by a seemingly capricious God. Reason was beautiful. And it was mystical. Literature is full of accounts of people transformed by words, ideas, and books—as a growing industry of popular novels taught both men and women that logic and literacy opened the way to full humanity. Priests and professors wore the same garb; the church and the college embraced a common mission. In early modern depictions of reason, angels often accompany reason, crowning it with laurels of wisdom and justice. Often personified as a god or goddess, reason bestowed divine gifts on humankind. Indeed, people were tempted to worship reason as she had opened for them a new way of understanding themselves and ordering society.

Our own age has conflicted views of reason, because we understand its limits, feel its inhumane touch, and doubt the power of pure reason to solve

---

66. Ibid., 288.
67. Ibid., 288.

our problems (indeed, we have witnessed how it has created quite a few). Long gone are the angels casting crowns; we now speak of the overly rational as "cold and calculating," possessed of "unyielding logic," people who "follow their ideas to the bitter end." As a result, education is devalued, and anti-intellectualism has taken hold. Experts are eyed with suspicion. Those who care about facts are derided as part of a "reality-based community." People make decisions "from their gut" or opine that something "just felt right" as they appeal to experience as the arbiter of personal, professional, and political choices. As our own age turns toward the authority of experience, it is good to remember that reason is not bad. Reason is part of human experience, often considered a reflection of God's image in humankind. To be spiritual *and* religious is to call for a new wholeness of experience and reason, to restitch experience with human wisdom and to renew reason through an experience of awe. Thus, the path of Christian faith in a postreligious age must be that of experiential belief in which the heart takes the lead in believing. As Parker Palmer writes,

> "Heart" comes from the Latin *cor* and points not merely to our emotions but to the core of the self, that center place where all of our ways of knowing converge—intellectual, emotional, sensory, intuitive, imaginative, experiential, relational, and bodily, among others. The heart is where we integrate what we know in our minds with what we know in our bones, the place where our knowledge can become more fully human.[68]

Experiential belief is integrated belief, that which brings back together capacities of knowing that modernity ripped apart. It is only in the territory of the heart where faith makes sense.

The Creed Revisited

More than a decade ago, I was part of an Episcopal congregation that loved asking questions. Indeed, many people made their way to that particular church because the community valued questions. We felt free to question everything—the creeds, the prayers, the scriptures. A member once moaned to me, "I just wish we could get everyone together on this monotheism thing."

On another occasion, we were having an argument about the resurrection, whether or not it had happened and whether or not it could be proved. One of my friends shared the story of how she had asked a liberal bishop if he actually believed in the resurrection. "Believe it?" he answered incredulously. "I've seen it too many times not to!"

The question "Do you believe in the resurrection?" often results in long, often tedious, explanations of creeds and councils, of texts and evidence, of arguments about historic and scientific facts and in disputes between liberals

---

68. Palmer, *Healing the Heart of Democracy*, 6.

and conservatives. Few, however, stop and ask what the real question might be. The question is not "What do you believe about the resurrection?" The question is simpler and more profound: "Do you trust in the resurrection?" The bishop was not interested in a doctrinal test, proving a historical event that happened many years ago. He believed—that is, he trusted and was loyal to—the resurrection, because he had witnessed it himself. "Do you trust in the resurrection?" is a much harder question than "Do you believe that Jesus was historically and scientifically raised from the dead?"

The bishop was pointing toward the same sort of belief that Jonathan Edwards suggested in the eighteenth century. He pushed the question out of the realm of scientific speculation toward experiential validation: How does the resurrection make things different in a discernable, practical way here and now in our lives, in our communities? Anyone can believe that a resurrection happened; the real question is whether one trusts the resurrection. The test for the bishop, as for Edwards, was a transformed heart and ethical action.

The bishop, however, pushed it one step farther than Edwards. Edwards was attempting to validate spiritual experience by appealing to the affections, but the bishop was trying to explain a theological idea, a classical Christian belief appealing to the heart. Edwards would have thought the resurrection a fact of history, one that needed little or no validation or explanation. It simply was. The bishop, however, lived in radically different times—when only a few question spiritual experience, but many question Christian doctrine. Although the two made the same links between Christian faith, character, and experience, the historical situation is inverted. The bishop needed to validate the central Christian idea of resurrection with an appeal to experiential belief.

Although some spiritual experiences appear as random insights or miraculous encounters, most are shaped by prayer. In stories, memoirs, and testimonies, saints, mystics, and ordinary people recount how speaking with God opened the way for an experience of God. It is in words, and in the territory immediately beyond our words, that human beings meet the divine. As John the Evangelist says, "In the beginning was the Word, and the Word was with God, and the Word was God" (1:1). The Jewish philosopher Martin Buber suggests that spirituality—a deep encounter with God—begins with trust-filled conversation. Prayer is not talking about God "in the third person," rather prayer means speaking to God as "You," a subjective person with the capacity for relationship. Buber claims that "in true prayer, cult and faith are unified and purified into living relation."[69] Prayer transforms religion, doctrine, and dogma into vital spirituality.

The ancient Christian tradition *Lex orandi, lex credendi*, or "The law of prayer is the law of belief," means that praying shapes believing. The first Christians prayed and worshipped for several generations before they had

---

69. Martin Buber, *I and Thou*, trans. R. G. Smith, 2nd ed. (London and New York: Continuum, 1958), 88–89.

a written creed, and they prayed for several hundred years before they had a canon of scripture. The liturgy of the Jesus communities and the prayers early followers uttered nurtured Christian theology, doctrine, and creeds.

"I don't want to be part of your church, because I don't believe in the Nicene Creed" is a common objection of those considering Christianity—or those considering leaving Christianity. But Christians do not worship a creed. The Nicene Creed was written some three centuries after Jesus taught his followers to love God and their neighbors. For the first three hundred years of church history the followers of Jesus worshipped God, served others, preached, taught, baptized, and evangelized the world without the benefit of a formal, universal doctrinal statement. The creeds developed in the context of a living, transformative, prayer-filled, risky, and active spiritual life—not the other way around. Indeed, a creed is considered a "symbol" of faith, not the faith itself. The words function as an icon, a linguistic picture of a divine reality beyond the ideas and concepts, a window into the world beyond words. Creeds are not unimportant; they are important only in the right order.

Creeds are essentially prayers of devotion that express a community's experience of encountering God. Indeed, the first creeds emerged from the Jewish experience of Jesus. The earliest Christians were Jews, men and women raised in a strictly monotheistic faith: "Hear, O Israel: The Lord is our God, the Lord alone" (Deut. 6: 4) and "You shall have no other gods before me" (Exod. 20: 3). Yet these same Jews worshipped Jesus as God, functionally making them bi-theists. Their experience of Jesus led them to rethink their understanding of God the Father and God's relationship to Jesus the Christ. The "rethinking" in context of experience took a very long time and eventuated in what we now know as creeds.

The experiential nature of the creeds can be seen in the Apostles' Creed (ca. 390), which begins with the words *Credo in Deum patrem*, translated into English as "I believe in God the Father." For those who read this through the modern lens of "belief," it seems as if this is an idea *about* God to which one must assent in order to join a Christian group—a question to answer correctly for entrance into heaven. But, if we grasp that the ancient sense of "believe" means "trust" or "devotion," the creed might be better translated thus:

> I trust in God the Father Almighty, Maker of heaven and earth. And [I trust] in Jesus Christ, his only Son, our Lord, who was conceived by the Holy Ghost, born of the Virgin Mary, suffered under Pontius Pilate, was crucified, died, and was buried. He descended into hell; the third day he rose again from the dead. He ascended into heaven, and sitteth on the right hand of God the Father Almighty. From thence he shall come to judge the quick and the dead. I trust in the Holy Ghost, the holy catholic church, the communion of saints, the forgiveness of sins, the resurrection of the body, and the life everlasting. Amen.

Notice that when we insert ourselves as the ones who must trust, the tone changes and the Apostles' Creed takes on the quality of a prayer. Instead of factual certainty, the creed evokes humility, hope, and a bit of faithful supplication. It moves the action of the creed from the brain to the heart. Changing a single word, "believe," to its original sense of "trust" transforms the text from a statement of dogma to an experience of God.

Since all creeds derive from the spiritual experience of the community, it is occasionally necessary and appropriate to rewrite them. Using the experiential language of belief, the Apostles' Creed could be rendered:

> I give my heart to God the all-powerful One, who created the universe, and Jesus Christ, God's Son, the Christ, who through the power of the Holy Spirit was born of the Virgin Mary. . . . And I give my heart to the Holy Spirit, devoting myself to the church and the communion of saints, trusting in the forgiveness of sins, the resurrection of the body, and life everlasting. Amen.

Notice that not all the intellectual problems of Christian doctrine are solved here—the language remains sexist and hierarchical, and we are still stuck with a virgin birth and a sin-filled church. You and your skeptical friends may not want to devote yourselves to this particular God.

But the emotional thrust is different from the one in the creeds recited in church. This no longer expresses philosophical ideas about God; rather, these words turn the affections toward what the early Christians experienced. They had found God, the One they called Father, Son, and Holy Spirit, to be the trustworthy Creator, Savior, and Sustainer of the universe, the beloved of their hearts. Through these words, contemporary followers continually remind themselves of the early Christian experience of God and Jesus, humbly dedicating themselves to a path of devotion and of beloving their God.

For people who have long recited the traditional creeds of the church, it can be hard to think of reinterpreting them or rewriting them. However, as Christianity expanded in the twentieth century, new believers found it necessary to rewrite the creeds in words and images that meshed with their cultures and their own experiences of God. In 1960, the Maasai people of East Africa, aided by Catholic missionaries, revised the creed in light of their encounter with Jesus:

> We believe in the one High God, who out of love created the beautiful world and everything good in it. He created Man and wanted Man to be happy in the world. God loves the world and every nation and tribe on the Earth. We have known this High God in darkness, and now we know Him in the light. God promised in the book of His word, the Bible, that He would save the world and all the nations and tribes.
>
> We believe that God made good His promise by sending His Son, Jesus Christ, a man in the flesh, a Jew by tribe, born poor in a little village, who left His home and was always on safari doing good, curing people by the power

of God, teaching about God and man, showing the meaning of religion is love. He was rejected by his people, tortured and nailed hands and feet to a cross, and died. He lay buried in the grave, but the hyenas did not touch him, and on the third day, He rose from the grave. He ascended to the skies. He is the Lord.

We believe that all our sins are forgiven through Him. All who have faith in Him must be sorry for their sins, be baptized in the Holy Spirit of God, live the rules of love and share the bread together in love, to announce the Good News to others until Jesus comes again. We are waiting for Him. He is alive. He lives. This we believe. Amen.

The Maasai creed invites us to go on a safari with Jesus. These are not just words about God; rather, these words welcome us into a story of God's hope for human happiness and healing.

Indeed, the word "doctrine," a word fallen on hard times in contemporary culture, actually means a "healing teaching," from the French word for "doctor." The creeds, as doctrinal statements, were intended as healing instruments, life-giving words that would draw God's people into a deeper engagement with divine things. When creeds become fences to mark the borders of heresy, they lose their spiritual energy. Doctrine is to be the balm of a healing experience of God, not a theological scalpel to wound and exclude people.

Rowan Williams, the Archbishop of Canterbury, pointed out in a recent book that the Christian creeds are similar to the Three Jewels of Buddhism, the vows that shape a Buddhist way of life: "I take refuge in the Buddha; I take refuge in the Dharma (Teaching); I take refuge in Sangha (Community)." The creed reminds us that Christians take refuge in God the Creator, take refuge in Jesus's teaching (forgiveness, love, and justice), take refuge in the life-giving Spirit, and take refuge in the church (the community). A vow. A prayer. An invitation. A living experience. Spiritual and religious. The heart of faith.

ALL YEARS: PREPARING FOR THE SEMINAR

Respond

Write a summary of Diana Butler Bass's considerations. What hope does she express? What does her writing indicate she "believes," i.e., trusts, loves, takes refuge in (her personal position)?

Write your responses to Diana Butler Bass's assertions. What hope do you express? What does your writing indicate you "believe," i.e., trust, love, take refuge in?

Practice

The diagram attempts to visualize something of the swirl of motives, intentions, beliefs, and actions alive in someone at any given time. The following exercise is designed to increase awareness of the belief, practice, and congruence gaps a person has experienced. Identify the different gaps you presently experience or have known sometime in your life:

Belief Gap: the separation between orthodox teachings and personal belief

Practice Gap: the separation between orthopraxis and personal behavior and practices

Congruence Gap: the disjunction between personal beliefs and personal action

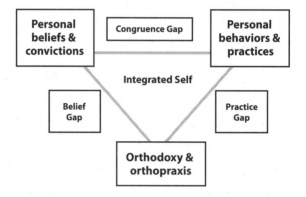

Belief Gap: Beliefs may be individually held or official positions held within a community (doctrines). Separation of personal belief and official doctrine can fragment a life and a community. A pastor of a church denomination that holds the belief that salvation is exclusively through Jesus Christ became ostracized when the pastor preached universal salvation. The gap between the pastor's belief and the denominational doctrine fragmented the community. A "belief gap" can disrupt harmony and force a decision for conformity or expulsion.

Practice Gap: A "practice gap" surfaces whenever a faith community advocates prescribed behavior and an individual does not conform to that behavior. A gap emerges as the mores of a community clash against individual actions and interests.

Congruence Gap: The gap phenomenon becomes internal when a person values something and behaves in conflict with that value. For example, honesty and truth-telling might be a high value but the person may habitually lie. The "congruence gap" generates internal conflicts that can become psychologically and spiritually destructive.

Wholeness, health, and holiness are closely related. Congruence intimates integrity. Living faithfully as a Christian, especially in a multicultural environment, entails facing and addressing the variety of "gaps" present. Unit Four directs attention toward wholeness by identifying and addressing the different "gaps" present in a person. Initially, you will be asked to become aware of the way you experience the different gaps. In subsequent weeks the gaps will be taken up one at a time to more carefully consider them.

Theological reflection is an important process of awareness, the first step toward wholeness, congruency, and integration. Often, those incidents that represent an occurrence "in the gap" are the ones most fruitful for theological reflection.

Review your writing in the preceding Respond section. Where are your "gaps?"

In the coming days and weeks, become mindful of those moments when you do/say something that goes against what you think you really believe. If there is such a moment that you can recall at this time, make note of it if you wish.

Week Twenty-three

YEAR ONE

Read

The books of Samuel and Kings provide one perspective on the history of the Kingdoms of Israel and Judah. The Chronicles (which you will read later) offer an alternative view of that history. Try not to be overwhelmed by the length of the reading or get bogged down in details, but attend to the sweep of the narrative.

1 Samuel
2 Samuel
Collins, Chapter 11, "First Samuel" and Chapter 12, "Second Samuel," pages 116–130

Focus

First and Second Samuel paint a picture of the formation of the Jewish faith. Identify the concepts, ideas, images, and actions that expressed knowledge of God, human nature, and the world as understood by the people of that time. Notice especially how various cultures participated in formation of the Jewish faith.

What "gaps" existed in the world Samuel engaged?

YEAR TWO

Read

Philemon
Jude
Powell, Chapter 22, "Philemon" and Chapter 28, "Jude," pages 415–425

Focus

Identify a common idea or theme in Philemon and Jude. Notice how Powell explores that idea or theme.

Analyze the idea or theme in Philemon and/or Jude. Begin by asking two or three theological perspective questions of wholeness, brokenness, recognition, reorientation, or restoration. For example, for brokenness, a question could be "from what did someone in the scripture of Philemon or Jude turn"; a wholeness perspective question might be, "What kind of world did the writer of Philemon or Jude believe God intended? What were to be the norms of that world?"

What "gaps" existed for the writer(s) of Philemon and Jude?

YEAR THREE

Read

MacCulloch, Chapter 16, "Perspectives on the True Church," pages 551–603

Focus

With this chapter, MacCulloch returns to Western Christianity. Events, especially tragic ones, impact how people think about and know God. Describe how the Black Death influenced behavior and belief. Notice especially how multicultural realities contributed to the perspectives described in the chapter.

YEAR FOUR

Read

Allen, Chapter 16, "The Holy Spirit, the Church, and the Sacraments," pages 171–182

Focus

Select an image Allen used, such as "the rush of a violent wind." Imagine what it is like to feel the wind's rush. What is the essence of the image you selected? What is it about?

Ask two or three theological perspective questions of the image from the perspectives of wholeness, brokenness, recognition, reorientation, or restoration.

Connect the reflection with something from literature or film. Look especially for material from cultures different from your own.

Recall a time when you experienced a gap between your belief and your behavior. Consider how Allen's chapter on sacraments addresses such a gap.

Finally, what do you believe about the matter under reflection?

ALL YEARS: PREPARING FOR THE SEMINAR

Respond

Read a couple of good online or printed magazine or news articles about something that you care about in the field of history, theology, literature, politics, or science.

Use the following outline to build the skill of reflecting theologically on something you read (or perhaps watched on TV or some other source).

Practice

THEOLOGICAL REFLECTION BEGINNING WITH A WIDE-ANGLE LENS

Why this title? The image of a wide-angle lens is used because this reflection begins with a variety of perspectives, then focuses on a thread/theme/idea/image that connects them. An individual starts by finding the threads or themes present—in this case in something he or she reads or watches. The key for use by an individual requires initiation from something that could produce several themes or ideas (in this case, two or more articles on a topic of interest). In an EfM group, the reflection's beginning point can be themes from the spiritual autobiographies, themes from the week's reading, themes from any on-board time of the group, or some other starting point from which a variety of perspectives can be elicited.

The key is first to list the themes in what is under consideration, then find a thread that runs through the themes.

Identify

FIND A COMMON THEME OR THREAD

Begin with the articles chosen for the Respond section above.

What are the common themes or elements which emerge?

Is there a central question, struggle, or issue contained in the articles?

State the central thread as a simple statement, image, metaphor, or issue.

For instance, a review of several articles could reveal themes of challenge of the *status quo,* support of a particular view, and/or revelation of something new. Asking "What ties some of those themes together" yields a thread that may have run through the articles.

Explore

THEOLOGICAL PERSPECTIVES

Write about what's going on in the image, issue, or statement you created in the Identify step above.

Sit quietly and let the image or statement and your writing rest in you.

What questions does your image or statement raise?

What questions does that image or statement answer?

Identify the perspectives contained in the questions, that is, wholeness, brokenness, recognition, reorientation, or restoration.

Connect

This is the point at which one looks at the various sources in life to help find meaning in matters of daily life and ministry. The object is to find connections between the image, statement, or issue and other aspects of our life that teach us something.

CONNECT TO CULTURE AND SOCIETY

Focus on one or two areas of your culture or society so that the reflection will not be too broad. These connections might come from your local community or the larger world: your work environment, the education system, the health care system, your grandmothers, movies, TV, literature, art, songs, artifacts, architecture, government, or the press, to name a few.

Pick just one area of our contemporary society with which to connect. For instance, what does the world of employment teach you about the theme you have identified? Or, what have you learned from the news media in your culture/society that helps you or challenges you regarding the theme?

How does the selected area of culture/society speak to or about this thread?

CONNECT TO CHRISTIAN TRADITION

- Identify biblical passages or other elements from Christian tradition (scripture, hymn, prayer, church history document) in which this common thread is evoked or brought to mind. Read the passages.

- Select one passage that seems to address the image, statement, or issue.

- Examine the passage:

  - Note how the passage offers insight into the image, statement, or issue you are considering.

  - Note how the passage challenges the image, statement, or issue.

  - What does the passage mean to you?

COMPARE AND CONTRAST CULTURE/SOCIETY AND CHRISTIAN TRADITION

From the perspectives of each, what kind of a world emerges?

Where do these perspectives join or compete? Where do they clash or contrast?

Note what seems to be "at stake" as you compare and contrast your Culture and Tradition connections.

CONNECT TO PERSONAL EXPERIENCE

When have you experienced something that relates to what seems to "be at stake" above?

CONNECT TO BELIEFS, POSITIONS, AND AFFIRMATIONS

What positions or affirmations do you hold in relation to what is at stake?

Identify how that belief formed for you. Was it from personal experience, from something you learned in your faith tradition, or from the cultural messages you have inherited or encountered?

What "gaps" are there for you between what you believe and how you act in relation to the theme considered in this reflection?

Apply

IDENTIFY INSIGHTS AND PERSONAL IMPLICATIONS

What have you learned about coherence of belief and behavior?

What are you personally called to do differently, to affirm, or to change?

What skills did this reflection help you learn in thinking theologically about something you read or watched?

DECIDE ON SOCIAL AND CIVIC CONSEQUENCES

What actions will you take to carry out the implications you have discovered?

Consider how this reflection supports you in living in a multicultural world.

Week Twenty-four   *Feb 21*

YEAR ONE

Read

1 Kings 2 Kings
Collins, Chapter 13, "First Kings 1–16: Solomon and the Divided Monarchy" and Chapter 14, "First Kings 17–Second Kings 25: Tales of Prophets and the End of the Kingdoms of Israel and Judah," pages 131–152

Focus

Prophets speak God's truth to those in power and frequently have the most to lose in speaking. Difficulties arise when prophetic voices do not agree on what the "truth" is. Two possible responses to the contradiction are to wait to see which was speaking truth or to decide in the midst of the uncertainty which is correct and act accordingly.

Reflect on how uncertainty impacts a consistency of belief and behavior.

YEAR TWO

Read

Philippians
Colossians
Powell, Chapter 17, "Philippians" and Chapter 18, "Colossians," pages 343–369

Focus

Note the passages Powell highlights from Philippians and/or Colossians. Which passages does he not include in his discussion, but that you think are important?

Identify any issues related to multicultural encounters that might have been present in the Philippians' and Colossians' experience.

YEAR THREE

Read

MacCulloch, Chapter 17, "A House Divided, pages 604–654

Focus

Describe the values that drove the actions of reformers. Think about how those values shape doctrines of God, humanity, and creation. How do those values relate to your personal experience and values? How are those values reflected in our contemporary society? What challenges or support are there for you in living faithfully with your values in a multicultural world?

YEAR FOUR

Read

Allen, Chapter 17, "Sin, Evil, and Hope for the Future" and the "Epilogue," pages 183–199

Focus

Allen presents several key ideas: Julian of Norwich's comparison of knowledge of God to wounds; a "colony of heaven"; and Simone Weil's "truth which is active in the soul [the whole person]" among others.

What other key ideas did you notice?

What significance, if any, do the ideas have to tensions between belief and behavior?

How do any of the ideas contribute to your living faithfully in a multicultural world?

ALL YEARS: PREPARING FOR THE SEMINAR

Respond

Identify the location of power–individuals, institutions–in the material you studied this week. Comment on the effects of power and powerlessness revealed in what you studied.

Practice

Reflecting theologically on dilemmas can move a person toward integrating beliefs and behaviors. Building a theology relies on the integration of beliefs with doctrines as professed in daily actions.

Try using the following to reflect theologically on a belief/behavior dilemma identified from your study or from the preceding session. Set aside an hour or so to work through the process.

THEOLOGICAL REFLECTION BEGINNING WITH A DILEMMA

Identify

Describe an incident for reflection–an experience in which you felt pulled in at least two directions over something, and for which there are no decisions pending, that is, the incident is over, though there still may be feelings. For example:

I had looked forward to my best friend's wedding for months and had my plane ticket and my new outfit. We had plans to enjoy the sights and catch up and just have fun. And then my surviving parent got sick, but told me I could go ahead with my plans. I felt so torn. There was no one else there.

Name the turning point in the incident.

What's the central moment of the incident? Where is the tension greatest? What was happening? What were you thinking and feeling at that moment?

Record the central moment in a short sentence and your thoughts and feelings at that moment.

State the issue.

Try to state what's at stake or what the central dilemma is at the moment of greatest tension.

To help get to the dilemma, list declarative statements about what you wanted at that moment or what interests were at stake at that moment. You may have several.

Record tension statements as "I wanted _____ and I wanted _____." For example:

I wanted to attend my best friend's wedding and I wanted to stay to take care of my ailing parent.

Select a pair of statements that best represent the central tension.

Record the central dilemma/what's at stake. For example:

Personal fun conflicting with caring for another. Dilemma: Plans affected by unforeseen circumstances.

Identify another time.

Clarify the dilemma by recalling another time when you experienced a similar tension.

Record your additional experience with the identified tension by completing the sentence: "It was a time when. . . ."

Explore
Explore the dilemma.

What is it like to live in that tension? Contrast the cost/promise of the dilemma.

Record your responses to the questions using either cost/promise or theological perspectives:

COST OF EACH SIDE OF THE TENSION	PROMISE OF EACH SIDE OF THE TENSION
Ex., Plans: caught off guard, decisions made that are hard to change	Ex., Know what is coming

OR use one or two theological perspective questions adapted from the Cycle of Gospel Living, developed by Eric Law (and used in Interlude One, Week 15).[70] This cycle focuses around power, loss or yielding up of power, and empowerment and moves through four phases.

• Give up power, choose the cross—This is a point of entry for the powerful

• Cross, death, powerless—This is a point of entry for the powerless

• Empowerment, endurance

• Empty tomb, resurrection, powerful

Here are examples of asking questions of the dilemma or image. Use only one or two when exploring your image or dilemma:

Give up power, choose the cross: What are the power dimensions of the dilemma or image? Who has power? What has to be yielded?

Cross, death, powerless: What sacrifice(s) might be called for? What are the temptations of the cross, of powerlessness? To whom or what is power yielded?

Empowerment, endurance: How is power transmitted to the powerless party? What is required in order to enter the cycle that leads to empowerment? What builds endurance?

Empty tomb, resurrection, powerful: What is left behind in the image or dilemma? How does resurrection occur in the image or dilemma? What is the hope of the power received?

Connect

TRADITION

Identify some stories from scripture or church history that relate to the dilemma or image. How or where does the Gospel Living cycle occur in our Christian story in scripture? In the lives of women and men of faith? Or perhaps some prayers or hymns come to mind that relate to this reflection.

DIALOGUE

Compare and contrast what your Christian tradition has to say about that dilemma or image. What choices would the tradition support? Not support? Why?

---

70. Law, *The Wolf Shall Dwell with the Lamb*, 74.

CULTURE AND POSITION

Where is that tension or dilemma experienced in our culture? Have there been news stories about it? Have you read a book or seen a movie that dealt with that dilemma? Is there a political dimension?

What do you believe about that dilemma? How was your belief in conflict within the dilemma? What do you hope for regarding the dilemma?

Apply

INSIGHTS AND QUESTIONS

What do you see in a new way now? What have you learned about facing this dilemma? What questions do you have about the dilemma in your life?

IMPLICATIONS

What do you want or need to do about this dilemma? Are there social implications? Are there actions you could take? Is there something more to learn? What support would help? Where will you find that support?

Week Twenty-five

YEAR ONE

Read

Ezra
Nehemiah
Collins, Chapter 21, "Ezra and Nehemiah," pages 220–228

Focus

The authors of Ezra and Nehemiah placed a high value on identity, security, and justice. Identify how these values shaped the understanding of God's promises for the people in your study. What stands out in Collins's chapter on these prophets?

YEAR TWO

Read

1 Timothy
2 Timothy
Titus
Powell, Chapter 21, "Pastoral Letters," pages 397–413

Focus

Think about Paul's struggle against "false teachings" and advocacy of "sound doctrines." Compare how the same issues exist in the contemporary church. What light does Powell shed on these letters?

YEAR THREE

Read

MacCulloch, Chapter 18, "Rome's Renewal," pages 655–688

Focus

Often, reforming produced examination and renewal among those against whom protestations were leveled. As you read through the chapter of the Roman Catholic counter-reformations, consider what is disclosed about God.

YEAR FOUR

Read

Sedgwick, "Introduction"; Chapter 1, "Describing the Christian Life"; and Chapter 2, "An Anglican Perspective," pages ix–51

Focus

Given Sedgwick's presentation, reflect on how the study of ethics contributes to the formation of theology. What are the creative aspects of Sedgwick's views? What choices do his views present to you? Reflect on how his views of ethics relate to what you see in our advertising today, or in our school systems. Note what you believe about the study and practice of ethics. What do you view in a new way after reading this week's assignment? State any implications that awareness has for what you will do any differently next week.

ALL YEARS: PREPARING FOR THE SEMINAR

Respond

Christian theologians over the centuries have developed a long list of doctrines. The table of contents of most theological textbooks reflects an author's arrangement of important doctrines. Often an author devotes an entire chapter to a particular doctrine or doctrines.

Each historical period prioritizes doctrines in response to the social and intellectual environment. For example, in the nineteenth and early twentieth centuries, most theology began with the doctrine of God, the characteristics and actions of God. By the end of the twentieth century Anglo-American theologians discussed the doctrine of human nature, the characteristics of humankind, how we act and who we are. John Macquarrie, a Scottish theologian who taught at Union Theological Seminary in New York City and at Oxford University, consistently asserted that contemporary theology must begin from the ground up. Thus, his *Principles of Christian Theology* begins with theological anthropology (i.e., the doctrine of human nature).

As a way to build a theology, create a list of fifteen or more doctrines. A denominational catechism would be a good place to start. For example, the 1979 Episcopal Book of Common Prayer (BCP) presents "An Outline of Faith" beginning on page 845. Each boldface heading names a doctrine.

Arrange your list of doctrines in an order that reflects your interest, beginning with what interests you the most. Using the first three or four doctrines, review your reading assignments over the past few sessions, noting how the author dealt with one or two of the doctrines of interest.

Practice

Try to locate doctrinal statements of several denominations (Anglican, Methodist, Christian Science, or any others) or faith traditions (Judaism, Islam, and so forth). Constructive theology is essentially a conversation among Christian doctrines and an individual's beliefs and actions (behaviors).

Select one doctrine from your list, for example, the doctrine of God. Write a statement from the Catechism of the 1979 Prayer Book that addresses the doctrine, such as human nature.

Make a personal statement of belief relative to the chosen doctrine.

Finally, recall your own personal behavior (describing an action or position) that reveals a stance relative to the doctrine.

For example,

BCP question: What are we by nature?

BCP answer: We are part of God's creation, made in the image of God.

Personal statement: I believe that we are all equal.

Behavior (action or position) that reveals an understanding of human nature:
   "The world is going to hell in a handbasket because of those _____."

Explore the connections, or disconnections, between the church doctrine, personal doctrine, and personal behavior. What do you see of wholeness or brokenness or restoration in those connections? What place does the empty tomb have in this conversation?

Reflect on images, emotions, or concepts that contribute to the threefold conversation.

What other doctrinal statements from the Christian tradition speak to the conversation?

What other position statements have you said or heard?

Describe how different actions contribute to the conversation.

What are the implications in a multicultural setting?

Week Twenty-six

YEAR ONE

Read

1 Chronicles
2 Chronicles
Collins, Chapter 22, "The Books of Chronicles," pages 229–235
Again, as with 1 and 2 Kings, try not to get caught up in detail, but read the Chronicles as a sweeping history, noting as you can any differences that stand out.

Focus

Compare the accounts of Israel's history in 1 and 2 Chronicles with that of 1 and 2 Kings. Who stands out in each of the accounts? What differences are there? What view of God comes clearer for you in reading these texts?

YEAR TWO

Read

1 Thessalonians
2 Thessalonians
Powell, Chapter 19, "1 Thessalonians" and Chapter 20, "2 Thessalonians," pages 371–385

Focus

Note which doctrines are either implicitly or explicitly mentioned in the two letters to the Thessalonians. What light does Powell shed on the doctrines?

YEAR THREE

Read

MacCulloch, Chapter 19, "A Worldwide Faith," pages 689–715

Focus

Well-crafted histories aid in understanding the social and intellectual period in which contemporary theology has developed. Name the primary factors that influence the building of theology for today's world.

YEAR FOUR

Read

Sedgwick, Chapter 3, "Incarnate Love" and Chapter 4, "Love and Justice," pages 53–101

Focus

In Chapter 3 Sedgwick uses sexuality, idolatry, and hospitality as elements to sketch a picture of incarnate love. In Chapter 4 he offers an important discussion of love and justice. Note which of the themes contribute most to the theology you are building.

ALL YEARS: PREPARING FOR THE SEMINAR

Respond

Prayer, worship, and study open one's heart to God. Ideally, all three frame theological reflection and all three contribute to developing a theology that stands one in good stead in the midst of life. Building an awareness of the theological "gaps" in one's life—and accepting that some will likely always exist for any given person—helps the Christian sojourner to walk with more steadiness in daily life. In this unit, Diana Butler Bass's work provides a frame for looking at aspects of believing and identifies some of the gaps that exist for individuals and institutions, both sacred and secular.

Use the scheme laid out in Week 21 to organize the material you studied this week in terms of the kinds of gaps that you might discern.

Belief Gap: the separation between orthodox (institutionally accepted) teachings and personal belief

Where did those gaps appear in what you studied?

Where did they appear in how you responded to some of the ideas you encountered in your study?

Practice Gap: the separation between orthopraxis (institutionally accepted behavior) and personal behavior and practices

Where did this gap occur in the material you studied and where has it occurred in your own experience?

Congruence Gap: the disjunction between personal beliefs and personal action

Where did this gap occur in your personal experience?

Practice

THEOLOGICAL REFLECTION BEGINNING WITH A WIDE-ANGLE LENS

Identify

After describing the gaps in the Respond section above, pick one gap and identify themes or threads that run through that gap.

What kinds of things does that gap seem to be about? Is it about civil disobedience, or punishment, or resistance–or something else?

Choose one thread (theme) as the focus for reflection.

Explore

The theme is descriptive of some kind of world, where "that's how things are." For example, the focus may be about an act of civil disobedience that represents personal behavior in the gap between orthopraxis and personal action. Deepen your reflection on the theme using two or three perspective questions to ask the focus:

- What temptations or dangers are present in such a world (of civil disobedience, or whatever the focus is about in your incident)?

- What is shown about human nature in this gap?

- What would wholeness look like?

Connect

Consider any or all of the following in any order:

What's at the "heart" of the selected gap?

Note your personal positions or beliefs about the matter under consideration. On what ground is your belief resting? What contributed to the formation of that belief?

Identify how the ground of your belief is watered by a faith tradition, by the world around you, or by personal experience.

Apply

What new ideas or understanding do you have now?

What are the implications for ministry in daily life in a multicultural environment?

Journal about how living with your Rule of Life has been going. Where have you encountered God?

Week Twenty-seven

YEAR ONE

Read

Amos
Hosea
Collins, Chapter 15, "Amos and Hosea," pages 153–163

Focus

Identify and describe behaviors or actions that upset Amos or Hosea and what they said about them. What was destructive in those actions? What could cause people or the prophets to become aware of the destructive aspects? When have you behaved in the same kind of way? What was the cost of that behavior? Compare and contrast your experience with the experience you identified in one of those prophetic books. How or when have you heard a "word of the Lord" that caused you to think again about your behavior? What actions in our contemporary world are similar to the destructive elements you identified in one of this week's prophetic books? What do you believe about the matter under reflection? Draw some conclusions that can direct you in living faithfully in a multicultural context.

YEAR TWO

Read

James
Powell, Chapter 24, "James," pages 445–461

Focus

Notice what Powell has to say about the Letter to James. What are the deep hungers of those to whom James wrote? What does the letter say about the need for congruence between belief and behavior?

YEAR THREE

Read

MacCulloch, Chapter 20, "Protestant Awakenings," pages 716–765

Focus

Describe how learning about "Protestant Awakenings" (especially pietism, Methodism, and the American Great Awakenings) contributes to living a life congruent with belief.

YEAR FOUR

Read

Sedgwick, Chapter 5, "The Practices of Faith"; Chapter 6, "The Call of God"; and the Appendix, pages 103–158

Focus

Record four or five ways in which Sedgwick's writings contribute to building your theology. Take special notice of the way Schleiermacher has influenced contemporary theology.

ALL YEARS: PREPARING FOR THE SEMINAR

Respond

Throughout this constructive theology unit, you have worked with various facets of building your own theology. Such work always is enriched when done within a learning community. Mark McIntosh, in *Mysteries of Faith*, notes three movements that a person or a community undergoes in building a life-giving theology: 1) seeing differently; 2) developing a habit of life; 3) ongoing conversation with God.[71]

Regularly practicing the discipline of theological reflection allows people to see things differently. Fresh visions, in turn, lead to developing a "habit of life" in which thinking theologically becomes routine. In McIntosh's words, "Learning to see the mystery of God's plan, to see in a way that illuminates the meaning of the world, requires you to develop some habits of mind and heart."[72]

EfM presents opportunities to develop habits of mind and heart—ways of seeing God's mystery and presence. McIntosh notes that "when theology becomes a habit, it becomes part of your character, a fundamental having and holding of who you are."[73] Theology opens a person to knowing about God and knowing God, and at the same time allows people to know more *about* themselves and, more importantly, to *know* themselves. The two-fold practice of knowing God and knowing oneself embodies the incarnational process. It is an interactive, dynamic, dance-like reality in which a person intentionally develops a "God-knowing" habit and simultaneously develops a *habitus* of self-knowing.

---

71. Mark McIntosh, *Mysteries of Faith* (Cambridge, MA: Cowley Publications, 2000), 5–20.

72. McIntosh, *Mysteries of Faith*, 12.

73. Ibid.

Review the work you have done throughout the unit and note what you have learned about yourself and about God. Assess where you are in the theological practice of knowing God and yourself.

Practice

Review your spiritual autobiography and your Rule of Life, considering how you would express your experience of God in terms of wholeness, broken-ness, empowerment, and/or resurrection.

Who are your theological or spiritual wisdom figures, drawing from the scriptures, your study of church history, and your life?

On what basis do you consider any of those figures to be sources of wisdom for you?

SECOND INTERLUDE UNIT

Globalization, Gender, and Interfaith Dialogue

Week Twenty-eight

ALL YEARS

Read

Kwok, *Globalization, Gender, and Peacebuilding*

Note: Professor Kwok uses the Eastern name order of her Chinese heritage in which the family name (Kwok) precedes the personal name (Pui-lan).

Focus

This book contains a lecture in three parts Kwok delivered as the 2011 Madeleva Lecture in Spirituality at the Center for Spirituality at St. Mary's College, Notre Dame, Indiana. Note that on page 2 she outlines the main points of her argument.

Notice Kwok's use of the following terms: the clash of civilizations; globalization; religion; *extra ecclesiam, nulla salus;* religious pluralism; Radical Orthodoxy; interfaith dialogue; fulfillment theology; *missio Dei;* exclusivist, inclusivist, and pluralist approaches to interfaith dialogue; interreligious and intrareligious dialogues; multiple religious belonging; syncretism; postcolonial; Orientalism; reciprocity; appropriation and misappropriation*; mujerista; Noble Sav*age stereotype; hybridity; self-in-reflection theory; dualism/binarism; polydoxy; divine multiplicity; religiou*s* violence as *performative* violence; interbeing

ALL YEARS: PREPARING FOR THE SEMINAR

Respond

Use the ABCD format to consider one or more of the divisions in Kwok's address:

- How globalization has impacted interreligious dialogue and relationships

- Voices missing in interfaith dialogue

- Peace-building as a basis for interfaith dialogue

A	B	C	D
What amazed you or gave you an "aha!" moment?	What bothered you?	What confused you?	What delighted you, or what did you discover?

Practice

Identify one of the passages you chose for the ABCD response above. Read it carefully and consider its context in Kwok's argument. Identify its focus in one sentence.

Explore the focus statement you wrote using some or all of the theological perspectives based on Bishop Tutu's terms:

- What constitutes wholeness/goodness?

- What is evidence of brokenness/separation from God?

- What brings recognition of that brokenness?

- What might make reorientation possible?

- What would be evidence of restoration to wholeness?

Connect to other sources. What is your personal position on this topic? What does the Christian tradition have to say in response to the focus of the passage? What does your culture/society say about this? What has been your personal experience on this subject?

Bring the theological perspective questions above into the conversation with at least one of these sources. Compare and contrast with the theological perspectives on the original focus statement.

Apply to your own current situation. What implications do you find for your own identity as a Christian in an increasingly intercultural and interfaith context? Is there an action you can or wish to take? Is there something you are called to change—in yourself, in a local situation, in a more global situation? Are there implications for your Rule of Life?

Week Twenty-nine

ALL YEARS

Read

Kwok, *Globalization, Gender, and Peacebuilding*

Focus

Review, as needed

ALL YEARS: PREPARING FOR THE SEMINAR

Respond

The following is an excerpt from an essay by Kwok, written originally for the Anglicanism in a Post-Colonial World conference held at Episcopal Divinity School in Cambridge, Massachusetts, in June 1998 and subsequently included in *Beyond Colonial Anglicism*.

The Anglican Church as a Cultural Hybrid[74]

An important characteristic of Anglicanism is comprehensiveness. The Lambeth Conference of 1968 report says:

> Comprehensiveness demands agreement of fundamentals, while tolerating disagreement on matters in which Christians may differ without feeling the necessity of breaking communion. In the mind of an Anglican, comprehensiveness is not compromise. Nor is it to bargain one truth for another. It is not a sophisticated word for syncretism. Rather it implies that the apprehension of truth is a growing thing: we only gradually succeed in "knowing the truth." It has been the tradition of Anglicanism to contain within one body both Protestant and Catholic elements.[75]

Many Anglicans value comprehensiveness, toleration of diversity, and the via media in their church, but few have thought about the cultural logic that makes these qualities possible. I suggest that Anglicanism was a cultural hybrid from the beginning, and this tradition should be celebrated in our postcolonial world. As a cultural hybrid of Catholicism and Protestantism, the

---

74. Kwok Pui-lan, "The Legacy of Cultural Hegemony in the Anglican Church," in *Beyond Colonial Anglicism: The Anglican Communion in the Twenty-first Century*, ed. Ian T. Douglas and Kwok (New York: Church Publishing, 2001), 56–59.

75. *The Lambeth Conference 1968: Resolutions and Reports* (New York: Seabury, 1968), 140.

Church of England in the sixteenth century assimilated elements from both traditions to create a very fluid identity. Adopting the via media approach, the Church of England was able to hold together the evangelicals and the anglo-catholics in the nineteenth century. The encounter with diverse cultures during colonial age presented both risks and opportunities to the cultural identity of Anglicanism. But instead of continuing the process of hybridity, Anglican churches were formed during the imperialistic period as mimicries of churches at the metropolitan center. The report of the Lambeth Conference of 1988 laments:

> Thus when Anglicanism was exported to other continents, it came not only with the "Englishness" of certain styles of clothing, music and worship, but with certain assumptions about who made decisions, who had authority in social life, who had ultimate control in economic affairs, markets, production, land ownership. The dominance of the English style . . . could be seen as a reflection of the plain facts of political and economic dominance.[76]

Although we have entered the postcolonial age, Anglican churches in many parts of the world remain cultural representations of the colonial era. Africans and Asians living in tropical climates continue to wear English clerical dress, even under the hot blazing sun. The African bishop is addressed as the Lord Bishop of Cape Coast or Freetown. John Pobee of Ghana has called this phenomenon the "Anglo-Saxon captivity of Ecclesia Anglicana."[77] In many cases, such mimicry of the "mother church" serves not as a mockery of colonial authority, but as a sign of privilege by association.

To get out of this captivity, the newer churches of the Anglican Communion must take seriously its hybrid identity as both Anglican on the one hand, and African, Asian, Latin American, or West Indian on the other. The 1966 Conference on World Mission and Evangelism with the theme "Called to One Hope: Gospel in Diverse Cultures" recognized the renewed quest for identity for oppressed people around the world. But as Christopher Duraisingh has observed, such an ethno-cultural quest for identity can lead to new forms of ethnic nationalism and cleansing, the oppression of religious minority groups, and the breakdown of community.[78] The urgent question is how to construct identity in community so that the result will not be fragmentation, fundamentalism, or balkanization. The Anglican Communion can offer a unique prophetic model. On the one hand, it should encourage the experimentation of new cultural forms among member churches. On the other hand, the different cultural hybrids are in communion with one

---

76. *The Truth Shall Make You Free: The Lambeth Conference 1988* (London: Church Publishing, 1988), 88.

77. John Pobee, "New Dioceses of the Anglican Communion," in *The Study of Anglicanism*, ed. Stephen Sykes and John Booty (London: SPCK, 1988), 395–398.

78. Christopher Duraisingh, "Editorial: Gospel and Identity in Community," *International Review of Mission* 85 (1966): 6–7.

another, so that each can serve as a mirror for others, without absolutizing one's specific cultural form.

ANGLICAN HISTORY FROM THE PERIPHERY

When Anglicans think of their tradition, they often trace it back to the ancient apostolic tradition, mediated through the Church of England, and later brought to different parts of the world. Most historical works on the Anglican tradition, including the recent book *The Transformation of Anglicanism*,[79] follow such a time frame. The influential book, *The Study of Anglicanism*, traces the history and authority of Anglicanism and dissects various aspects of the church, sacraments, and ministry, but devotes only two chapters out of thirty to the younger churches.[80] From a post-colonial perspective, this is reading history from the metropolitan center, relegating the histories of other peoples to the periphery.

If colonization is a transnational and transcultural process, affecting both the colonized and the colonizers, how can we reinterpret the history of Anglicanism as a continued interaction between "the center" and "the periphery," thereby destabilizing both? Furthermore, how can we reimagine a different temporality so that we can resurrect the histories and stories of people not represented in metropolitan history? This requires a multicultural interpretation of the history of Anglicanism, a task that has hardly begun.

I will offer a few examples as several possible directions this multicultural interpretation can take. During the colonial days, the Anglican congregations in America had to coexist with those of other denominations, especially with the strong presence of Puritans in the northeast. After the Episcopal Church USA separated from the Church of England, it could not follow the model of the religious establishment. The Episcopal Church adopted a national structure which paralleled that of the government. The General Convention was divided into two houses: the House of Bishops and the House of Deputies that included clergy and laity. It drew its members from the middle and upper class, and included leaders in the public sector.[81] The Episcopal Church offers the longest historical example of the relationship between the church and state in a postcolonial setting. It will be especially enlightening to analyze the role of the Episcopal Church USA when the United States became a colonial power, following Britan, in the nineteenth century, and the sole superpower in the twentieth.

Another example is discerning racial politics in the Anglican Communion, especially in its important gatherings. In the Lambeth Conference of 1948, black bishops made up only 6 percent of the 37 bishops from Africa,

---

79. William L. Sachs, *The Transformation of Anglicanism* (Cambridge: Cambridge University Press, 1993).

80. Sykes and Booty, eds., *The Study of Anglicanism*.

81. Sachs, *The Transformation of Anglicanism*, 67–68.

but by 1978, they made up 80 percent of the 102 African bishops, representing almost 20 percent of all participants.[82] Most recently the increased presence and influence of bishops from the South during the 1998 Lambeth Conference was evident. The first Anglican Consultative Council, which met in 1971 in Limuru, Kenya, was perhaps the first time that a world council with non-whites as the majority had met since before the Council of Nicea.[83] During the Lambeth Conference of 1867, churches in the Third World were referred to as "Colonial Churches," but many have become fully autonomous provinces since 1950. Bishop Desmond Tutu was the chair of a Section in Lambeth in 1978, and Bishop James Ottley served in that capacity in 1988. Christiopher Duraisingh, Emilio Castro, and John Pobee have each played significant roles in recent Lambeth Conferences. The contributions of these bishops and theologians in Anglican gatherings have to be lifted up, since the official reports failed to highlight them.

The third example regards the inclusion of women in the ordained ministry within Anglicanism. As always, such in innovative attempt began at the periphery, but had rippling effects in the whole church. Because of war circumstances, Bishop R.O. Hall ordained Florence Li Tim-Oi to the priesthood in China in 1944. Later, in Hong Kong, Bishop Gilbert Baker officially ordained Jane Hwang Hseenyuin and Joyce Bennett to be the first two women priests in 1971. When the matter was discussed, Professor John Mbiti and Archdeacon Jabex Bryce of Fiji spoke approvingly of women's leadership in their African and Polynesian cultures.[84] The ordination of these pioneering women opened the doors to the consecration of women to the episcopate. The 1998 Lambeth Conference welcomed eleven women bishops for the first time. The ordination of women symbolized the long struggle of women to gain access to full ministry in the church. After a quarter of a century, the Church of England finally decided to follow a practice, first adopted in a tiny British colony, to recognize the leadership of women in ordained ministry.

Practice

When many Episcopalians (and others) think of Anglicanism, often the images that first come to mind are from England: an English village church, Westminster Abbey, the Archbishop of Canterbury, the Vicar of Dibley. What other Anglican images from tradition and culture come to mind for you?

Describe a typical Anglican Christian in your own context. In the United States, the typical Episcopalian for some time has been affluent (by world standards), white, and over sixty, although this is rapidly changing in many

---

82. John Howe, *Anglicanism and the Universal Church* (Toronto: Anglican Book Centre, 1990), 14.

83. Ibid., 19.

84. Joyce M. Bennett, *Hasten Slowly* (Chichester: Little London Associates Publishing, 1991), 16.

areas. And yet, statistically, the average Anglican worldwide is a poor African woman in her twenties with young children.

One resource for examining the breadth of Anglicanism is the Anglican Communion News (ACN) website. Spend some time, if possible, exploring this site. Notice its organization, the featured stories on the front page, the top stories in each of the global divisions.

Kwok calls on the newer churches in the Anglican Communion to embrace a "hybrid identity as both Anglican on the one hand, and African, Asian, Latin American, or West Indian on the other" while avoiding "new forms of ethnic nationalism and cleansing, the oppression of religious minority groups, and the breakdown of community" that sometimes arise in the quest for identity in a diverse community.

What evidence do you find on the ACN website of member churches embracing hybridity? Where do you see remnants of their Anglican colonial heritage? What are the central concerns in the different world divisions, as evidenced in the news stories that appear on the site? What seem to be the challenges?

Choose one or two of the member churches, or an area, and search for additional information outside the ACN website. Note their challenges as churches in multifaith and multicultural contexts. What information that you find challenges your assumptions? What inspires you? What implications arise for understanding your own sense of identity as an Anglican, if you are such? If you identify with another denomination, what implications arise for your understanding of your own denominational heritage and its history with globalization?

Vocation— Hearing and Responding to God's Call

Week Thirty

ALL YEARS

Read

"It is a continual theme of Christian theology that every new generation must take up the task of 'faith in search of understanding' with fresh vigor and creativity."[85] The essay selected to introduce this unit on vocation comes from a book that is the work of a group of theologians who set about the task of doing theology in today's multicultural world. They describe themselves as "a committed, diverse group of theologians who stand at the beginning of a new millennium and in the center of the world's most powerful empire and ask again: How should the Christian faith be understood today, here and now, in this place and time?"[86] The book covers the classical theological themes of God, human beings, sin and evil, Jesus Christ, church, and spirit. Their work on the theology of the church (ecclesiology) culminates in presenting a theology of mission (missiology).

Paul Lakeland is the "Aloysius P. Kelley, S. J., Professor of Catholic Studies" at Fairfield University in Connecticut. Among his works are *The Liberation of the Laity: In Search of an Accountable Church* (Continuum, 2003) and *Postmodernity: Christian Identity in a Fragmented Age* (Fortress Press, 1997)."[87]

Lakeland's essay sets a context for discerning one's vocation in a post-colonial, multicultural world. It provides a launching point for a discussion of Christian mission and vocation, intended to provoke discussion and raise basic questions that push EfM participants to examine their theological foundations and to think through their own understandings of the relationships between Christology, missiology, and ecclesiology. Carefully read and note your own responses: disagreement, challenge, or agreement.

The Mission of the Church[88]

Mission means "sending" or "being sent." The mission of the church is thus that for which it is sent, those purposes for which Christ commissioned it. To understand the full complexity of the term *mission*, however, we have to approach it from at least three different perspectives. First, *who* is sent?

---

85. Serene Jones and Paul Lakeland, eds., *Constructive Theology: A Contemporary Approach to Classic Themes*. A project of The Workgroup on Constructive Christian Theology (Minneapolis: Fortress, 2005), 1.

86. Ibid., 1.

87. Ibid., xii.

88. Ibid., 230–238.

Second, *to whom* is the church sent? Third, *what* is the church sent to do? In actual fact, the questions need to be asked in reverse order. That being said, there is a preliminary question that we need to address: What is the relationship between the mission of the church and the larger question of the *missio dei*, "God's mission," or what we might better understand as the divine purpose or creative will of God? These four questions will guide our examination of the mission of the church.

God's Mission and the Mission of the Church

God's purposes in and for the world are revealed to us through the Bible, but also through looking around us at the world. The world, in its goodness, is the expression of God's creative will, filled with the Spirit and offering glory to its Creator. Of course, there is abounding sin, suffering, and evil in this world, but the person of faith cannot see these as God's responsibility. In the Book of Genesis, God looks upon the creation and sees that it is good. As the early chapters of Genesis unfold, it becomes clear that God's purpose for the world is precisely that it shall be itself, a created reflection of divine goodness. God wills that all creatures, including human beings, be fully what they are—no more and no less. In the case of human beings, being fully what they are, made in the image of God, is made clear in God's commission of Adam and Eve for stewardship. On God's behalf, human beings will cherish creation. In a sense, they are commissioned as "cocreators" and "copreservers" of God's handiwork. Their tragedy, and that of creation, of course, is that they are not equal to the task. Moreover, it is apparent from the very beginning that their principal failure is their inability to recognize that their freedom does not mean autonomy. Their success in carrying out their mission is directly connected to their awareness that they depend on God, not on themselves, for their achievements.

From the beginning, then, God's mission and human purposes are closely intertwined, though there is tension between them. God's commission to human beings to share in the divine creativity is addressed, too, to the whole human race. Adam and Eve are not Hebrews, still less Christians. They represent all humankind. Their failure is our failure. Their task is our task. The Hebrew scriptures tell the story of God's continuing faithfulness to the task of creation and the new initiative that God takes with the covenant people. It is as if God is trying again to enlist human beings in the task of cocreation, this time choosing Abraham and his descendants. Once again, as in the Genesis account, human beings take up the task and are unequal to it. Time after time, the heroes of the Hebrew scriptures reveal their prideful egos; Moses, Saul, and David are good examples of the failure to do what God has called them to do, while Israel itself is another.

Christian scripture sees God's initiative in and through Jesus Christ to be a further effort to engage the human race in God's mission. Jesus is sent into the world to show the way in which a human being can conform his or her life to God's mission. The way of the cross is the way of conformity to the will of God. Jesus Christ is the perfect instrument of God's mission. He proclaims the kingdom of God. But he is also the perfect exemplar of the one who is called to mission. Discipleship, then, is mission, but only because discipleship is, like Christ, outwardly directed in response to God's call to share in God's mission. Discipleship, in other words, is commitment to the mission of Christ, which is in its turn carrying out God's mission. And God's mission is expressed in the creative will as it shows itself in the world. Thus, to complete the circle, the divine creative will is to a degree dependent on the faithfulness of human beings to the divine purpose. For Christians, this means faithfulness to their discipleship of Christ.

What Is the Church Sent to Do?

Given that God invites all human beings to cooperate in the work of cocreation, what is the specific mission of the disciples of Christ, the community called church? Formally, of course, there is no difference. That is, all human beings take up their mission insofar as they live out lives that respect and foster the integrity of God's creation, whether they know it or not, whether they know God or not. Through revelation, all the children of Abraham know more about God's purposes and are aware of their call to mission in ways that others are not. This is both a privilege and an enormous responsibility. However, there is a material specificity to the call of Christ to his church, one that historically Christians have understood as a more perfect revelation of truth but that might better be expressed as a clearer call to participation in the mission of God. When Jesus commissions the disciples to go out like sheep among wolves, when he calls his apostles, when he charges his followers to "preach the gospel to all nations," his commission to them is to spread the Good News of the gospel, to proclaim the imminence of the reign of God.

To talk of the mission of the Christian community, then, is to talk about being called to further the reign of God. But this calling is one that is always subject to historical conditioning and that must be asked and answered anew for every generation. Alongside the scriptural message that we have so far focused upon, there is also the need to "read the signs of the times." Reading the signs of the times is a vital dimension of contemporary religious reflection. It is a kind of lectio divina that focuses not upon the text of scripture but upon creation and human history as texts, in which the call of God and the challenges of meeting that call are always there to be seen. It is also a hazardous enterprise, since it requires an attention to the prejudices and ideology that we may bring to the reading through our own social location, gender, race, and so on, and that may distort our reading or lead us to find exactly what we are looking for. But it is a necessary activity, since without this prayerful and spirit-filled act of divination, the mission of the Christian community will be pursued naively, and thus ineffectually.

The Christian tradition, like other religions, cherishes a specific vision of what it is to be a human being and, since "ought" follows "is," sees itself as called to foster and protect that vision. To read the signs of the times, then, is to search our moment in history for all that seems to threaten the human and for those special people and places where the defense of the human and the world in which we live has been especially promoted. The anti-human will be the challenge that defines mission today. People and movements that struggle against the anti-human are our resources and our guides in the struggle.

There are many candidates for the label of "anti-human" in our world to-day: world poverty, disease, malnutrition, drugs, violence, terrorism, military and corporate greed, environmental collapse, and so on and so on. These are all signs of the anti-human. Reading these signs is a challenge, but one very persuasive contemporary reading of them unifies the problems under the heading of globalization. Readings of the phenomenon of globalization range from canonizing it to demonizing it, with many shades between. But there can be little doubt that the phenomenon of globalization offers the possibility of ameliorating the condition of the world's hopeless masses on the one hand, while apparently exacerbating their misery on the other. It may very well be the case that globalization is an unstoppable social force, if we mean by it the collapse of distance and the homogenization of values, which seem to follow inexorably in the wake of the miniaturization of the world brought about by the communications explosion in general and the World Wide Web in particular. But if we simply acquiesce in its inexorable advance, we abandon the Good News of the gospel. The gospel, of course, stands against evil, not against globalization. But it must stand today against those antihuman forces that gain power and momentum through the communications explosion, whether they be "savage" capitalism, power politics, or the contempt for the human that all forms of violence evince.

Mission will never stop being partially about little things, binding up the wounds of those close to hand, comforting the dying, visiting the sick. But in the face of globalization we also need to be aware that so much of what we are called to attend to close at hand is occasioned or intensified by much grander and less visible forces. The "wretched of the earth" and the "masters of the universe" are linked together. In the gospel vision, the linkage is one of a love that does justice. What are the concrete changes to which we must be committed if that relationship is to be marked by love, justice, and solidarity? Answering that question is a way of defining the face of mission today, not the whole of mission, perhaps, but that part of the mission of the church that is distinctive of our moment in history.

To Whom Is the Church Sent?

This question can be answered in fairly traditional terms. The church is sent to "all the nations," to preach the Good News. But given the nature of the contemporary mission as we have determined it above, the way in which it is sent differs remarkably from past understandings. In traditional understandings of mission, the church is the body that possesses the truth, and it is divinely commissioned to preach that truth to the ignorant of all other religions and none. This work of evangelization is successful when those who hear the message are moved to accept it and to become part of the body that proclaims it. The conversion of the world to Christ is the objective of Christian mission traditionally understood. In our contemporary approach, these assumptions have to be challenged.

If the core of the Christian gospel is the message that God loves and cares for the divine creation and wills human fulfillment, then the church is called to proclaim this truth and to struggle against everything in our world that militates against it. However, the other great world religions also maintain this same truth in their different ways, and while Christians find Jesus Christ to be the exemplar and guarantor of God's love of the world, Jews and Buddhists and Hindus have other ways of expressing their commitments to the project of human liberation from all forms of bondage. The need for mission to be effective would suggest, then, that in addressing those of other faiths, it is the message of Jesus rather than Jesus as the message that ought to be stressed. In the end, the Christian claim that Jesus is savior means that through discipleship of Jesus, the church is led to faithfulness to God's call. Successful mission needs to be measured by its effectiveness in leading people to faithfulness to the call of God as they hear it in their lives, not by its success in persuading people to abandon their own faiths and choose Jesus as the one who is exemplar and guarantor of God's love. Thus is the mission of the church fulfilled, while the integrity of the great world religions is respected.

If Christian mission can be conducted in an atmosphere of respect for the wisdom of the world's religions, then a posture of solidarity and indeed of listening can and should be adopted. Mission today has to be collaborative and humble. In the face of globalization, a solidarity of those who will work to protect the human race and our world is a necessity. But once we understand that God wills the salvation of human beings more than God wills the worldly success of Christ's church, it is also a theological responsibility. If the mission of the church is to succeed through alliances that lessen the sense that the church is privileged, and through a humble posture of listening to the wisdom of the world that is not the church, it can only conform the church more fully to Christ, who is its head, the one who was faithful to God in and through apparent human failure.

he is confronting us?

Who Is Called to Mission?

Different branches of the Christian church have answered this question in different ways, some stressing that mission is primarily the responsibility of ministers or clergy, others seeing mission at least as witness as a responsibility of the whole church. Typically, however, across the denominational divides, Christians have tended to distinguish between mission narrowly understood, which is conducted primarily through preaching the gospel, and mission more broadly construed as the exemplary lives of Christians in the world. Today we have to rethink this division of responsibilities. If mission is primarily conducted through the church's active concern for God's world and in a struggle against the forces of the antihuman, then "preaching the gospel" in the narrow sense is more properly to be understood as a responsibility of "internal mission." Preaching the gospel is above all the way that Christians are reminded of their responsibility to mission and inspired to the cost of discipleship. The work of priests and ministers, in other words, is instrumental to the mission of the church, but not itself the mission of the church. The mission of the church is the work of the whole community, as it engages in a praxis of defense of the human, the contemporary proclamation of the Good News. In traditional categories we could call this "witness." But it is not so much witness to discipleship as it is witness that discipleship entails solidarity with suffering humanity, in the cause of faithfulness to God's love for the world. In the ancient world, those outside the young Christian community marveled at their praxis, exclaiming, "See how those Christians love one another." In our world, our mission will be successful if the world beyond the church looks at us and says, "See how those Christians love us!"

ALL YEARS: PREPARING FOR THE SEMINAR

Respond

Consider your entire time in EfM and name some views that you have discovered in your study of the EfM material regarding the mission of Israel or of the church.

Locate what your denomination or faith tradition says is the mission of the church or of people of faith, corporately or individually.

What do you believe God is up to in the world, the nation, the region, and the neighborhood in which you live, and/or in your personal life?

Practice

Reflect on your beliefs about the mission of the church and of your individual mission in the world.

Identify

From whom is the church's mission or your mission received?

a model How is Christ associated with the church's mission? With your understanding of your mission? *help the needy*

Name one context where you especially feel a sense of mission in your life. *Street van Tithing*

Explore

There are a variety of theological perspective questions that relate to doctrines of creation, sin, judgment, repentance, or redemption and that can be used to reflect on a personal experience or belief, a scripture passage or other article from a faith tradition, or messages and actions of the culture in which one lives.

Use *any* of the following that may help personal reflection on the statements you listed in the preceding Identify phase.

Creation/Wholeness: What is good or creative in the statements? How do your statements reflect or reveal a notion of wholeness or goodness? Where might power, powerlessness, or empowerment in the world be affected by your statements?

Sin: What do your statements indicate is broken or may be a cause of separation from God? How might acting on your statement cause or support brokenness?

Judgment/Recognition: How would action on your stated belief(s) about a personal or corporate mission in faith provide opportunity for a change of direction?

Reorientation/Repentance: What would need to change if you carry out the mission you believe you or the faith community has? What power may need to be relinquished? Who might need to relinquish that power?

Restoration/Empowerment/Resurrection: How might the mission you assent to contribute to restoration of wholeness between God and creation or between human beings and our world?

Connect

Who, what, when, or where are the contributing factors to your beliefs about personal and corporate mission? How did those beliefs come into being? Does your belief conflict with something you learned through experience or the world around you?

Apply

What or whose freedom is possible if your mission is fulfilled in any aspect of your life?

What do you need to learn in order to better live out your sense of mission?

What has already helped to prepare you to take up that mission?

Week Thirty-one

YEAR ONE

Read

Micah
Isaiah 1–39
Excerpt on Micah from Collins's longer work, *Introduction to the Hebrew Bible*, found in Part II of the Guide, pages 242–245
Collins, Chapter 16, "Isaiah," pages 164–173

Focus

Micah and Isaiah contain familiar passages that have been often quoted. Identify key verses from both prophets that speak to vocation, mission, and ministry.

YEAR TWO

Read

Galatians
Powell, Chapter 15, "Galatians," pages 307–321

Focus

Galatians, known as Paul's "angry" letter, brings emotion center stage in developing a theology. Consider how Paul's anger shows the creating of his theology. Explore what working with his anger led Paul to do. What light might be shed on Paul's view of gifts?

YEAR THREE

Read

MacCulloch, Chapter 21, "Enlightenment: Ally or Enemy?," pages 769–816

Focus

The Enlightenment produced a sea change in Western Christianity that continues well into the contemporary social and intellectual context. In what ways has the Enlightenment revolutionized the understanding of human nature? Think about the positive and negative impact the altered views of humanity have had on understanding vocational development.

YEAR FOUR

Read

Peace, Rose, and Mobley, Foreword, Introduction, and "Part I: Encountering the Neighbor," pages xi–44

Focus

In the Foreword to *My Neighbor's Faith*, Joan Chittister aptly describes what the book intends and why: "In this book all the languages of God are spoken–Hindu, Buddhist, Jewish, Christian and Muslim–so that we can learn from one another."[89] Much is to be learned about God's "commonwealth of love and justice," also known as God's Reign or the Kingdom of God. Identify the ways the essays in "Part I: Encountering the Neighbor" contribute to developing a theology of mission and ministry in a pluralistic world. Also, what specific ideas, images, or stories foster vocational development?

ALL YEARS: PREPARING FOR THE SEMINAR

Respond

Look for ways that multicultural experience impacted the people and institutions you read about in this week's assigned reading.

Particularly remark on how multicultural experiences shaped or impacted the church's understanding of its mission.

Make notes for discussion in the seminar.

Practice

Identify

Eric Law guides men and women to reflect on their perceptions and actions in light of increasing multicultural dynamics in much of the world. His work presents a model of human community and interaction that may be useful in theological reflection as a means of encouraging deeper insights and implications for ministry. His Cycle of Gospel Living, introduced in Interlude One, considers human relationship in terms of the dynamics of power.

---

89. Jennifer Howe Peace, Or N. Rose, and Gregory Mobley, eds., *My Neighbor's Faith: Stories of Interreligious Encounter, Growth, and Transformation* (Maryknoll, NY: Orbis Books, 2012), xii.

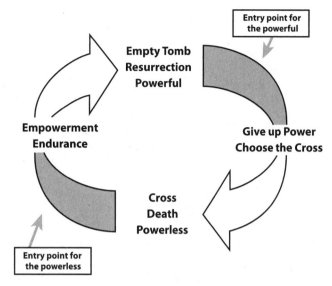

Cycle of Gospel Living

Explore

Imagine Law's model as an overlay on the EfM material you studied this week:

Where or how does the model fit?

Who had power?

Did anyone relinquish power? How?

Was anyone empowered? How did that empowerment occur?

Where is brokenness in the model? Where is restoration? At what point(s) might there be recognition that something needs to change?

Connect

Relate the model to your life and make notes about your connections from personal experience.

What aspects of your societal dimension relate to the model?

Apply

In what ways are you sent into the world to participate in Law's dynamic?

What is the relationship between the mission of the church and the larger question of the *missio Dei*?

Make notes for discussion in the seminar.

Week Thirty-two

YEAR ONE

Read

Jeremiah
Lamentations
Collins, Chapter 17, "The Babylonian Era: Jeremiah and Lamentations,"
pages 174–184

Focus

How does Jeremiah respond to his multicultural context? Note two instances when Jeremiah enacts his prophetic message. How would you describe Jeremiah's understanding of his own vocation?

YEAR TWO

Read

1 Corinthians
2 Corinthians
Powell, Chapter 13, "1 Corinthians" and Chapter 14, "2 Corinthians,"
pages 273–305

Focus

How does Powell's discussion of the Letters to the Corinthians illuminate the theology of mission, ministry, and vocation?

YEAR THREE

Read

MacCulloch, Chapter 22, "Europe Re-Enchanted or Disenchanted?,"
pages 817–865

Focus

This chapter lays out necessary components for setting the context of contemporary Anglo-American and European theology. Note the specific persons or ideas that interest you, and how what you identify correlates with your gifts and passions.

YEAR FOUR

Read

Peace, Rose, and Mobley, "Part II: Viewing Home Anew" and "Part III: Redrawing Our Maps," pages 45–124

Focus

When someone openly embraces the differences in another culture, that person sees home as through a different lens. Cultural dissonance may arise that requires re-drawing of familiar boundaries. What implications are there for mission in that circumstance? How do the stories affect your sense of self?

ALL YEARS: PREPARING FOR THE SEMINAR

Respond

Members of the theological team that worked with Paul Lakeland on the theme of "church" in *Constructive Theology* provide two short articles that flesh out the longer essay.[90] The following underscores the tensions around universalism and mission:

Mission and Christian Universalism[91]

Based on Christianity's own experience with universalism, Christians can discern both graces and problems that globalism entails. Throughout the ages, universalism has led many Christians to the insight that what deserves their ultimate loyalty is not any nation, ideology, race, culture, or other "local" affiliation, but only God's creation as a whole. Christian faith in a universal God has nurtured radical ideas of human dignity and equality; today, that same faith helps to define and defend human rights internationally. Christian universalism can have salutary effects on the advancement of knowledge. If the truth of the gospel knows no limits,

---

90. Serene Jones and Paul Lakeland, eds., *Constructive Theology* (Minneapolis: Fortress Press, 2005), 234–235. Amy Platiinga Pauw, the "Church" chapter editor, along with James. H. Evans, Mary McClintock Fulkerson, Roger Haight, Bradford E. Hinze, Leonard M. Hummel, Paul Lakeland, M. Douglas Meeks, Jamie T. Phelps, Kathleen M. Sands, Craig Stein, and Kathryn Tanner, collaborated around the theme (doctrine) of church. They augmented Lakeland's statement on mission (missiology) highlighting the effects of globalization.

91. Universalism is defined in the glossary contained in *Constructive Theology* as "the theological position that all people are saved by God." Jones and Lakeland, *Constructive Theology*, 304.

then the gospel can and must be reconciled with the best science and most profound thinking available.

Unfortunately, Christian universalism also has produced the opposite effects. Rather than a basis for equality, Christianity more often has built hierarchies of domination and submission. In relation to non-Christians, universalism has been a rationale for conquest and persecution. Confidence in the universality of the gospel too often has produced not open-mindedness but a lethal combination of ignorance about and arrogance toward knowledge that comes from other sources.

Universalism, then, can be emancipatory and redemptive. But it also can be destructive and imperialist. For Christian mission, both *ad intra* and *ad extra*, a great deal depends on telling the difference. If Christian mission is nothing more (or less) than the restoration of creation, criteria for discerning emancipatory universalism can be found in four features that the Bible ascribes to the world as God's creation: the world is good, free, historical, and participatory.

The goodness of creation implies, first and foremost, the material goodness of these bodies and this planet designed by God. Universalism can only be emancipatory if, first and foremost, it protects and promotes the physical well-being of humans, other life-forms, and the earth itself. An emancipatory globalization must create worldwide standards for wages, health care, and environmental protection. When globalization refuses these standards it shows the oppressive face of universalism.

The freedom of creation is the divine intention for each being and each community to be themselves. An emancipatory globalization can lead the peoples of the world to unprecedented levels of appreciation, encounter, and engagement with each other. But when globalization results in the homogenization or "Coca-colonization" of the world, this is cultural imperialism, not emancipatory universalism.

As a historical phenomenon, creation does not end "in the beginning." It continues through time, blending into the process of redemption. The process of redemption in history is not to be mistaken for the myth of progress, in which "developed" cultures are superior in every way to traditional cultures. A redemptive globalization will not impose the values of the modern West on other cultures but will emerge from multisided dialogue and sometimes struggle among the peoples of the world.

Finally, creation is participatory; all of humanity has both the right and the responsibility to be creatures who create. As globalization weaves information into a single web and economies into a single market, it can enable more and more people to take substantive part in the decisions that shape their lives. When globalization expands everyone's access to information and ideas, when it includes and empowers, then it is functioning as an emancipatory force. But when globalization takes decisions that ought be public and gives them over to the hands of private interests, then it becomes not a grace but a problem, a destructive expression of universalism.

What are the theological positions asserted in the short article?

Describe how your experience with Christians challenges or confirms the positions.

What support and challenge to the assertions do you find in your EfM reading throughout the year?

Practice

Identify a focus.

A mind map is a tool, similar to brainstorming and sometimes referred to as radiant thinking, that uses a graphical format to illustrate the connections between ideas and themes. The main idea is put in the center and secondary, tertiary, and so on, relationships are shown branching out from each level of connection.

More information about and illustrations of mind maps can be found at

http://www.mindmapping.com

http://mindmap.nu/how-to-do-radiant-thinking-based-on-mindmapping/

http://www.mindtools.com/pages/article/newISS_01.htm

You may find other sources of information on this process.

Construct a mind map by making associations with a centering theme or word. Write associations around the theme, anything that comes to mind in association with that theme. A mind map usually has at least three main branches.

The mind-mapping technique can be used to start a theological reflection from a theme from Lakeland's essay, "universalism."

EXAMPLE:

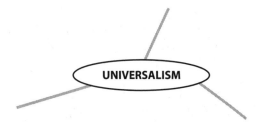

After making several associations, study the entire map.

What images or metaphors express the nature of "universalism"?

Select one to explore.

Explore the world of the metaphor/image:

Identify a specific point from which to explore the chosen image.

For example, if an image is "open doors," identify a standpoint—from inside or from outside. Stay with just one standpoint during the reflection.

Other standpoints can be the source of additional theological reflections.

What questions does the image raise for you? For example, what questions come up when considering an "open door" image from the standpoint of being outside the door?

Write down two or three questions and explore the image through those perspectives.

Connect with other areas of life.

Briefly state when you experienced the world depicted in the image/metaphor you are working with. Remember to work from the standpoint previously identified.

For example, in a "standing outside an open door" metaphor, someone would connect to times when they have "stood outside an open door."

Connect with other sources, such as contemporary culture and the Christian tradition. You may find that something from your reading over the past few weeks comes to mind. Essentially, consider how the culture in which you live or the Christian tradition you experience engages in an experience like your image.

Bring in your personal beliefs about "universalism." What do you believe? What do you hold to be true?

Apply

Notice how what you learn from the reflection applies to your life. For example, what light does this reflection shed on how you engage opportunities for ministry? What mission might your image be directing you towards?

Write a prayer about the learning or insight you have gained as a result of your reflection.

Note: There may be opportunity during the group's seminar time to explore the theological reflections of various group members, and/or to create a mind map to generate a reflection around a central theme of the group's choosing.

Week Thirty-three

YEAR ONE

Read

Ezekiel
Collins, Chapter 18, "Ezekiel," pages 185–196

Focus

Identify a concept drawn from this week's readings. Write one or two descriptive sentences that capture the idea. Explore the dimensions of the topic, such as what is assumed and valued; name the destructive elements that are present in the topic; examine the explicit and implicit hopes for the future. Ask, "What light do ideas and voices from contemporary literature, television productions, or Internet blogs shed on the reflection?" Note what position or beliefs you hold in relation to the topic. Consider the importance and implications your thinking has for serving and ministering to those among whom you live and work.

YEAR TWO

Read

Ephesians
Powell, Chapter 16, "Ephesians," pages 323–341

Focus

Where is Ephesus and what is its significance in Paul's journeys?

What is the mission of the church according to this letter to the Christians in Ephesus?

What do you believe about living "a life worthy of your calling"?

YEAR THREE

Read

MacCulloch, Chapter 23, "To Make the World Protestant," pages 866–914

Focus

MacCulloch's chapter covers over two hundred years of history that is likely familiar. As the historian's work comes closer to the present, the line between history and journalism blurs. Identify a thread that runs through the chapter. In one or two sentences, describe it. Examine the thread using questions framed from theological standpoints: human nature; creation, sin, judgment, repentance, and redemption; the way God is disclosed; the kind of future desired. Develop associations with concepts, images, or stories from current culture and society. Uncover what truths and beliefs you hold. What do you see that you have seen before? Describe what implications your reflection has for your daily life as a Christian seeking to serve the world in Christ's name.

YEAR FOUR

Read

Peace, Rose, and Mobley, "Part IV: Unpacking Our Belongings" and "Part V: Stepping across the Line," pages 127–206

Focus

"Interfaith encounter forces its practitioners to assume responsibility for both the actual and perceived histories of their groups."[92] Reflect on the significance of what the authors in Parts IV and V dealt with in such encounters and recall what you have experienced whenever you have encountered "the hospitality of your neighbor's faith."

ALL YEARS: PREPARING FOR THE SEMINAR

Respond

To whom is the church called at the time you have been studying and at the present time?

Pay attention to signs on churches in your vicinity or visit their buildings and notice their bulletin boards or visit their web sites.

What can you identify about what the sense of mission might be in these churches?

Practice

Alan Jones, Episcopal priest, author, and spiritual director, offers a description of the spiritual journey as engagement with three great imperatives of the desert tradition: Look! Weep! Live! This mode offers still another way to guide and deepen theological reflection.

The first imperative is, *Look!* Looking means a contemplative willingness to see what is there in front of us without prematurely interpreting what we see. The desert tradition claims that if we look long and accurately enough, the tears will begin to flow. Thus the second imperative is, *Weep!* The fruit of honest contemplation is "the gift of tears"; and the sure sign that our attentiveness has

---

92. Peace, Rose, and Mobley, eds., *My Neighbor's Faith*, 125.

been focused and honest and the tears cleansing is joy. Joy is the fruit of desert patience. Thus, the third imperative, *Live!*

The pattern is simple. We look. We weep. We live. This pattern is repeated throughout the believer's life. It echoes and reverberates both in and out of the Christian tradition.[93]

When we Identify a focus from which to begin reflection and Explore that focus, we respond to the imperative to *Look!*, noticing how the world is. Exploring also takes us into the *Weep!* imperative as a sense of what brings about separation from God and others begins to dawn. We enact the imperative to *Live!* as we explore that which restores wholeness and identify Insights and Implications that take us back into the action of life.

Practice reflecting with Jones's model on the various mission indicators you noted in the Respond section of this week's preparation. How does that sense of mission represent what the congregation appears to believe is "broken" in the world, and what represents their call to "*Live!*"?

Apply Jones's desert imperatives to your life as you have reflected on it during your experience in EfM. What have you looked at and seen as a result of EfM? What have you wept over? What have you lived in a new way?

Note: The preference is to work with actual evidence from local church statements—explicit or implicit—rather than just imagining what such statements or views might be. What are some ways that the seminar group might identify the sense of mission of churches in the area if there was not time for individuals to do this work before the seminar meeting?

---

93. Alan W. Jones, *Soul Making—The Desert Way of Spirituality* (San Francisco: Harper & Row, 1975), 22.

Week Thirty-four

YEAR ONE

Read

Isaiah 40–66
Collins, Chapter 19, "The Additions to the Book of Isaiah" and Chapter 20, "Postexilic Prophecy" pages 197–219

Focus

The additions to the Book of Isaiah contain the very familiar Servant songs. Reflect on how the imagery of the suffering servant has contributed to Christian theology and worship. What words and images seem most familiar to you?

Identify a story, image, and/or idea that affected you from your reading about the postexilic prophets. How do you define the vocation of prophet? A discussion of how prophecy in the Hebrew Bible has been interpreted in Christian contexts may be found in the article "Forthtelling, Not Foretelling" on the Oxford Biblical Studies Online website at http://oxfordbiblical studies.com/article/book/obso-9780195161496/obso-9780195161496-chapterFrontMatter-2

YEAR TWO

Read

1 John
2 John
3 John
Powell, Chapter 27, "The Johannine Letters: 1 John, 2 John, 3 John," pages 493–507

Focus

Reflect on how the theme of "God is love" relates to your interests and passions.

YEAR THREE

Read

MacCulloch, Chapter 24, "Not Peace but a Sword," pages 915–916

Focus

Look for the themes that interest you in the chapter and explore one using a couple of the theological perspective questions that have been offered this year from Bishop Tutu's, Alan Jones's, or Eric Law's approaches. Notice what connections you make with your experience and culture. What do you believe about the theme? Reflect on the implications your line of thought holds for living as a Christian in the various contexts of your life.

YEAR FOUR

Read

Peace, Rose, and Mobley, "Part VI: Finding Fellow Travelers," pages 207–242

Focus

Identify a theme that runs through the essays presented in Part VI. State the theme in writing. Examine the dimensions of the theme using the theological perspectives, such as how God discloses God's self; the quality and characteristics of humanity revealed in how the theme is developed in the essays; how the viewpoints of creation, sin, judgment, repentance and/or redemption are discussed. Relate content from contemporary society and culture to the theme. Ask what you believe, value, and affirm as true. Draw out the significance for your ministry.

ALL YEARS: PREPARING FOR THE SEMINAR

Respond

A second short article from Jones and Lakeland adds the following thoughts on mission.

Post-colonial Critiques of Mission[94]

Although it is a call to spread good news, the "Great Commission" of Matthew's Gospel has done considerable damage. This is the judgment of post-colonial criticisms, which interrogate the effects of the past 500 years of Western expansion, in which Western values, including Christianity, were brought to every corner of the globe. Christian mission was woven into mercantile trading routes and imperial expansion from the very beginning. However, post-colonialists focus on the medium of Western colonialism, an economic and political relation between nations in which the sovereignty of one was dependent upon the power of the other "empire" nation. Emerging in the mercantile imperialism of the late 1400s to 1800s and accompanying missionary movements, colonialist forms of Western power were later

---

94. Jones and Lakeland, *Constructive Theology*, 236–237.

enhanced through the force of monopoly capitalism in the late nineteenth through the mid-twentieth century.

Post-colonialist criticism reveals that missionary expansion has been inextricably complicit with forces of expanding power and the inevitable complexities of dominance and submission that attend them. Missionary literature of these centuries unabashedly brands the objects of mission as inferior in status. They were "the Heathen," according to a 1792 pamphlet. Africans were "savages" or "barbarians" practicing "primitive" religion. Even the "affirmation" in the 1537 papal announcement that Amerindians were human was rooted in an economy of Western superiority. Paradoxically founded in ostensibly well-intentioned desire to share good news, Christian mission's imaginaries for the Other and the practices that accompanied them effectively obliterated the dignity and agency of many populations in colonized territories.

Although the "Colonial period" has passed, the "post" of post-colonial criticism is not a chronological indicator, signaling that Christianity and the world have moved beyond the problems of Western dominance. Even with the coming of political independence for most colonized nations and the end of official colonial relationships by mid-twentieth century, new forms of global economic, military, and cultural dominance associated with global capitalism have emerged, frequently termed neocolonialism. Coinage of such terms as coloniality to refer to the continued residual effects of colonialism also reminds us that grave problems persist.

Despite universal renunciation of the dehumanizing terms of the past, what is problematic in continuing forms of coloniality remains unresolved. Some would argue that the more egregious treatments of "natives" as barbarian or pagan are corrected by recognizing the legitimacy of indigenous cultures. The missionary task is to adapt the gospel to a local culture—a process known as indigenization for Protestants and inculturation for Roman Catholics. The problem of colonized consciousness is, for example, solved by a recovery of traditional African religion, or at least by empowering indigenous African theologians. Others, however, insist that not only is a search for pure origins impossible, but inculturation and its terms (for example, culture as "clothing" or "soil" for the gospel) are themselves a species of post-colonialist Western discourse. However it is understood, post-colonialist discourse about mission constitutes a formidable search for the power of gospel as God's justice and will be vital to ecclesiology in the new millennium.

Notice the emotions and thoughts that the article evokes in you. Identify what experiences you have had that impact your response.

How do you think other authors that you have read in EfM would respond to the article?

Practice

Identify a focus.

For this Practice, work with the personal emotions, thoughts, and experiences you noted in the Respond section.

Explore the focus/Look!

As you think about your thoughts, feelings, and personal experience, what image or word might capture your sense of things?

Make some notes about the following:
Questions that arise for you as you consider the image or word.

What question(s) makes you *Weep!*?

How does your image or word address separation from God or others?

How does your image or word relate to power/powerlessness/empowerment?

Connect

How do you answer those questions?

Where do you turn for the answers?

Whose "voice" speaks answers to you?

Apply/Live!

State any sense of restoration to wholeness you experience in the reflection and/or how you are going to foster such a restoration in your daily life.

Week Thirty-five

YEAR ONE

Read

Daniel
Collins, Chapter 27, "Daniel, 1-2 Maccabees," Chapter 28, "The Deutero-canonical Wisdom Books," and Chapter 29, "From Tradition to Canon," pages 278–306

Focus

Daniel, the final book in the Christian ordering of the Hebrew scriptures, is believed to have influenced apocalyptic imagery in the New Testament, including the "little apocalypses" in Matthew 24-25, Mark 13, and Luke 21 as well as the Revelation to John. As you read the biblical text, notice familiar imagery such as monsters rising from the sea, the "Ancient of Days," "son of man," etc. Note the influence of Daniel on predictions of the "end times" in the boxed text on page 281 in Collins. What examples from culture/society of concern about the end of the world can you recall? How do they compare to the visions of Daniel?

As Collins says in his Introduction, the Deuterocanonical literature is not included in all editions of the Christian Bible. The Anglican tradition generally includes these books, but in a separate section. Note the following in Collins' analysis of Ben Sira and the Wisdom of Solomon: problematic images of women; the identification of Wisdom with Logos and Torah; the problem of theodicy; the immortality of the soul.

Consider Collins's description of the Hebrew scriptures as "a collection of writings marked by lively internal debate and by a remarkable spirit of self-criticism, directed not only at the people of Israel but sometimes at the myths and certainties of the tradition."[95] Note a few examples from your reading over the course of this year in EfM.

YEAR TWO

Read

The Revelation of John
Powell, Chapter 29, "Revelation," pages 519–537

Focus

State one new understanding and one thing that bothers you about the Revelation of John.

---

95. John J. Collins, *A Short Introduction to the Hebrew Bible* (Minneapolis: Fortress Press, 2007), 305.

YEAR THREE

Read

MacCulloch, Chapter 25, "Culture Wars," pages 967–1016

Focus

Reflect on how MacCulloch's context as an Oxford-trained British citizen shapes his understanding of history. How does his understanding compare with yours and the cultural context out of which you read history?

YEAR FOUR

Read

Peace, Rose, and Mobley, "Part VII: Repairing Our Shared World," pages 241–266

Focus

Describe the sense of God's call that comes through the essays you read this week.

ALL YEARS: PREPARING FOR THE SEMINAR

Respond

This unit brings attention to one's vocation as hearing and responding to God's call. State your deepest sense at this moment of what God is calling you to do to contribute to the restoration of wholeness in the world.

Practice

Describe how you experience something as a call from God.

What practices best help you attend to God and be available to experience a call?

What would hold you back from that practice?

Either in employment or a volunteer capacity, what activity most engages you in a sense of God's call to you?

What wholeness does that work contribute to?

What brokenness does it address?

How are you transformed in doing that work?

Describe your understanding of ministry for yourself.

Week Thirty-six:
Revisiting and Closing the Year

Individual responses to the material in the following Read, Focus, Respond, and Practice sections will be shared when the group gathers for the last meeting of the seminar year. The mentor and group will decide how they want to incorporate this work and the sharing into a celebration of the year.

ALL YEARS

Read

REVISITING SOME POINTS OF THE YEAR

The *Guide* invited us this year to use theological reflection perspectives of restoration and wholeness and perspectives of power, powerlessness, and empowerment, in addition to other familiar perspectives of the world, sin, judgment, repentance, and redemption. We also were invited to develop a personal Rule of Life.

Review the theological perspectives of Bishop Tutu's cycle of Wholeness-Restoration.

- Wholeness/goodness
  What is revealed about wholeness or goodness of creation?

- Brokenness/separation from God
  What constitutes threats to wholeness or goodness or as brokenness or separation from God?

- Recognition
  What is a threat to goodness or to a relationship to God? How would you recognize such a threat?

- Reorientation
  What reveals a reorientation to relationship with God, if any? What would such a reorientation cost? What would it promise?

- Restoration to wholeness
  Where is there a possibility of restoration to wholeness?

Review theological perspectives based on Eric Law's Cycle of Gospel Living: being powerful, loss or yielding up of power, and empowerment.

- Give up power: choose the cross
  This is a point of entry for the powerful. Who has power? What has to be yielded?

- Cross: death, powerlessness
  This is a point of entry for the powerless. What sacrifice(s) might be called for? What are the temptations of the cross, of powerlessness? To whom or what is power yielded?

- Empowerment: endurance
  How is power transmitted to the powerless party? What is required in order to enter the cycle that leads to empowerment? What builds endurance?

- Empty tomb: resurrection, power
  What is left behind? How does resurrection occur? What is the hope of the power received?

A Rule can reflect decisions about prayer, study, and action related to these categories.

- Listening

- Commitment

- Time

- Hospitality

- Reflection

Focus

Closure is a time to acknowledge what has been, to celebrate what now is, and to anticipate what will come. The time given to this depends on the length of time the group has been together and the personal styles of group members and the mentor. EfM provides an opportunity to form a close and supportive community that cannot be easily replaced. It is important for the group to plan appropriate ways for students to acknowledge the blessing of the group's time together, while also helping each other shift to new forms of emotional, spiritual, and intellectual support for their ministry.

Closure includes telling stories about significant events in the life of the group and the ways the group has affected each person. Name any regrets or frustrations people have, look ahead to what steps seem to be in view, and help one another plan for alternative forms of support for future life and ministry. The following design combines closure with a focus on ministry.[96]

---

96. Adapted from EfM, *Common Lessons and Supporting Materials* (Sewanee, TN: The University of the South, June 2005), 6-16-1 to 6-16-2.

ALL YEARS: PREPARING FOR THE SEMINAR

Respond

The theme for Volume B of the *Reading and Reflection Guide* is Living Faithfully in a Multicultural World. Keeping that theme in mind and reviewing your EfM work this year, respond to the following.

1. Experience in EfM has helped me:

   • give up . . .

   • take on . . .

   • change . . .

   • affirm . . .

   • focus . . .

   On this day I am a point of God's loving presence in this world and my purpose is to . . .

   What is the relationship between your responses to the previous two topics?

2. A metaphor describing me is . . .

   As a minister, what do I intend for myself? For others?

   How might I resist my intentions?

   Identify themes, insights, and surprises.

3. Contrast "doing ministry" with being ministers.

Practice[97]

Looking back from this moment, recall your original motives, intentions, and expectations for committing to EfM.

Name some ways the EfM experience has conformed to your original motives, intentions, and expectations.

In what ways has it differed?

How has the EfM experience confirmed and supported you?

How has it posed a challenge or discomfort?

Name other significant challenges and discomforts that face you right now.

Assuming that God's call always comes in some degree as challenge and discomfort, how and toward what might God be calling you through any present challenge?

---

97. Adapted from a design created by EfM trainer Bill Coolidge.

Identify your present motives, intentions, and expectations for committing to a life of ministry.

Have you changed? Are you changing? How?

If God chose to speak directly to you at this moment, what would you hear?

Reflecting on your time in EfM, consider your experience:

• as part of the group's life

• regarding personal relationships

• regarding educational input

Identify valuable supports for you and your ministry in the future as you are graduating from this program.

My personal ministry goals:

• For the next three months

• For the next year

• For the next five years

Complete the thought, "I plan to access support and supervision by . . ."

Explore your overall responses with any of the following perspectives: Notice how your responses reveal something about

Wholeness/goodness of creation

Brokenness/separation from God

Recognition

Reorientation

Restoration to wholeness

Giving up power (choose the cross)

Powerlessness (cross, death)

Empowerment (endurance)

Power (empty tomb, resurrection)

What Rule of Life will help carry you forward from this beginning made in EfM?

PART II

Resources

Overview of the Year: Reading Assignments for Volume B

Notes

1. Common readings at the beginning of each unit are read by all years.

2. Assignments for years one and two marked with an asterisk are readings in the Bible. Chapters in the survey text are numbered. Please note that chapters are sometimes read out of sequence. When both are assigned, it is suggested that the Bible be read before the survey text chapters.

3. Readings in the each of the three texts for Year Four are indicated by name of the author(s).

WEEK	UNIT	YEAR ONE	YEAR TWO	YEAR THREE	YEAR FOUR
		Collins	Powell	MacCulloch	Allen, Sedgwick, Peace
1	**Introductory Meeting**	Norms, Books, Housekeeping, Orientation and Planning	Norms, Books, Housekeeping, Orientation and Planning	Norms, Books, Housekeeping, Orientation and Planning	Norms, Books, Housekeeping, Orientation and Planning
2	**Unit One** Spiritual Autobiography and Listening	Common Readings: Living in a Multicultural World Why Listen?	Common Readings: Living in a Multicultural World Why Listen?	Common Readings: Living in a Multicultural World Why Listen?	Common Readings: Living in a Multicultural World Why Listen?
3		Preface, Introduction 1 The Near Eastern Context 2 The Nature of the Pentateuchal Narrative	Preface 1 The New Testament World 2 The New Testament Writings	Acknowledgements, Introduction 1 Greece and Rome	Allen Preface Introduction: What is Theology?
4		* Genesis 1–11 3 The Primeval History	3 Jesus 4 Gospels	2 Israel	Allen 1 The Holy One of Israel
5		The Priestly Creation Story	* Matthew	3 A Crucified Messiah	Allen 2 Holiness for Today
6		* Genesis 12–50 4 The Patriarchs	5 Matthew	4 Boundaries Defined	Allen 3 The Maker of Heaven and Earth 4 Limits of Science
7		* Exodus 1–15 5 The Exodus from Egypt	* Mark 6 Mark	5 The Prince: Ally or Enemy?	Allen 5 What Is Meant by "God"

WEEK	UNIT	YEAR ONE	YEAR TWO	YEAR THREE	YEAR FOUR
8	**Unit Two** Theological Reflection as a Life Skill	Common Reading: Last Words	Common Reading: Last Words	Common Reading: Last Words	Common Reading: Last Words
9		* Exodus 16–40 6 Revelation at Sinai	* Luke	6 The Imperial Church	Allen 6 Nature as Witness and Innocent Suffering
10		* Leviticus * Numbers 7 Priestly Theology: Exodus 25–40, Leviticus and Numbers	7 Luke	7 Defying Chalcedon: Asia and Africa	Allen 7 Innocent Suffering and Life beyond Death
11		* Deuteronomy 8 Deuteronomy	* John	8 Islam: The Great Realignment	Allen 8 Suffering from Nature and Extreme Human Cruelty
12		* Joshua * Judges	8 John	9 The Making of Latin Christianity	Allen 9 The Sacrifice in Creation The Trinity
13		9 Joshua 10 Judges	* Acts of the Apostles 9 Acts	10 Latin Christendom: New Frontiers	Allen 10 The Incarnation as Sacrifice
14	**First Interlude**	Common Reading: Law Preface Chapters 1–8	Common Reading: Law Preface Chapters 1–8	Common Reading: Law Preface Chapters 1–8	Common Reading: Law Preface Chapters 1–8
15	**First Interlude**	Common Reading: Law Chapters 9–13	Common Reading: Law Chapters 9–13	Common Reading: Law Chapters 9–13	Common Reading: Law Chapters 9–13
16	**Unit Three** Developing a Sustaining Spirituality	Common Reading: A Graph of Spirituality	Common Reading: A Graph of Spirituality	Common Reading: A Graph of Spirituality	Common Reading: A Graph of Spirituality
17		* Psalms	10 New Testament Letters 11 Paul	11 The West: Universal Emperor or Universal Pope?	Allen 11 The Temptation in the Wilderness
18		* Song of Songs 23 Psalms and Song of Songs	* Romans	12 A Church for All People?	Allen 12 The Sacrifice of the Cross
19		* Proverbs 24 Proverbs	12 Romans	13 Faith in a New Rome	Allen 13 The Resurrection of Jesus and Eternal Life
20		* Job * Ecclesiastes (Qoheleth) 25 Job and Qoheleth	* Hebrews 23 Hebrews	14 Orthodoxy: More Than an Empire	Allen 14 Jesus as Lord and Jesus as Servant

WEEK	UNIT	YEAR ONE	YEAR TWO	YEAR THREE	YEAR FOUR
21		* Ruth * Jonah * Esther 26 The Hebrew Short Story	* 1 Peter * 2 Peter 25 1 Peter 26 2 Peter	15 Russia: The Third Rome	Allen 15 Revelation and Faith
22	**Unit Four** Integrating Belief, Behavior, and Doctrine in a Multicultural World	Common Reading: Attending to the Gaps Believing	Common Reading: Attending to the Gaps Believing	Common Reading: Attending to the Gaps Believing	Common Reading: Attending to the Gaps Believing
23		* 1 Samuel * 2 Samuel 11 First Samuel 12 Second Samuel	* Philemon * Jude 22 Philemon 28 Jude	16 Perspectives on the True Church	Allen 16 The Holy Spirit, the Church, and the Sacraments
24		* 1 Kings * 2 Kings 13 First Kings 1–16 14 First Kings 17–2 Kings 25	* Philippians * Colossians 17 Philippians 18 Colossians	17 A House Divided	Allen 17 Sin, Evil, and Hope for the Future Epilogue
25		* Ezra * Nehemiah 21 Ezra and Nehemiah	* 1 Timothy * 2 Timothy * Titus 21 Pastoral Letters	18 Rome's Renewal	Sedgwick Preface, Introduction 1 Describing the Christian Life 2 An Anglican Perspective
26		* 1 Chronicles * 2 Chronicles 22 The Books of Chronicles	* 1 Thessalonians * 2 Thessalonians 19 1 Thessalonians 20 2 Thessalonians	19 A Worldwide Faith	Sedgwick 3 Incarnate Love 4 Love and Justice
27		* Amos * Hosea 15 Amos and Hosea	* James 24 James	20 Protestant Awakenings	Sedgwick 5 The Practices of Faith 6 The Call of God Appendix
28	**Second Interlude**	Common Reading: Kwok Parts 1–3	Common Reading: Kwok Parts 1–3	Common Reading: Kwok Parts 1–3	Common Reading: Kwok Parts 1–3
29	**Second Interlude**	Common Reading: Kwok (review)	Common Reading: Kwok (review)	Common Reading: Kwok (review)	Common Reading: Kwok (review)
30	**Unit Five** Hearing and Responding to God's Call	Common Reading: The Mission of the Church	Common Reading: The Mission of the Church	Common Reading: The Mission of the Church	Common Reading: The Mission of the Church
31		* Micah * Isaiah 1–39 Collins on Micah 16 Isaiah	* Galatians 15 Galatians	21 Enlightenment: Ally or Enemy?	Peace, Rose, Mobley Foreword Introduction 1 Encountering the Neighbor

WEEK	UNIT	YEAR ONE	YEAR TWO	YEAR THREE	YEAR FOUR
32		* Jeremiah * Lamentations 17 The Babylonian Era	* 1 Corinthians * 2 Corinthians 13 1 Corinthians 14 2 Corinthians	22 Europe Re-enchanted or Disenchanted?	Peace, Rose, Mobley 2 Viewing Home Anew 3 Redrawing Our Maps
33		* Ezekiel 18 Ezekiel	* Ephesians 16 Ephesians	23 To Make the World Protestant	Peace, Rose, Mobley 4 Unpacking Our Belongings 5 Stepping Across the Line
34		* Isaiah 40–66 19 Additions to the Book of Isaiah 20 Postexilic Prophecy	* 1 John * 2 John * 3 John 27 Johannine Letters	24 Not Peace but a Sword	Peace, Rose, Mobley 6 Finding Fellow Travelers
35		*Daniel 27 Daniel, 1–2 Macabees 28 The Deuterocanonical Wisdom Books 29 From Tradition to Canon	* The Revelation to John 29 Revelation	25 Culture Wars	Peace, Rose, Mobley 7 Repairing Our Shared World
36	**Final Meeting**	Revisiting and Closing the Year	Revisiting and Closing the Year	Revisiting and Closing the Year	Revisiting and Closing the Year

Terms in the New EfM Curriculum

Common Reading   A common reading is assigned to all year levels. Each unit begins with an introductory essay read by all participants. Interlude texts are also assigned for common reading.

Identify, Explore, Connect, Apply   Theological reflection is described in four movements: Identify, Explore, Connect, Apply. This pattern also underlies the Read, Focus, Respond, Practice pattern of the Reading and Reflection Guide.

Interlude   An interlude is a two-week session in which all participants in a group read and respond to a common text chosen in relation to the theme of the Reading and Reflection Guide. There are two interludes in each program year.

Interlude Text   The text assigned to an interlude session is called an interlude text or interlude book. Two interlude books are read each year. The books address special topics that reinforce the theme of the Reading and Reflection Guide for that program year.

Participants   Those enrolled in a seminar group are generally referred to as participants or group members.

Program Year   The approximately nine-month period (thirty-six sessions) during which the group seminar meets is its program year.

Read, Focus, Respond, Practice   The guide for each session follows the sequence of Read (assigned reading), Focus (questions or terms specific to the assigned reading), Respond (connects the reading to the unit theme), and Practice (suggested application for individual and/or group work). This sequence provides a four-fold discipline for the practice of ministry.

Reading and Reflection Guides

These guides outline what is needed for participants to prepare for each of the thirty-six seminar meetings in a program year, including individual reading assignments and suggested ways to focus, respond, and practice what is being learned. There will be four volumes, A–D, used in a cycle. All groups will use the same Reading and Reflection Guide volume in a program year.

Readings in the Christian Tradition

The textbooks that replace previous chapters in the red notebooks provide participants with their weekly readings in the Christian tradition: the Hebrew Bible in Year One; the New Testament in Year Two; church history in Year Three; and theology, ethics, and interfaith encounters in Year Four.

Theme

Each volume of the Reading and Reflection Guide has a central theme that is carried through each of the units and interludes. Volume A's theme is ministry in your own particular context. Themes for the subsequent volumes are (B) ministry in an intercultural and interfaith context, (C) growth into Christian maturity, and (D) the journey into a deepening relationship with God.

Expectations and Purpose

The Participants

You, the participants in an EfM seminar group, are all adults. You set your own learning goals and need the latitude to learn as each individual does best. This requires a certain commitment to the program, but every participant does not need to work in the same way or with the same intensity. EfM has the flexibility for each of you to work in his or her own way.

There are some basic expectations of each participant:

- Attend the seminar sessions or at least maintain the community by letting others know when you will be absent.

- Read the materials and complete the work assigned to the best of your ability.

- Participate in the discussions, reflections, and worship of your seminar group.

The Mentor

The role of the mentor is crucial to the life of the group. The term "mentor" originates in Greek mythology. Mentor was a friend of Odysseus who remained in charge of his household while he was away. "Wisdom" in the form of Athena took shape in Mentor to be the guide and teacher of Telemachus. A teacher who guides is a description of an EfM mentor.

The EfM mentor brings skills in working effectively with small groups of people. The responsibility for the life of the group belongs to everyone, but the mentor is the initial convener. The mentor works to allow everyone an opportunity to learn, to share, to discover. At the same time, the mentor is also a member of the group. The mentor is also there to learn, to share, and to discover. The mentor has a second role, that of administrator for the group. The mentor handles registrations, receives and distributes materials, files reports, and is accountable to the administrative staff in Sewanee.

The mentor serves the group, neither as a teacher whose most important task is to provide information, nor as a therapist. The mentor is a guide in a journey of discovery. Some groups have co-mentors who work together as a team. This can be very helpful to the process since it can be very difficult to lead and participate simultaneously.

Mentor training and accreditation by an EfM trainer is required. It is an important component of the EfM program. Mentors must renew their accreditation every eighteen months.

The Seminar Group

The EfM seminar group is the crucible for learning in the EfM program. Each seminar group usually contains no fewer than six and no more than twelve participants and a mentor (or two co-mentors). The group provides an environment that supports the exploration and expression of ideas so that discovery and learning occur. It is a place of trust and confidentiality as participants in the seminar reflect upon ways to pursue a life of faith on a daily basis.

Seminars usually meet for two-and-a-half to three hours once a week over a period of thirty-six weeks during the academic cycle. For many of us this cycle begins in September and ends in June, but the group may decide to meet more frequently for shorter periods of time or less frequently for longer periods of time. Less frequent meetings can be very helpful when participants are scattered or they live in a region where bad weather can make travel difficult for extended periods. Some seminar groups meet online.

EfM seminars regularly engage in three different aspects of learning. These may not all be done in any one session, but attention needs to be given to all three aspects.

- There is time for social and spiritual needs to be addressed. This is a way to build trust, friendship, and community. It is an opportunity to support each other and maintain the freedom we all need to express our thoughts and feelings.

- There is time to discuss the materials which participants read in the texts. It is not a time for classroom presentations, rather an occasion to raise questions, wrestle with the materials, obtain clarifications, and generally share impressions about what has been read.

- There is an opportunity to engage in reflective activity. This may come in the form of a spiritual autobiography, one of many forms of theological reflections, studying and following a spiritual discipline, or exploring the meaning of the ministries we have.

The Program

The EfM Program expects participants, mentors, and trainers to remain faithful to the program. EfM is a program for adults and one expectation of the program is that adults take responsibility for their lives, set their own goals, and seek the support necessary to move forward. The program asks participants and mentors to provide an arena in which learning can take place on a mature adult level.

The relationship of EfM and The University of the South to the local church and to the judicatory/diocese is one of collaboration. Together we join to provide a program of theological education for the laity that carries a number of benefits.

- Portability—Participants can begin in one location and continue their work in another one.

- Accreditation—EfM grants Continuing Education Units to indicate completion of the work.

- Access to an international network

- A training opportunity for the laity

- Connection with The University of the South and its School of Theology

- Basic theological education to support the laity in responding to the call to ministry in daily life. For some the theological groundwork in EfM may be supplemented with additional opportunities to prepare for ecclesial roles such as that of lay reader, vocational deacon, or educator.

Providing the program is something in which various agencies participate. The local church provides a setting and may offer some financial assistance to participants. The diocese may contract with EfM, which lowers the tuition for participants. When there is a contract with the local jurisdiction, a function of that contract is the appointment of a coordinator who maintains a liaison with the EfM program in Sewanee, arranges for mentor training locally, acts as a communicator for EfM, and promotes the program.

What EfM Is NOT

- *EfM is not only Bible study.*

    EfM participants study what the Bible says, but they also learn how to understand the Bible within its historical context and literary setting. Biblical studies form the primary work of the first two years. EfM is more than a Bible study in which one reads the Bible, seeks to understand it, and then applies it to daily life. EfM takes seriously God's revelation through all of Christian tradition, from the earliest biblical messages, through the development of liturgy and theology, and even in the context of the challenges we face in our own times.

- *EfM is not a program in personal therapy or problem solving.*

    While EfM groups develop a close community in order to delve deeply into matters of faith and theology, the group does not exist as a problem-solving agency or as a setting for analyzing or addressing personal and social problems. In an EfM group, members may wish to share various aspects of their lives, but EfM is not a place to probe or press individuals to talk about those things they would prefer to leave unexamined.

- *EfM is not a closed community.*

    The content of EfM materials and the processes we use for reflection are not secrets. A group may invite a guest such as someone who brings some special information or someone who would like to participate for a session in order to decide if he or she might like to join. On the other hand, we do respect one another's privacy. This means that we expect the group to maintain confidentiality about personal matters. The rule of thumb is: secrets—no; privacy—yes. Participants may share with others what they have learned and how that was learned, but they are expected to retain in confidence specific personal aspects of their colleagues' lives which may have been shared during the course of the program.

- *EfM is not an academic program leading to a degree or an ordination program.*

    Local arrangements may permit EfM to become part of the work leading to a degree or to ordination, but the School of Theology of The University of the South makes no recommendations about ordination nor does it grant course credit for completing the Education for Ministry program.

Purpose Statements for the Five Units

Unit One, Spiritual Autobiography and Listening: to develop the theme of ministry in personal context through creating a spiritual autobiography using contextual lenses and to approach listening as a fundamental skill for ministry.

Unit Two, Theological Reflection as a Life Skill: to learn how to use theological reflection models and methods as a means for integrating experience and content and to develop the discipline of theological reflection as a life skill for ministry in daily life.

Unit Three, Developing a Sustaining Spirituality: to guide the work of developing a personal spirituality through prayer and worship which, when combined with study and theological reflection, offer a four-fold spiritual discipline that can help sustain us in the practice of ministry.

Unit Four, Attending to the Gaps—Integrating Belief, Behavior, and Doctrine in a Multicultural World: to provide means by which a person can examine and build a personal theology through the integration of belief, behavior, and doctrine.

Unit Five, Vocation—Hearing and Responding to God's Call: to offer a Vocational Development Model for use in discerning and responding to God's call; and, second, to provide a framework for reviewing the year's work.

Supplemental Readings in the Christian Tradition

Week Five, Reading Assignment for Year One

The Priestly Creation Story

The Priestly creation story in Genesis 1–2:4a is one of the shortest and yet most tightly packed theological statements in the Bible. In its present form it dates from the time of the Restoration in the fifth century BCE. It had developed, however, over a much longer period and had been polished smooth by the time P gave it its final working. We must study it line by line in order to unpack the many levels of meaning in it.

Let us go over the main points.

First read **Genesis 1–2:4a**.

Then read again the biblical reference for each point in conjunction with the discussion.

1. God alone is the creator of all, with no divine helpers. The world is not simply shaped by God. (1:1)

2. God creates by speaking; God simply says, "Let there be . . . ," and what is spoken comes to be. (1:3, 6, 9, etc.)

3. God creates light; it is not the gift of the sun, which shines only with the light God has given it. (1:3)

4. God keeps the waters of chaos in their place by calling for a firm dome to keep out the waters that are above and by gathering the waters below into the seas so that the dry land appears. (1:6–10)

5. The heavenly bodies—sun, moon, planets, and stars—which were thought to be gods by many cultures in the ancient Near East, are only creatures of God. (1:14–18)

6. The earth shares in the task of creation, though only at God's command: the earth brings forth vegetation. The waters also bring forth sea creatures and the earth, animal life, but not in the same way as the earth brings forth vegetation. God creates the higher forms of life. (1:11, 20–21, 24–25)

7. God creates humankind in God's own image and gives it dominion over all the creation. (1:26)

8. God creates humankind male and female, and this fact is connected closely with humankind's creation in the divine image. (1:27)

9. God blesses humankind with sexuality and the gift of children. (1:28)

10. The final work of creation is God's rest on the seventh day. (2:2)

The First Words

Even from this brief outline we can see some of the things that were on the mind of the author. First, one important aspect of this story cannot be seen in most English translations. Grammatically, the Hebrew begins in the middle of a sentence. What could this mean? Is it a mistake? Was the first corner of a manuscript lost? No, there is a theological meaning. Beginning a sentence in the middle is a way of saying, "We do not know what God was doing before our world came into being. Our knowledge cannot pry before the beginning of our world; God's beginning is unknowable to us."

God and Creation

Next, it is important to say, above all else, that God is completely different from everything else. Other religions may have said that there were all sorts of divine beings: animal monsters, heavenly bodies, the seas, storms—anything that seemed powerful or mysterious. For the P writer, nothing in the world is divine. Rather, the whole universe is God's creation. Some religions may have thought of at least part of the universe as being made out of the substance of the divine, flowing forth out of the god. For P, nothing of God flows into the universe; God is God, and all else that exists is not God and is not divine.

Third, there is no need to look to lesser gods for the fertility of the earth. Vegetable crops and animals are included in God's design for the world, and the earth brings forth her increase at God's command. The worship of Baals (fertility gods), with all the gross practices that went with it, is not necessary; indeed to worship them would be to deny the power of the one Creator.

Fourth, the whole creation leads up to the creation of humanity. Life has not been created in order to provide playthings for the gods nor to act as slave-servants to the gods. Humanity, man and woman, is created to be God's representative in governing creation. It is a position of great dignity and worth.

Israel, the Chosen People

Each of these points was important in the life of Israel. She had been chosen to be God's people; God had made a covenant with her and had promised that, through Israel, all the nations of the earth would be blessed. The covenant was the basis for all of Israel's religious faith. After the Israelites had settled in Canaan, they were tempted and led away from God to the worship of the Baals and the *astral deities*—the sun, moon, planets, and stars—which the other nations worshiped. The prophets constantly tried to overcome the worship of these false gods so that Israel would be faithful to the covenant. When the northern kingdom was destroyed and the leaders of Judah (the southern kingdom) were carried into exile, the warnings of the prophets were shown to have been correct. Thus we can see the P writer—in the circumstance of exile—expressing in this story the true dignity of human-kind and the complete sovereignty of God as these facts had been learned in Israel's life and taught by the prophets. All of what Israel stood for was expressed by the covenant. This was how Israel knew God; God was the God who had made the covenant with Abraham, Isaac, and Jacob and who had sealed it at Sinai through Moses. This God, and this God alone, had created the nation of Israel, and this God alone had created the heavens and the earth and all things.

The creation story expresses the faith of Israel learned by her experience as the people of God's covenant. Just as God had made Israel God's people at Sinai, so also God had made all of humanity in God's own image at creation. Both the covenant story and the creation story say the same thing: God has given humanity dignity and worth and dominion; therefore, the creation story reaches its climax in the creation of humankind.

The Sabbath

The P author does not end the story with the creation of humanity. The final day of creation is not the sixth, on which human beings are created, but the seventh, on which God rests. This rest does not mean only a mere recuperation from the exhaustion of creation. Rather it is a cessation of regular work in order to enjoy the fruits of that labor. God rests in order to enjoy creation. The P author, with special interest in the *cult*—the practices of worship—leads us to the practice of the Sabbath. This is not, however, a contradiction of what we have just said about the creation of humanity as the climax. The covenant, the basis of Israel's faith in the dignity of all people, is what the Sabbath is all about. The Sabbath is the celebration of the covenant. Therefore, the story leads to two ends, both of which refer to the same central point of Israel's faith: (1) God's gift of life and authority—a people under God—and (2) the Sabbath, which is the celebration of this people under God through the covenant.

You are not expected at this point in your studies to be able to feel all that is involved in the covenant. The point you should be able to grasp at this stage is that the P creation story sums up the experience of Israel and is not a simple childish story. You will come back to this story again and again, and the more you become familiar with the rest of the Old Testament, the more you will feel the power of it. Now look back again to the beginning of the story, and we will go over it more closely.

The Priestly Creation Story

This verse, which looks so simple in the English translation, is very strange in the Hebrew because it begins mid-sentence. The text can be translated, carrying it on through verse three, in several ways. (1) "In the beginning God created the heavens and the earth. The earth was without form and void, and darkness. . . ." (2) "When God began to create the heavens and the earth, the earth was without form and void, and darkness. . . ." (3) "In the beginning of God's creating of the heavens and the earth–(when) the earth was without form and void, and darkness was upon the face of the deep, and the wind of God was moving over the face of the waters–God said, 'Let there be. . . .'" None of these translations really fits the text as we have it, but each one is possible. Somewhat closer might be to start with an ellipsis ". . . " and then use the wording of option 3 above.

What difference would it make which translation we pick? Some people have argued that if we use the first one, there is nothing before God creates. God creates the heavens and the earth, and they are formless and empty until God then shapes and fills them. While it is fine theology to believe God created from nothing–*ex nihilo* is the Latin phrase that is used–Genesis 1 does not make such a claim. If we take the second or third translation, there is already a formless empty abyss and God begins to create; God shapes and fills a chaos that already existed.

Dualism

Later theology, especially Christian theology, has insisted that God created out of nothing not simply as a way of choosing one of these translations over the other. Theologians have been trying to oppose a point of view which was very common in the world of the first few centuries of the Christian era and is still very much with us. This point of view is called *dualism*. It says that there are two aspects of the world: the material and the nonmaterial, sometimes called the "spiritual." The material is usually regarded as less good, sometimes evil. Theologians have not wanted to say that there was something, anything, already existing when God began creation, because this already existing something, chaos, could be used by the dualists to refer to matter, the material stuff, which God shaped. They could then say that this matter is the source of evil. So the theologians said that God created *ex nihilo*, out of nothing; anything and everything that is, matter included, is created by God and is good. You can begin to see here that many beliefs, many truths, are not stated explicitly by every biblical passage on a similar theme.

Dualism had a great effect on the thinking of the early church. It came from eastern roots. In Persia the religion of Zoroastrianism taught that there were two gods, one evil and one good. The good god was the god of light; the evil god, the god of darkness. (The name of the god of light, Mazda, is known to many people although they may not know where it originated.) A man named Mani, who was greatly influenced by Zoroastrianism, developed a religion, dualistic in nature, that prescribed ways of combating the power of the material world and escaping into the world of spirit and light. His religion, usually called *Manichaeism,* flourished in the third and fourth centuries, especially in North Africa, and influenced many Christians. St. Augustine, one of the greatest theologians of the church, was a Manichee before he converted to Christianity.

Plato

The teachings of the great pre-Christian philosopher Plato have also led to dualistic conclusions. Plato taught that, although individual things in this world come and go—they are born and they die, they come into being and they decay—there lie behind the individual things the *ideas* of them. There are many individual trees, each different to some degree from the others and each destined to die and decay, but each is a partial representation of the idea Tree. The idea contains all that it is possible for a tree to be; it is complete and single, not needing many separate examples of itself to express its completeness; it lasts forever, eternally existing while the individual representations of it come and go. Why Plato said this, what problems he was trying to understand, we shall look at later. The fact that he said it, however, allowed people of a later time—during the third through the fifth centuries CE—to develop a religion that was dualistic in a much more subtle and sophisticated way than was Manichaeism. The Neo-Platonists taught that the ultimate One lies beyond all things, and it is impossible to speak of that One at all. The *via negativa* is all that is possible. From the One all the rest of the universe emanates as light emanates, flows, or shines from a light bulb or a candle. The farther away from the source, the less like the One a thing becomes, until finally, at the farthest remove, there is matter. A human being, according to Neo-Platonism, is really spirit, akin to the One, but the spirit is trapped in a material body. Below humanity there is no spirit; all is merely material. Only by mystical exercises can humankind rise above the material body and reach union with the One. This point of view has influenced much of Christian piety. Augustine was also a Neo-Platonist before becoming a Christian.

Whatever the correct translation of this verse may be, theologians were right in thinking that the Old Testament opposed dualism. The Hebrews did *not* make a distinction between matter and "spirit." As we shall see in the JE (Yahwist-Elohist) creation story, the first human being is made from the dust of the earth and has life breathed into him so that he becomes "a living being." The entire creature, without division into body and spirit, is a living being. When the Christian church said that Jesus is the word of God made flesh, it also spoke against any kind of dualism.

This is why many theologians prefer the reading of verse one that says, "In the beginning God created the heavens and the earth." But there is no way to decide on the basis of the text itself. The P writer has other ways of dealing with the problem of dualism.

Genesis 1:2

Whichever way you translate the first verse, when the earth appears it is without form and void—that is, it is chaotic, empty of all form, design, or meaning—and darkness is upon the face of "the deep." "The deep" is a translation of the Hebrew word *tehom*. Behind this word there lies a whole mythic tradition. In the ancient world of the Mesopotamian basin there existed a story of the creation of the world by means of a great battle between a warrior god and a dragon, a sea-monster, who represented watery *chaos*. To many peoples who lived in desert lands far from the sea, the sea was fearsome. Its great storms were powerful and destroyed ships and houses built close to the shores. Stories of sea monsters were told by returning sailors. So "the deep," the waters of the sea with its monsters, was a symbol of chaos to the ancient people.

The Babylonian creation myth is a long story about the birth of various gods and about the eventual conflict between the god Marduk and the goddess Tiamat. In the course of the conflict, Tiamat is slain, and it is from her body that the firmament, the great dome of heaven, is made. It is worth noting here that the name Tiamat is closely related linguistically to *tehom*. By slaying Tiamat, the chaos monster, the monster of the deep, Marduk makes it possible for order to reign.

Much has been made of the common background out of which the Babylonian and the Hebrew creation stories come. The differences between the stories are more important—and more instructive—than their similarities. The Babylonian myth is an involved story of the birth of the gods and of the struggles among them for supremacy. Human beings are created almost as an afterthought, to serve as slaves for the gods, tending the earth so that the gods might have leisure. In the P story, the reference to "the deep" is virtually the sole remnant of this older myth. There is no birth of God; God is there before the story begins. Only by taking a broad meaning of myth as we have done can the P story be called a myth at all. P has stripped the narrative of all features of a "story about the gods" and has reduced it to a statement of doctrine, using the older myth as a framework only. By using an older framework with which people were familiar, the writer is also able to "start where they are" and show them greater truth.

The capriciousness of the gods and the denigration of humanity in the Babylonian myth stand in complete contrast to the picture of the sovereign and loving God of the Hebrew story. Nothing is told of God except God's acts toward the world he is creating. No questions of God's origins are raised; no relationship to any other god is assumed (until we get to the plural pronouns in verse 26); and the dignity of humankind toward which the whole story moves is a contradiction of the Babylonian estimate of human worth.

Still, the symbol of chaos, tehom, the deep, like Tiamat—the monster of the deep—is important. Chaos, or the threat of chaos, is always present in life. We know that we are insecure in the world we live in. We feel the threat of destruction. The world itself is not secure. The ancients felt this, too, in the dark, a storm at sea, a tornado, wild forces of any kind. As the P story of creation unfolds, by bringing order to chaos, God takes possession of it and subdues it. In Hebrew thought, it is God alone who keeps chaos under control. In the story of Jonah, a man who refuses to obey the word of God finds himself thrown back into chaos where he is swallowed up by the very monster of the deep herself. Jonah returns to dry land when he promises to obey God.

There is an additional level of meaning in the use of tehom/Tiamat. Since the Priestly account comes to us through the experience of exile, using the term may be a subtle way for the Israelites to remember that ultimately the Lord and not the Babylonian gods is the source of all creation. (We see another example of this with the creation of the sun and moon.)

The wind or storm of God was moving over the chaos. The word that the English Bible translates "spirit" is *ruach* (pronounced ROO-ahk). This word can mean "spirit," but also means "wind, breath, or storm." In this verse, the picture is that of the great divine wind blowing storm-like over the sea, or "hovering" over the deep like a great bird about to light on its nest, especially one incubating its eggs. The "spirit" of God here should not be thought of as acting to create; it is simply there, a storm, almost part of the chaos itself in wildness, yet showing forth the presence of God about to create, to bring order into the chaos. The image of the "hovering" of the spirit is one of almost-life, of the care and tending immediately before birth.

Genesis 1:3

Light is created. It is not some god-like stuff that flows from God into the darkness. Some religions have thought of light itself as a god. With the fear of darkness that most people have, it is understandable that light should be thought of as divine, as saving in some way and giving safety. In Genesis light is from God. God alone is the source of the safety that light brings. Notice also that light is created before the sun, stars, and moon. Light does not come from them, according to this story, but directly from God.

The form of words in verse 3 is important: "God said . . . ." God creates by his word. In the P account God creates by speech alone. This shows God separated from his creation and speaking to it. It portrays God with such immense power that it takes only a word for there to be a creative response. Later philosophers and theologians speak of both the transcendence of God and immanence of God. Transcendence refers to the separateness of God from God's creation; immanence refers to God's nearness. The creation-by-speech here in Genesis 1 shows God's transcendence. In Genesis 2 the immanence of God is evident in the manner of creation, for God shapes the clay.

Thought about God swings between these two poles. On the one hand, if God is not transcendent, God tends to become confused with the rest of the world. Pantheism is a form of religion that overemphasizes the immanence of God at the expense of transcendence. The term means literally "all is God." Stoicism is an ancient religion, prominent in the world of the first few centuries of the Christian era, which is pantheistic. Much modern thought tends also toward pantheism, confusing nature with God. Unless God is not the world, God loses the dimension of divinity.

On the other hand, if God is not immanent, near to us, then God is irrelevant. A merely transcendent god who was not accessible to his people could not even be known, let alone worshiped. In the eighteenth century, when people were supremely confident in the power of human reason to know and understand all things, a view of the world developed that did not allow God to have any significant relationships with the world. The universe was thought to be like a huge machine, operating according to the laws inherent in it. A theological school of thought called deism pictured God as a clockmaker. God designed the universe and made it as a clockmaker makes a clock, in such a way that it could continue to run on its own. Then God withdrew from it, allowing it to run in accordance with its inherent laws, never intervening again. This is a doctrine of God that overemphasizes the divine transcendence. If it be true, there is no point in praying to God or expecting any relationship with God other than adoration for the work that the almighty has done in time long past.

By saying that God creates both by the word and by handling the stuff of creation, the biblical writers express both the transcendence and the immanence of God. God is the one who stands over against us, completely different from us, and speaks the divine word to us; God is also the one who is immersed deeply in the world with the stuff of it clinging to God's hands. God is not the world, but God is deeply involved in it.

There is one further point that P wants to make: the world is "good." It is like a refrain in a song. Here, God declares the light to be good. This does not simply mean that it is pleasant or beautiful. God also creates the great sea monsters and creeping things and calls them good. When God calls them all good, the meaning is that they fit in with the great overall purpose of creation. They have their place in the grand design. The goodness of creation is based on God's purpose, not on our sense of beauty.

Genesis 1:4–5

Notice that although God creates the light, darkness is not created. God separates the light from the darkness, but darkness continues. Primitive people, like many of us moderns, feared the darkness, especially when there was no moon or when it was cloudy so that there were no stars. Evil spirits—and evil people—can work their wills in the darkness.

Notice also that, even though God does not create darkness, God calls the light "day" and the darkness "night." In naming the darkness God takes possession of it. Throughout our study of the Old Testament we become aware of the power that ancient people ascribed to the act of naming. If you were able to name something, you had power over it. Even today we see something of this. A parent gives a newborn child her or his name; the child has nothing to say about it. When children grow up, they can legally change their names, but while they are children, it is the parents who decide what they shall be called. It may be that the custom that teenage children have of taking a nickname by which their friends know them is an unconscious attempt to break loose from the bonds of parental control. A remnant of this control-by-naming can also be seen in the care with which some people try to ensure that coworkers never discover that childhood nickname. To know someone's embarrassing nickname would be tantamount to having a certain degree of control over the person.

In the Old Testament we see events in which God changes a person's name: Abram is changed to Abraham, Jacob to Israel. The meaning of the name is not as important as the fact that God has changed it and has thereby claimed the person. When God names the darkness "night," God claims it, takes possession of it, and thereby restrains it by his power. We said earlier, in discussing the first verse, that P had ways of combating dualism: This is one of them. The possibility of chaos taking control of God's creation is overcome because God takes possession of darkness and is Lord of the night as well as of the day.

The final sentence in verse 5 shows the Hebrew system for counting the days: A day goes from evening to evening, not from morning to morning as ours does. In Jewish custom this is still so; the Sabbath, for example, does not begin on Saturday morning, but on Friday evening at sundown. In the Christian church holy days are first celebrated on the evening before. Christmas eve and Hallowe'en (which is "All Hallows' Eve," the eve of All Saints' Day) are well-known examples, but the rule applies in all cases. Worship services held on such "eves" characteristically contain prayers and scripture readings concerned with the theme of the holy day itself.

Genesis 1:6–8

The word translated "firmament" means a hammered metal bowl; the firmament is like a great upside-down metal bowl that separates the waters. In this imagery we have the ancient view of a three-tiered universe, which was held, with modifications, until the sixteenth century CE when Copernicus put forth his theory of the motion of the planets around the sun. In the Genesis picture, the earth is a disk with waters beneath it and the firmament above it holding back the waters. So the three tiers are the waters under the earth, the earth, and the waters above the firmament. We see this cosmology (picture of the earth) again in the second of the Ten Commandments, when we read, "You shall not make for yourself an idol, whether in anything that is in heaven above, or that is on the earth beneath, or that is in the water under the earth. . . ." The reason for this commandment is that all the things in this three-tiered universe are creatures, not God.

Notice that heaven is not the sacred dwelling-place of God; it is simply the firmament. God dwells above heaven. The important point about this is not that it tells us where God is, but that it says God is not to be localized in any point within creation.

The creation of the firmament to keep the waters in their proper place reflects the ancient fear of water in large quantities; a deluge of water symbolizes chaos. Once again, the P writer deals with chaos and dualism. Chaos is held in check by the firmament, which God has made. Humankind is dependent only on the good God for safety. In the P account of the story of Noah and the flood, God opens the windows of heaven and the springs of the deep and releases the waters of chaos to destroy a large part of creation. As we see when we study that story, God makes a covenant with Noah promising never to do that again—God's creation shall stand and the watery chaos be held back forever.

Genesis 1:9–10

Again we see the fear of water, and God sets the proper limits of the seas so that the dry land appears. This is a different form of the creative act of God of withholding the power of chaos.

By having God name the dry land "Earth" and the waters that were gathered together "seas," the P writer is using the names of powerful gods in ancient religions. Because God both creates and names these, we are to see that they are merely creatures, not gods. The P writer thus combats the influence of polytheism (belief in many gods). Once again comes the refrain: "And God saw that it was good."

Notice that the refrain did not occur at the end of the second day when the firmament was constructed. This formula of approbation does not reappear until the seas and the dry land are created. This is because the creation of the firmament is only part of the complex work of creating the world of cosmos within which the rest of creation will take place. The formula of approbation designates the completion of an act. On the second day a creative act is left incomplete, and on the third day two acts occur. The fact that two days are spanned shows that P is using older traditional material, fitting it, sometimes awkwardly, into a seven-day scheme. The liturgical interest of P, the concern that the whole story leads up to the Sabbath, compels the use of a seven-day scheme and the fitting of material into that scheme as neatly as possible.

Genesis 1:11–13

In the ancient world, wherever the growing of crops took the place of hunting or herding as the chief means of life and livelihood, people became concerned about the fertility of the earth. Without the proper mixture of good soil, water, and sunlight, the crops would not grow. Almost all agricultural societies have religions that try to bring about the fertility of the earth. In the ancient Near East these religions often tried to do this by practicing sacred prostitution. By having sexual relations with a temple prostitute, one guaranteed that the land would be fertile. In these verses the P writer combats this kind of religion.

Plant life is created by God. But notice how this happens. Previously, God has created by his word. Here God speaks to the earth, commanding it to "put forth" vegetation. P does not try to deny the obvious fertility of the earth. The wonder of the seasonal rebirth of green things from the earth is too clear to be denied. But P has the earth act at God's command. The earth's fertility is God's gift.

The reference to "plants yielding seed and fruit trees of every kind on earth that bear fruit in it" is to grasses and herbs that yield seed directly, and those plants and trees that have their seed inside a fruit or nut. That is, all kinds of plants have within them the means of reproduction. The earth is fertile and plants have the power to reproduce, due to the command of the word of God. The self-contained powers of nature to bring forth life are not nature's own; nature is a creature. And it is good.

Agricultural fertility cults frequently have in their mythology a dying and rising god. When scholars of the history of religion noticed this, and especially when they saw the forms it took in the Near East, many of them suggested that this accounted for the Christian belief in the death and resurrection of Jesus. This, they thought, was simply a variant on the dying and rising god of the agricultural fertility cults. In fact there is much of the symbolism of the rebirth of nature in the proper celebrations of Easter. The lily, the rabbits, Easter eggs, all speak of the rebirth of natural life. (But for those of us who live in the northern hemisphere, it is too easy to drift into a belief that Jesus' resurrection was somehow part of the natural order, rather than a gracious act of a loving God.)

The ancient Hebrews were surrounded by these kinds of religions, particularly in the myths surrounding Baal, the Canaanite god of fertility, and Anath, his sister. The myth tells of the death of Baal. The god of death, Mot, holds Baal in the prison of death. Anath goes to Mot, slays him and cuts up his body, casting it about over the land, and Baal comes back to life. The prophets of Israel constantly fought against Baal worship. Israel had been created as a nation by God and must remain faithful to him. Still, the need for successful agriculture was obvious. In the P creation story the author maintains that the God of the deliverance from Egypt is also the one who gives fertility to the earth. Faithfulness to the covenant will suffice to ensure the fertility of the land.

The figure of Jesus comes out of this kind of background. There can be no possibility of adequately describing his death and resurrection in the terms of the fertility cults. His death was a once-for-all event and his resurrection has its meaning only in connection with the promises God made to Israel in the covenant. It speaks not of life coming naturally out of death, but of God being faithful to God's promises.

Genesis 1:14–19

On the fourth day the heavenly bodies are created. Worship of the astral deities—the sun, moon, stars, and planets—was widespread in the ancient world. Indeed, almost anywhere you go around the world you will find evidence of such worship. The stars and planets are one feature of nature that is there for all to see. Hunting tribes may not be concerned with growing crops;

different animals that have been worshiped may not be known in places far from where they live; oceans may be unknown to inland dwellers, and deserts with their sandstorms may be unfamiliar to people who live along the coasts. But the lights of the heavens can be seen anywhere in the world.

One of the things about the stars that impresses people who pay close attention is that they move with such regularity. We are sometimes amazed that our astronomers can predict with accuracy where a particular planet will be at a specific time, but the ancient astronomers could do this, too. Ancient people were impressed with the fact that, although much in life was uncertain, the movement of the stars was always the same.

Because of the regularity of the heavenly bodies, many believed that the stars controlled everything else and determined what was to happen on earth. Even today astrology, the study of the stars to see what they tell of life, is popular. Some people really believe what their horoscopes say. Others may view astrology as mere superstition, but in ancient times it was a serious matter. All of life was thought to be governed by the astral deities. Men and women, in this view, simply live out lives that have already been determined at the time of their birth. They have no freedom and nothing much matters, since all is determined in advance.

For Israel, however, this could not be so. God had called the people Israel and made a covenant with them. God would be their God and bless them, and they were to keep God's commandments. Israel could be faithful to God or unfaithful. Israel was free–to obey or disobey. Therefore, Israel was responsible for what she did. To believe in the astral deities and their control over life was a denial both of the lordship of God and of human responsibility.

The P editor says that God created the lights in the firmament–they are not gods. Although P used the names of the gods Earth and Sea, "Sun" and "Moon" are not used. By using the clumsy expressions "greater light" and "lesser light," P makes it plain that these, too, are creatures of God. We may have here another example of the exiled Israelites being able to find a "safe" way to jeer at their captors. "You worship 'big light' and 'little light,'" they are saying, "while we worship the creator of all that is."

The heavenly bodies are creatures of God, and they have quite simple jobs to do. They do not control the lives of people: they are the means by which to tell time! They divide the day from the night and they mark off the seasons and the years. They also give light on the earth, but it is not their own light, but the light that God created first of all creatures. This, too, is good; another act of creation is completed. With this, the cosmos (the universe itself) is finished.

Genesis 1:20–23

On the fifth day living beings are created, beginning with those that are least like humans and moving, on the sixth day, to humankind, which is created in the image and likeness of God. Living creatures are treated in a special way in this story. The plants, which were brought forth from the earth, are not thought to be forms of life. They have their seed and reproduce, but they are not called living creatures. When we look at this first creation story, we see that humans were allowed to eat vegetables but not meat. The life given to God's creatures is sacred and is not to be taken away by any other creature.

There is a Hebrew word used in this chapter that is not translated into English in every instance. When used of human beings, the word *nephesh* is usually translated "soul." But when used of other members of the animal world, it is often left out. This is unfortunate, for the P writer's use of nephesh makes some important theological points. There is no simple English word or phrase to cover the two aspects of nephesh. It refers to the life force that separates animals from rocks, for instance, or stars, and also from plants. Nephesh also refers to the individuality of each creature. We are accustomed to recognizing each human being as unique; the P writer believes every animal—even the "creepy crawlies"—is unique to God.

Of the living creatures, first the sea monsters are created, then the rest of the sea creatures and the birds. The seas have been separated from the dry land and held in their place—chaos has been controlled. Now even the fearsome monsters of chaos are discovered to be creatures of God and are called good; they are nothing to fear. These living creatures are then given the gift of procreation as a blessing. Even for living creatures, fertility is not simply a power contained within them but is a special gift from God. Only God is the source of creativity.

Verse 21 uses the verb *bara*: create. This is a different verb from those used before, except in verse 1 when bara is used for the whole process of creation. This verb never has anyone or anything except God as subject. Both God and people can "make," "shape," "form," and so on; only God is said to bara.

Genesis 1:24–25

On the sixth day the earth brings forth living creatures: domestic animals (cattle), wild animals (beasts), and creeping things—all the forms of life on dry land. All are connected very closely with the earth, which acts as mediator of God's creation. There is no blessing or command to be fruitful; apparently, as with the plants, this is part of their nature. Perhaps the blessing was necessary for the creatures which came from the sea because the sea was not given the ability to give power to reproduce. This is the suggestion that Gerhard von Rad makes in his book Genesis. He says, The absence here of divine blessing is intentional. Only indirectly do the animals receive the power of procreation from God; they receive it directly from the earth, the creative potency of which is acknowledged throughout. Water, by creation, stands lower in rank than the earth; it could not be summoned by God to creative participation.

Yet in verse 20 it seems that the same command is given to the waters as was given to the earth: "Let the waters bring forth. . . ." This is a case in which the English translation is somewhat misleading. In the Hebrew three different verbs are used in those places where the English reads "bring forth." In verse 11 the verb is *dasha*, "to yield tender grass," and it is in the causative form–"cause to yield tender grass." In verse 12, the verb is *yatsa*, "to go out," again in the causative–"cause to go out." Thus in the case of the earth's "bringing forth" vegetation, the verb is in the causative: the earth causes the grass to come forth. In verse 2 also the verb is yatsa in the causative, so the earth causes the living creatures to come forth. In verse 20, however, the verb is *sharats*, "to swarm," and it is in the simple form not indicating causation. Verse 20, therefore, means, "Let the waters swarm with living creatures. . . ." God created them directly, without the mediation of the waters, and gave them the power to reproduce.

The real significant contrast seems to be not so much between the creatures of the water, the birds of the air, and the animals of the dry land, but between the animals and human beings. The animals are closely tied to the earth, whereas humans are more intimately related to their creator.

Genesis 1:26–28

This is the climax of the story. In all the other acts of creation the form of words is very direct: "Let there be . . ."; "Let the earth put forth . . . ." Here, God takes counsel with God's self for a more deliberate and important act: "Let us make man in our image, after our likeness." This is a very strange expression. The name for God in this story is Elohim. When we discussed this before, noting that it is the name which the E writer uses and also the P writer at this point in the story, we mentioned that the word is in the plural: the gods. We also said that there was no doubt that both E and P believed in only one God. All through this story of creation the word Elohim has been translated "God," but now, in verse 26, the plural is used: "Let us . . . in our. . . ."

In the ancient world the idea of a heavenly court was common. The main god was surrounded by other heavenly beings the way a king or queen is attended by the members of an earthly court. In most of the old religions the court was made up of lesser gods. In the Old Testament there was only one God, but God was frequently pictured as being served by a court. In some present-day eucharistic liturgies this same imagery occurs: "Therefore with Angels and Archangels, and with all the company of heaven. . . ."

God is submerging God's self in the heavenly court. "Man" is made in God's image. "Man" is like God, but is also quite distinct from God. The P writer in this whole section seems to be saying these two things about humankind. On the one hand P uses the words "image" and "likeness": An "image" is a copy of the original, like a statue, and a "likeness" is an outline or silhouette. This would indicate a very close likeness to God, even in a physical sense. On the other hand, God is submerged into the heavenly court, so the likeness to God must be somewhat blurred.

In addition, the Hebrew word for man used here is *'adam* (the same word which later will be used as a proper name, Adam). This word is closely related to the word for earth, *'adamah*. Thus P also shows that though humankind differs from the animals, it remains tied to the earth and therefore to the animals and indeed the rest of creation.

The result of this very subtle use of words is to give a picture of humankind ("man," male and female: see below) as a being who is very much a creature, not to be confused with God, but one who stands in a very special relationship to God and is very much like God. It would seem that the point here is not so much to say that humanity, as the image of God, can give us an idea of what God is like, as it is to say that humanity is to act like God in the world: God gives human beings dominion over all the living things in the world. Their purpose is not to rule, but to act as God's agent or steward.

It was a common practice in the ancient world for statues of a king to be set up throughout his realm. These were not regarded simply as carved statues, but as the king's representatives, looking out for his interests in those places where the king himself could not always be. This seems to be the idea expressed here: Humankind is God's representative, looking after God's interests in the world. This authority, dominion over God's creation, is given in the creation.

'Adam is not a sexually specific word. There is another word for a male person: *'ish*. In spite of the male domination of ancient society, P means both "man" and "woman" when he uses *'adam*. (Notice the change of pronouns in v. 27: "In the image of God he created them, male and female he created them.") In the P account, sexuality, male and female together making up *'adam*, is a direct creation by God from the outset. (The JE story has woman made after man.) God blesses and commands humankind to procreate: "Be fruitful and multiply, and fill the earth and subdue it." Sexuality, then, is a gift of creation, a blessing, and a command.

Genesis 1:29–31

Notice that there is a limit to human dominion: Only vegetables may be eaten. Both humans and beasts are given vegetables for their food, though to humans both herbs and fruit are allowed while the animals have only herbs (green plants). The shedding of blood is not part of the divine plan for creation. In the Old Testament it is a basic belief that "in the blood is the life." God alone gives life, and it is not to be taken. Those who spill blood put an end to what cannot be revived. Later visions of the perfect time that will come when God brings in the kingdom show animals and humans living without shedding blood. The P writer, of course, knows that both animals and humans eat flesh, but a complete respect for life leads the writer to say that this is not part of God's plan. We shall see that P has God give animals to humans for food at the time of Noah. Even then the blood is not to be eaten. It is to be poured out to God as giver of life.

The final refrain is emphatic: ". . . indeed, it was very good." The world as it comes from the hand of God is perfect. This is the basic faith expressed in the Old Testament: whatever evil there is now in the world is not due to God. As God created the world there was no evil in it, and no dualistic power of evil. As the JE account will go on to show, evil comes when human beings overreach their assigned role. Not content to be God's representatives in the world, humans aspire to be as gods themselves.

Genesis 2:1–3

We would expect the P writer to say that creation ended on the sixth day, but this does not happen. God finished the work by resting on the seventh day. Rest is part of creation. To us rest sounds like doing nothing. To those who have to work until they are exhausted, to fight for the very possibility of life, leaving the old to die by themselves because there is no time to tend to them and still carry on the struggle for life, rest is an activity of sheer bliss. This is the kind of life that was usual for the ancient people, and is still true for most of the earth's people now. Rest, for them, is a necessary activity of life; without it, life is ground down into death. Thus the seventh day is not a day apart from creation, but the time of the creation of the act of rest. The Sabbath, in the Israelite calendar, is not a day of inactivity, but a day when work is not done so that rest may be done. As a celebration of the covenant, the Sabbath was especially seen as the day of recreation, of being restored to the very basis of life. God has hallowed, set apart, this day for this use. Verse 4a says that all this is a genealogy, the generations of the heavens and the earth. P usually puts this kind of verse first as a title. Here, since the creation story has its own introduction, it had to be put at the end.

Summary

1) *Dualism is rejected.* Light is created and comes from God. Though light is good and necessary, it is not to be worshiped. Darkness, though it is fearsome because it conceals evil action and makes it easier to commit evil, is not in itself to be feared; God claimed it and is Lord of it when God named it "night." The waters of chaos are set within their proper limits by God: the waters above are held out by the firmament and the other waters are gathered together as the seas and kept in their place by God's command. The monsters of the deep are like playthings to God, who created them and gave them the seas in which to roam. All this may sound very far from our way of thinking, but its message to us is clear. Biblical faith does not allow us to call anything that God has made evil or unclean, nor does it support our fears of the unknown. God is behind all that is, and we need fear nothing but God's absence.

2) *God is both transcendent and immanent.* God is the absolute Lord over creation. Nothing else is to be mistaken for God and worshiped. This means that we need not bow down before anything in the world! But God is also very near to everything in the world. God is involved in creation, so that we cannot treat anything that God has made as though it did not matter. The immanent side of God is presented more explicitly in the creation account of Genesis 2.

3) *There is freedom in the world.* Nature acts as God has created it to act, but it does so in respect to God's command to it. Human beings are given a role to play in God's design, but they must respond from their own freedom. The sun, moon, and stars do not control the things that happen. Nothing is decreed beforehand and sealed in fate. The astral bodies measure time, but they do not control it.

4) *Creation is fertile by the gift of God.* Ancient people thought that the powers of nature that gave or withheld fertility had to be worshiped. P says that fertility is from God, and God alone is to be worshiped. This belief, by assuring us that nature is not sacred, has allowed us to subdue it and bring it under our control. Much mischief has been done under the auspices of this word "subdue." The notion is one of responsible stewardship, not at all one of exploitation. We need now to remember that it belongs to God and brings its resources to us as a gift; ours to control, it is not ours to plunder.

5) *Humanity is in the image of God.* Humankind is shaped after the pattern of the elohim. This strange imagery both expresses the dignity of humankind and sets its limits. "Man," male and female, is like God, but is not to be confused with God.

6) *"Man" includes woman.* Sexuality is not simply a sign of our kinship with the animals and therefore a lower bestial function to be concealed and denied as unworthy of us. Humankind, 'adam, is not complete as male or female; neither is humankind originally a complete being, solitary and alone, who later "falls" into sexuality. From the outset God created humankind so that both sexes were needed for completeness. The modern notion of the self-sufficient individual is ruled out by this, as is the idea of male superiority. (This is quite remarkable since the place of women in ancient society, Hebrew included, was definitely lower than that of men. We can see this, and how it was made somewhat better, when we turn to the JE creation story.)

7) *Human beings are God's representatives.* Although the blessing of reproduction is given to humankind and animals alike, only human beings are commanded to fill the earth and subdue it. This has sometimes been taken to mean that we are given complete ownership of the world, but this is not the case. Humanity is God's steward. It is to fill the earth so that God may be

represented everywhere and to subdue the earth for the purposes of God. In spite of being made in God's image and being given the dominion, 'adam is still connected to 'adamah: that is, 'adam is of the earth and thus has limits set.

In these terms the P writer sees a perfection in humanity's original relationship to God and to the world. There is no downgrading of humanity as a mere puppet or slave to a tyrannical God; "man" (male and female) has great dignity and value. The terms of human dignity are clearly spelled out. The P writer was well aware of the fact that humankind had sunk to a level lower than that of the beasts, that we had denied our own dignity and taken it away from others, that we were such as to be worthy of complete condemnation before the righteousness of God. This merely points up the rightness of the terms of human life which humankind has violated. All, even the downfall of humankind, is set within the order which God has created.

Week Twelve, Reading Assignment for Year Four

The Trinity[98]

The truth takes its own forms and expresses itself in its own ways. Our efforts at defining, proving, or establishing it are all acts after the event. It is what it is, and not what we make it. Christianity prevails in the world in a fact which we have called Trinity, and which is Trinity, however inadequate and unsatisfactory our explanations of the term or our analyses of the thing may be. I would describe Christianity in its largest sense to be the fulfilment of God in the world through the fulfilment of the world in God. This assumes that the world is completed in man, in whom also God is completed in the world. And so, God, the world, and man are at once completed in Jesus Christ who, as He was the *logos* or thought of all in the divine foreknowledge of the past, so also is He the *telos* or end of all in the predestination of the future. That is to say, the perfect psychical, moral, and spiritual manhood of which Jesus Christ is to us the realization and the expression is the end of God in creation, or in evolution. I hold that neither science, philosophy, nor religion can come to any higher or other, either conjecture or conclusion, than that. But now, when we come to the actual terms or elements of God's self-realization in us and ours in Him, we cannot think or express the process otherwise than in the threefold form of the divine love, the divine grace, and the divine fellowship, in operation or action. Putting it into scriptural phrase, we speak as exactly as popularly in defining the matter of the Gospel to be, The love of the Father, the grace of the Son, and the fellowship of the Spirit. As our spiritual life is dependent upon each and all of these three constituents, so we can know God at all only as we know Him in the actual threefold relation to us of Father, Son, and Spirit.

The first element in the essential constitution of the Gospel is the fact in itself that God is love. That God is love means that He is so not only in Himself but in every activity that proceeds from Him. The very phrase the love of the Father expresses the whole principle of the universe. That God is Father means that it is His nature, or His essential activity, to reproduce Himself, to produce in all other that which He Himself is. That God in Himself is love carries with it the truth that from the beginning all things

---

98. This essay concludes *The Gospel in the Gospels* published in 1906 by William Porcher DuBose, the first dean of the School of Theology of The University of the South, Sewanee, Tennessee. You will find more information about him at http://liturgyandmusic.wordpress.com/2010/08/18/august-18-william-porcher-dubose-priest-1918/

else mean, and are destined to come to, love in the end. The mystery on the way that somehow light must come out of darkness, that love must needs conquer hate, and that in everything good seems to be only the final and far off goal of ill, may puzzle us but it does not disturb the principle itself. When we come to enter fairly upon the evolution of the future, the higher not merely psychical or social or moral but spiritual life and destiny of man, all the truth gradually dawns upon us in the following discoveries, which are already established facts of spiritual experience: The truth of all spirit is love; the matter of all law is goodness; God is not creator or cause only, nor lord or lawgiver only, but Father of all things, since all things through man are destined to share His spirit, to be partakers of His nature, and to reproduce Himself as Father in themselves as children. In order to be sons of God through actual participation in the divine nature there stands in the way indeed the need of a mighty redemption from sin and an as yet far off completion in holiness; but no matter how unredeemed or incomplete, we know beyond further question that all our salvation lies in redemption and completion, and that we shall be ourselves and the world will come to its meaning only when the self-realization of God as Father shall have accomplished itself in our self-realization as His children. If we knew the fact only that God in Himself is love, it would be to us a gospel indeed of great joy, because it would carry in it the assurance of the highest good, whatever that might be. But it would be but a partial gospel, and in fact only a gospel at all through its certainty of proceeding further.

The phrase Grace of the Son expresses that which perfectly complements and completes all that is meant by the Love of the Father. What is Fatherhood without a correlative Sonship? And what is all love even in God as its subject apart from its actuality and activity as grace in man as its object? The divine propriety of the terms Father and Son as applied to God cannot be too much magnified. The distinction between God as He is in Himself and God as He is in all possible expressions of Himself is one that we cannot think Him at all without making. The most perfect expression of love is contained in the statement, that Love loves love. Its nature is to produce, to reproduce, to multiply itself. Itself is forever the true object of itself, at the same time that it is ever a going forth from itself into that which is not itself. This essential principle of love or self-reproduction is what makes God eternally Father. But the eternal Fatherhood is actualized only in an eternal Sonship. Nothing proceeds from the Father which is not reproduction of the Father, and is not therefore Son. Man sees himself now in nature and destinature son of God. He feels his call and obligation to fulfil God in him as Father by realizing himself in God as son. His spiritual end and impulse is to know as also he is known, to love in return as he is first loved, to apprehend that for which he is apprehended of God in Christ. In proportion as he finds the meaning and truth of his own being in the reproduction of God, in being son of God, he finds the meaning and truth of the whole creation realized and expressed in his own sonship as heir of all and end of all. And in proportion again as he thus finds all things meaning and ending in sonship, he comes at last to see God Himself as realized in the universal sonship Himself therein realized as Eternal Father. So it is that in Jesus Christ we see everything expressed, because everything realized or fulfilled. He is all truth, because He is the truth of all things God, Creation, Man. And because He is thus truth and expression of all, He is Logos of all. What else could the Logos of all be but Son, or the Son but Logos? What could perfectly express God but that which is the perfect reproduction of Himself, or what is perfect sonship but perfect likeness?

The Grace of the Son is the divine gift of sonship. How could we have known God only in Himself? How could God have been actually our Father without the actuality of our sonship to Him? And could we have known, could we have wanted, could we have willed, could we have accomplished or attained our sonship without the gift or grace of sonship in Jesus Christ? God, we are told, predestinated us unto sonship through Jesus Christ unto himself. He predestinated us to be conformed to the image of His Son, that He might be the first born among many brethren. In bringing many sons to glory, He gave to us a Captain of our salvation, an Author and Finisher of the faith of sonship and so of the sonship of faith, who was Himself perfected as Son through the sufferings that are necessary to the perfecting of sonship in us. We see in Jesus Christ all that is meant, involved, or implied, in the fact that He is the divine Fatherhood realized and expressed in human sonship.

If that fact, viewed in its totality, signifies not only a human act, nor only a divine act, but a divine-human act, an act of God in man which is equally an act of man in God, then we say that Jesus Christ is not only as well the humanity as the divinity in that act, but He is the divinity as well as the humanity. He is not only the *gratia gratiata* in it but the *gratia gratians*—not only the manhood infinitely graced but the Godhead infinitely gracing.

Jesus Christ is therefore to us no mere sample or example of divine sonship. He is no mere one man who more successfully than others has grasped and expressed the ideal of a divine sonship. Neither is He a single individual of our race whom God has elected from among equally possible others, in whom as mere revelation or example to all others to manifest the truth of God in man and man in God. On the contrary, Jesus Christ is Himself the reality of all that is manifested or expressed in Him. He is as God the grace communicating and as man the grace communicated. He is both Generator and generated with reference to the life incarnate in Him both the sonship eternally in God to be begotten and the sonship actually begotten in man. As He was in the beginning with God and was God, so is He universally with man and is universal man.

When we have thus adequately conceived Christ as the universal truth and reality of ourselves, and in ourselves of all creation, and in creation and ourselves of God, then we are prepared for the conclusion that we know God at all, or are sons to Him as our Father, or are capable in that relation of partaking of His nature or entering into His Spirit or living His life, only in and through Jesus Christ; because Jesus Christ is the incarnation or human expression to us of the whole Logos of God that is to say, of God Himself as in any way whatever knowable or communicable. We cannot get at God to know or possess Him otherwise than as He reveals and imparts Himself; and He reveals Himself through His own Word and imparts Himself in His own Son. There and there alone is He to be known, and there He is all our own. The Logos who is the eternal Self-revelation of God manifests Himself as ideal principle, first and final cause, meaning and end, of creation; and the end of the whole creation which manifests God is realized through spiritual humanity in the imparted sonship of the Everlasting Son of the Father.

There is yet one other condition of truly knowing or really possessing God as wholly our God. As God is unknowable and incommunicable but through Christ, so is Christ, however perfectly He is in Himself the self-revelation and self-communication of God, not so to us but through the coequal action of the Holy Ghost. There is no knowledge of God in Himself only, there is no knowledge of God in creation only, or in others, or even in Christ only, without the answering knowledge of God in ourselves also. It is only like that answers to like. The deep that answers to deep must be the same deep. Jesus Christ expected in every son of man not only the answer of the man in him to Himself as eternal and universal Son of man, but the answer of the God in him to the perfect God head in Himself. Ye cannot see God in me, He says, because ye have not God in you. No man cometh unto me except the Father draw Him. I do not wish to urge the mere conventional language of Christianity, true as I believe it and helpful as I may find it to myself. I would if possible speak in the common language of common experience. When we speak of knowing God, and having God, it must mean knowing Him where He is to be known and having Him as He is to be had. Now, whatever God is in Himself, He is knowable to us only in Jesus Christ, and He can be our God only as He is conceived in us by the operation of the Spirit of God and born of the want which He implants and the faith which He generates.

The doctrine of the Trinity is ordinarily thought of as the very extreme of speculative reasoning upon the nature of God. But let us remember that practical faith in the Trinity antedated any speculative thought or doctrine of the Trinity. And behind that faith the fact itself of the Trinity is all that makes God knowable by us or us capable of knowing God. Before there was the word Trinity, the new world of Christianity had come to know God in Christ, and to know Christ in itself. The entire doctrine developed out of that actual experience was nothing but a positive affirmation and a determined defence of the fulness of the truth of God in Christ and Christ in us. We can do no better than conclude this entire exposition of the Gospel with an interpretation of it in the only terms in which it is expressible, viz.: in terms of the Trinity.

We have to do now with the Trinity, not as matter of doctrine nor as object of faith, but as fact in itself. But at the same time we neither forget nor minimize the essential Christian conviction that the fact of the Trinity through the actual operation of God's Word and Spirit has been so made matter of spiritual observation and experience as to be legitimate object of faith and material for doctrine. Our object at present, however, is not to define God but to define the Gospel, and our contention is that the Gospel is definable in facts that taken together make up the truth of the Trinity.

The first condition and constituent of the Gospel is the fact that God in Himself is love. How do we know that God is love? I believe that actually or historically we know it in Christ in whom the fact of the divine love is consummated and manifested. But in the light now of Christianity I believe that it is also philosophically demonstrable that goodness or love is the essential principle and the ultimate end of the universe. How God is love, not only in antecedent nature but in the actuality of self-fulfilment in the world, may be readable too in nature, after the light thrown upon it by Christianity, but in fact it is known in its reality only in Christ. Love is no more in God than in us an abstract disposition or affection. All the love we know is in concrete relations and the forms of affection determined by the character of those relations. Human love is marital, parental, filial, etc. out to the wider and widest forms of national, racial, and human affinity and affection. The concrete form in which alone we can know God as love is expressed by our designation of Him as eternal Father. That gives shape and definiteness to not only our conception, but the reality itself of His relation to us and ours to Him, and no less of how that relation is to be fulfilled. The full reality of fatherhood comes about in actuality only in the full realization of sonship, and that therefore must be God s meaning and end for all that is in the universe of His self-expression. We begin so to anticipate the truth that is to be expressed in such statements as that God has foreordained or predestined us to sonship through Jesus Christ unto Himself, that God has foreordained us to be conformed to the image of His Son, and many others to the same effect. But before we come to these unfoldings of the divine nature and purpose, let us reflect upon the following antecedent truth.

The beginning of all distinction between a pantheistic and a theistic conception of the world lies in recognizing the world as the expression, not of God Himself or, as we say, "of His substance," but of His Logos, His Thought, Will, Word. The Logos of God, then, is not God (*a theos*); we distinguish Him. And yet certainly the Logos is God (*theos*); we identify Him. Moreover, when once we have conceived and accepted God as eternal Father, we are in position to assume that the Logos, not merely as the principle of the divine self-expression but as God Himself self-expressed, must manifest Himself universally as Son or in sonship; since universal and everlasting Sonship is the only self- expression of eternal and essential Fatherhood.

The first constituent, therefore, of the Gospel is the fact in itself of the divine Love in Fatherhood. The second is, the equal fact in itself of the actualization of the divine Fatherhood in creature—or, definitely, in human— Sonship. The love of the Father fulfills and manifests itself in the grace of the Son. Love is grace *potentid*; Grace is love *actu*,—just as Fatherhood itself is Sonship potential, and Sonship is Fatherhood actualized. When we have once seen all humanity perfected as son in Jesus Christ, it is not hard to see in Him the whole creation so perfected in man as its head and as heir of its destiny. And then still less hard is it to see how we could never have known God as Father if He had not so fulfilled and manifested Himself as Son.

The hesitation and reluctance to see all God, and highest God, not only in the humanity but in the deepest human humiliation of Jesus Christ, is part of the disposition to measure exaltation by outward circumstance and condition instead of by inward quality and character. We find it impossible to recognize or acknowledge God in the highest act of His highest attribute. We cannot listen to the thought that it is with God as it is with us, that it only is with us because it is with God, that self-humiliation is self-exaltation. Not only in this way do we refuse to know God Himself as love, but we refuse to understand the universe as love. If we would but surrender our reason as well as our heart and will to God in Christ, we should cease to prate as we do of the mystery and the incomprehensibility of things. We could see how our Lord could say of the cross itself, Father, the hour is come. Glorify thy Son, that the Son may glorify thee. We lose thus the supreme lesson of human experience: Not merely to conjecture that somehow good is the final goal of ill; but to know by actual trial just how the supremest ills are the necessary steps to the highest goods. As St. Paul says, the cross of Christ is foolishness and a stumbling block only to the earthly wise and the self-righteous. To them that are saved, or are ever so little being saved, it is the wisdom of God and the power of God. To know God in Jesus Christ is to know the divine Logos, through whom alone God is knowable. It is to know him, not in His inferior activities of physical creation, nor yet in His higher capacity of lawgiver and law in a world of intelligent reason and free will. Rather is it to know Him in the act and process of that self-communication of love, grace, and fellowship, which is the basis and condition of the only real knowledge.

The third constituent of the Gospel is the fact in itself of the fellowship of the Spirit. Truly, our fellowship is with the Father and with His Son Jesus Christ. The possibility or potentiality of such a real unity and community with God must exist somehow beforehand in our nature as spirit, or in the natural relation of our finite spirits to the Father of spirits. But the actuality of spiritual relation or intercommunication which we call fellowship is no fact of nature but an act or interaction of spirits. It is not for us to say how, theoretically, spirit can act upon spirit; all that we can do is to understand how, practically and actually, spirit does act upon spirit. The most perfect expression of the actual action of the divine upon the human spirit is contained in the words, The Spirit beareth witness with our spirit, that we are the sons of God. Let us assume the objectivity or truth in itself of the eternal Fatherhood that is to say, not only Father-relation but Father-spirit, love, will, purpose or predestination, etc. of God in Himself. Let us also assume the objective reality as matter of fact of all that we have claimed to have happened in Jesus Christ: viz., that in Him as Logos God revealed Himself in the universe, and that in Him as Son God fulfilled Himself in humanity. In other words, let us assume that all that God is in Himself as Father has evolved itself through nature and man in the universal and everlasting Son-ship realized in Jesus Christ; God in Christ as Son is *actu* all that He is *potentia* in Himself as Father. When we have assumed all that body of objective truth the truth in itself of the Father and the Son what remains still to make it the Gospel to ourselves? Undoubtedly something remains. All the reality in the universe can be no Gospel to us so long as it remains objective, or until it enters into living relation with ourselves. Of course, it can never so enter unless there is in us the natural potentiality of entering into relation with it. But equally certainly that potentiality can only be actualized by ourselves. What is necessary within ourselves to give effect to all that is true without us is a corresponding response, or a response of correspondence, on our part. That correspondence is, I repeat, not a fact of natural relationship, but an act of spiritual communication or self-impartation. When the Spirit bears witness with our spirit, that we are sons of God, it is not only God who communicates the gracious fact, but it is God who awakens the humble and grateful response, and puts it into our heart to say, Abba, Father. If we cannot thus know God subjectively in ourselves, we cannot know God objectively in Jesus Christ. And if we cannot know Him in His Word and by His Spirit, we cannot know Him at all.

As we can know the eternal and universal Sonship incarnate in Jesus Christ only in the perfection of the human sonship realized in Him in other words, as we can know the Word or Son of God only in the man Christ Jesus, so we can know the Spirit of God only in ourselves or in our own spirit. We cannot know any spirit other than our own otherwise than through a certain oneness or identity of it with our own. There must be both an inter-penetration of the two as distinct and the identification of them as one. Hence the common demand upon men to be of one spirit. What a subject of reflection then, and of realization or actualization, is there for us in the fact of our fellowship, our participation, with the Father and the Son in the unity and identity of a common Spirit. It is in this eternal Spirit that God Himself is God and is Love. It was in this eternal Spirit that the whole creation in humanity offered itself without spot to God in the person of Jesus Christ; and in that consummate act fulfilled His relation to it through realizing its own relation with Him. It is through this eternal Spirit, which is God's and Christ's and ours, that we pass from ourselves into Christ and through Christ into God.

We have seen that there could have been no Gospel of God to us except one of objective Word and subjective Spirit. All life is defined as internal correspondence with external environment. We saw, I think, long ago that as it is the function of the divine Word aptare *Deum homini*, so is it that of the divine Spirit *aptare hominem Deo*. On the same line we may say, that as eternal life is given to us in Jesus Christ to be received, so is it given to us by the Holy Ghost to receive the life. Our Lord said of the promised Spirit, that its function should be to bring us to Him. There would be nothing to which to come if there were no objective fact and gift of life, there would be no coming to the life if there were no subjective preparing for and drawing to the life. How then finally does the Spirit fit us for Christ and fit us to Christ? It is the act and operation of the Spirit, first, that from the beginning, though yet a very far off, we can already know Christ as our own. That is the power of faith, which lives by God's Word and takes what that says as though it were. To faith Jesus Christ is the divine, not only revelation but reality of itself from the beginning of the foreknowledge of God in the eternity of the past to the end of the predestination of God in the eternity of the future. To faith Jesus Christ is all the eternal love, the all-sufficient grace, the perfect fellowship or oneness-with-it of God, which is salvation ex parte *Dei* or *salvailo salvans*; and no less in Jesus Christ the perfection of our own faith, hope, and love, our own holiness, righteousness, and life, our own death to sin, and our own life to God, which is salvation *ex parte hominis* or salvatio *salvata*. The Spirit thus brings us first to a perfect correspondence of faith with the fact of our life of God in Christ. But just because faith means life, that is, knows, desires, wills, and intends it therefore it is it. God already imputes, as He will impart, and faith already appropriates, as it will possess, the life which is so believed in. So believing in it we have it already in faith, and as surely shall have it at last in fact. Attuned to Christ by the anticipatory spell of faith, hope, and love, we shall be by a natural process of spiritual assimilation transformed into His likeness in act, character, and life, until coming to see Him perfectly as He is we shall be wholly what He is.

It has not been my object to add to the solution of the speculative problem of the Trinity. I have only aimed to show practically and spiritually that if at all we are to know and worship God in reality as our God, we must do so as Christianity has always done in Trinity. We must worship God in the Father, and the Son, and the Holy Ghost. Because God is, and is operative for us, not alone in one but in all these. We cannot but distinguish the Three; it is only in the completeness of their threefold operation that we can perfectly know the One.

Week Thirty-one, Reading Assignment for Year One

Micah[99]

This section on Michah is extracted from John J. Collins's longer text, *Introduction to the Hebrew Bible*, because Michah is not addressed in the *Shorter Introduction to the Hebrew Bible*, our current text for Year One.

Roughly contemporary with Isaiah was Micah of Moresheth, a small town about twenty-three miles southwest of Jerusalem. According to the superscription of the book, he prophesied in the days of Jotham, Ahaz, and Hezekiah, and his oracles concerned both Samaria and Jerusalem. In contrast to Isaiah, Micah was a rural prophet and not so closely engaged with the Davidic dynasty. As in the case of all the prophetic books, however, we must reckon with a process of edition and supplementation that may have gone on for centuries. A clear example of this is found in Mic 4:10, where Zion is told to writhe like a woman in labor, "for now you shall go forth from the city and camp in the open country; you shall go to Babylon. There you shall be rescued, there the Lord will redeem you from the hands of your enemies." The initial prophecy that the city would be undone, and that its inhabitants would have to camp in the open country, may well have been uttered by Micah. It is quite compatible with the critique of the ruling powers by the rural prophet. The extension of the prophecy to include the Babylonian exile and the subsequent restoration must have been added by a postexilic scribe, who felt impelled to update the oracle in the light of subsequent history.

The actual extent of the supplementation of the oracles of Micah is a matter of controversy. One scholarly tradition, developed in Germany in the late nineteenth century and still widely influential, attributes only material in chapters 1–3 to the eighth-century prophet, and that with minor exceptions, most notably the prophecy of restoration in 2:12–13. These chapters consist primarily of judgment Oracles. The more hopeful oracles in chapters 4–5 are usually dated to the early postexilic period. Chapters 6–7 are also regarded as later additions. At least the conclusion in 7:8–20 was added to adapt the collection to liturgical use. This kind of analysis may go too far in denying the prophet any hope for the future. At least a few passages in chapters 4–7 are likely to come from the eighth century. In contrast to this approach, some recent commentaries have tried to defend the essential unity

---

99. John J. Collins, *Introduction to the Hebrew Bible* (Minneapolis: Augsburg Fortress, 2004), 321–324.

of the book (Hillers, Andersen and Freedman). There can be little doubt, however, that the oracles underwent a process of transmission and that the book, like those of the other pre-exilic prophets, was given its present form after the Babylonian exile.

The Social Critique

The opening oracle invokes an old tradition of the theophany of the divine warrior. In Judges 5 the imagery of storm and earthquake were used to express the terror caused by YHWH going to help his people in battle. In Micah they describe the terror of YHWH coming to judge his people. The wrath is directed against both Samaria and Jerusalem. The focus on the capital cities is significant. The offenses are primarily charged to the ruling class. Jerusalem is derisively called a "high place." Micah makes no distinction between the guilt of the two kingdoms. In 1:6 he prophesies that Samaria will be made a heap. In 3:12 he predicts that "Zion shall be plowed as a field; Jerusalem shall become a heap of ruins." The latter prophecy is cited in Jer 26:18, where its nonfulfillment is explained by the fact that Hezekiah repented. Micah says that he will go naked and barefoot as Isaiah did, but where Isaiah symbolized the captivity of Egyptians and Ethiopians, Micah's action is a gesture of mourning for the destruction of Judah. The statement that "it has reached the gate of my people" recalls the invasion of Sennacherib (cf. Isaiah 1), but it more likely refers to the Syro-Ephraimite war, in view of the date ascribed to Micah and his concern for Samaria as well as Jerusalem.

The initial charge against Samaria and Jerusalem is idolatry. Jerusalem is compared to a high place; Samaria is accused of prostitution (cf. Hosea). More typical of Micah, however, is the accusation of injustice. The statement that "they covet fields, and seize them; houses and take them away," refers to the same phenomenon noted in Isa 5:8, which is addressed to those who add house to house and field to field. The punishment will fit the crime. Their own houses and fields will be seized by the invaders. Micah's condemnation of the exploitation of the poor is more biting even than that of Amos. The rich "tear the skin off my people and the flesh off their bones; eat the flesh of my people. . . chop them up like meat in a kettle" (3:2–3). The punishment to come will be a response of YHWH to the cry of the poor. Like Amos, Micah disassociates himself from the professional prophets (nebî'îm, 3:5–12). These people, we are told, give oracles for money (3:11; rulers and priests are similarly venal). They cry "peace" when they have enough to eat, and mislead the people by saying "surely, the Lord is with us" (3:11). If Isaiah saw this Davidic slogan as ambiguous, Micah sees it as a misleading illusion. We have no narrative of the call of Micah as we have of Amos. It seems safe to assume that he did not consider himself to be a nābî'. Like Amos, his preaching encountered opposition and some people tried to suppress it (2:6). It has been noted that the formula "thus says the Lord" occurs only once in chapters 1–3, and that Micah sometimes speaks in his own name (3:1). Nonetheless, he also speaks in the name of the Lord (e.g., 1:6: "I will make Samaria a heap"), and he claims to be filled with power, with the spirit of the Lord, to denounce the sin of Israel (3:8).

The critique of the cult in chapter 6 is also in line with what we have seen in the other eighth-century prophets and is plausibly attributed to Micah. This passage is cast in the form of a rib, or legal disputation, and can be viewed as a covenant lawsuit. God reminds his people Israel that he brought them up from the land of Egypt and redeemed them from slavery. There is a clear implication that Israel should have responded by serving the Lord with justice and has failed to do so, but the offenses and consequent punishment are not spelled out. While the exodus played no part in the preaching of Isaiah of Jerusalem, it figured prominently in the oracles of Amos and Hosea, even though Amos, like Micah, came from the southern kingdom. Micah too addressed Israel as well as Judah. Many scholars assume that the appeal to the exodus here is the work of a Deuteronomistic editor, but this is not necessarily so.

Micah 6:6–8 considers the misguided reasoning of an Israelite, or Judean, worshiper. The assumption is that God will be impressed by the cost of the sacrifice. Even human sacrifice is contemplated. As we have seen in connection with Genesis 22, human sacrifice was practiced in ancient Israel and Judah. King Manasseh of Judah, son of Hezekiah, was said to have made his son "pass through fire," which is to say that he sacrificed him as a burnt offering (2 Kgs 21:6). Human sacrifice, however, is much less likely to have been an option in the postexilic period. Micah's critique of sacrifice is essentially the same as that of the other prophets we have considered. It indicates a misunderstanding of what YHWH wants, which is "to do justice, and to love kindness, and to walk humbly with your God" (6:8). Most of the positive oracles in chapters 4–5 are likely to have been added by postexilic editors, when the time of judgment had passed and the need was for consolation and hope. Micah 4:1–5 repeats an oracle found in Isaiah 2:1–5, with a variation in the concluding verse. The imagery of tôrāh going forth from Jerusalem and the peoples streaming thereto fits better with the aspirations of Second Temple Judaism than with what we know of the eighth century. The oracle probably circulated anonymously. That it is associated with two eighth-century prophets is striking, but probably coincidental. A more difficult case is presented by Micah 5:2–5, which predicts the advent of a ruler from Bethlehem of Judah, the ancestral home of David. Many scholars take this as a postexilic prediction of a restoration of the Davidic line, and the obscure statement in v. 3, "the rest of his kindred shall return," can be read as supporting this interpretation. But the focus on Bethlehem, as opposed to Zion, may be significant. Micah of Moresheth may have felt that the Davidic monarchy could be redeemed if it returned to the humble roots symbolized by the ancestral village. The prediction of a ruler from

Bethlehem would then be a rejection of the ruling king and the Jerusalem court, but not of the Davidic line. The oracle would still have been read in a messianic sense in the postexilic period. In the later context Assyria would be understood as the archetypical enemy. The fantasy of a final defeat of invading nations appears frequently in the later prophetic and apocalyptic books (e.g., the prophecy of Gog in Ezekiel 38–39).

Resources for Spiritual Autobiography and Listening

Spiritual Autobiographies—Some Guidelines

A spiritual autobiography is your life story—the telling of your journey told with the purpose of discerning and proclaiming how your experience has shaped your relationship with God. Each year in the program you are asked to recall your life story. Later, you are given an opportunity to share what you think is appropriate with your seminar group. A different structure is provided for your use for each of the four years of the program. These structured methods allow you to look at the whole sweep of your life. Constructing your autobiography provides a firm foundation for the continuing work of integrating the content of your year's study with the events of your life. Your experience is a primary resource for your theological education; the yearly review of your life story enables you to hear how the timbre and direction of that story has changed in the last twelve months. Your call, discernment, vocation, and ministry are imbedded in your spiritual journey. This process of telling and retelling your story helps those themes come more clearly into your consciousness.

A spiritual autobiography may contain both religious material—significant people or times within the religious community—and everyday material like people and times in your life that have influenced who you are now and how you understand God's presence or absence in your life.

The work you do on your spiritual autobiography is private, "for your eyes only." This allows you to be free, without concern about how others will interpret either the context or expression.

Preparing a spiritual autobiography each year provides a way to deepen your understanding of both the Christian life and ministry. By virtue of your baptism you were called to ministry, guided and pushed by personal gifts, passions, skills, experiences, and interests.

Once you prepare your spiritual autobiography, you need to decide what you want to share with your seminar group. Martin Buber, a twentieth-century philosopher and Jewish theologian, is reputed to have said that he could never hold a significant conversation with another person until he had heard the other's life story. The purpose of sharing autobiographies is to build trust and understanding within the group and to begin to make connections within your own story. We need the experience of hearing other life stories to know that we are not alone in God's world. By sharing appropriate stories of our lives we form learning communities that can challenge and support us throughout our lives.

Your mentor will relate her or his own story and help the group structure the time for sharing of autobiographies. Most groups give each member **around ten minutes** to tell his or her story, followed by time for the rest of the group to respond. Spiritual autobiographies are the focus of most of the seminar time for the first few meetings of the year. This is a special time for your group. This component of your group's life will carry you to the next phase of your year together. This may be the first time to tell your story in this way. It may seem a bit daunting at first. Remember that you should offer what you feel comfortable sharing in the group. This is not an opportunity for "group therapy" or psychologizing, so the group should not engage in raising questions about motives or probe for information beyond what you share. Feel free to say "no" or to say that you do not wish to explore questions that others may raise out of curiosity or concern.

Sharing your "spiritual autobiography" is a way to say, "Here I am," and to join your EfM group as a full participant. Over the years in EfM you will probably find that your spiritual autobiography changes. You may find yourself free to talk about things which were previously guarded. You also may find that your freedom to "be yourself" will grow as your personal story, the life of the group, and the story of God's people relate to each other.

Holy Listening

VocationCARE is a program in ministry discernment and design, a sister program to EfM in the Beecken Center at The School of Theology/Sewanee. The method incorporates two rounds of storytelling and encourages deep listening. The acronym CARE stands for

- CREATE *space to explore Christian vocation together;*
- ASK *self-awakening questions together;*
- REFLECT *theologically on self and community; and*
- ENACT *the next faithful step.*

VocationCARE Model for Storytelling/Holy Listening

Tips for First Storytelling

EXAMPLE:

Tell a story about why you do what you do, love what you love, care about what you care about.

BE SPECIFIC

Talk about what actually happened. It helps to begin stories with "One time . . . " or "I remember a time when. . . . "

BE DESCRIPTIVE

Use images, feelings, and places to provide texture, color, and thick description to your story. Use the 5Ws: who, what, when, where, and why.

BE SELF-REFLECTIVE

What was the occasion of your discovering that *this* was what you loved, cared about, or loved doing? Was there anyone with whom you shared this discovery? How did it feel to know this about yourself?

Tips for First Hearing of Another's Story

UNDIVIDED ATTENTION

Make eye contact with the storyteller and give him or her your full attention as if there was nothing else more important than listening to his/her story.

HOLY LISTENING

Listen reverently as if you were in the presence of the Holy and witness the truth of this sacred story. Hold the space with your presence and receive the precious gift in this story. Imagine you are listening with God's ears.

JOURNALING

As you journal: What images, key words, or phrases stand out as meaningful to you? Is there a question you might ask your partner that would move the conversation deeper into "the heart of the matter"? What did you enjoy or find yourself wondering about?

Tips for Second Storytelling

EXAMPLE:

Tell a story about a time when you found a note to sing that was unique and God-given, a time when you heard the echo of the Word in your life.

BE SPECIFIC

Talk about what actually happened. It helps to begin stories with "One time . . . " or "I remember a time when . . . "

BE DESCRIPTIVE

Use words, images, feelings, and places to provide texture and color to your story description. Cover the 5Ws: who, what when, where, and why.

BE SELF-REFLECTIVE

Where was I? What was I doing?

What happened? Was there any risk or challenge in claiming this inner harmony?

Were there any companions in this discovery? Anyone who could share this joy with me?

Tips for Second Hearing of Another's Story

UNDIVIDED ATTENTION

Make eye contact with the storyteller and give him or her your full attention as if there was nothing else more important than listening to his/her story.

HOLY LISTENING

Listen reverently as if you were in the presence of the Holy and witness the truth of this sacred story. Hold the space with your presence and receive the precious gift in this story. Imagine you are listening with God's ears.

JOURNALING

As you journal: What images, key words, or phrases stand out as meaningful to you? Is there a question you might ask your partner that would move the conversation deeper into "the heart of the matter"? What did you enjoy or find yourself wondering about?

Adapted from Fund for Theological Education's *FTE Guide to VocationCARE* © 2012, 18–19. Used with permission.

Resources for Reflecting Theologically

The EfM Four-source Model of Theological Reflection

Terms

Movement: primary steps of theological reflection—*identify* something that matters, *explore* the topic, *connect* to other areas of life and meaning (Sources, Voices), and *apply* learning to ministry.

Source/Category/Voice: interior and exterior areas of life from which a person draws when making sense out of something that has happened: *personal experience/action, faith tradition, culture/society (contemporary and/or traditional)*, and *personal beliefs/positions*. For instance, a person's belief forms in relationship to something that happened, something that was read, something that was learned. Each of those areas speaks with some kind of voice, contributing to how a person makes sense out of what has occurred. A belief about the sanctity of life can be explored to discover what formed that belief in a search for deeper awareness of God and of meaning.

Theological Perspective: questions asked in applying a theological lens to the reflection commonly use traditional terms developed in systematic theology (*creation, sin, judgment, repentance, redemption*); reframing or rephrasing them can bring out subtle differences in understanding. For example, in this volume you will be asked to consider the perspective questions in terms of *wholeness, brokenness, recognition, reorientation,* and *restoration.*

Every person uses images, ideas (concepts), feelings (intuitions), values, and behavior (action) as the substantive content for reflecting. Whenever one's thought process engages the heritage of the faith tradition in which one was raised, the reflection becomes theological in tone. While thoughts cannot be separated into discrete isolated units for consciousness, clarifying distinctions can be useful. The EfM program draws on or listens to four primary categories or sources/voices in theological reflection: **Faith Tradition; Culture/Society; Personal Experience/Action;** and **Personal Belief/Position**. Each of these categories emerged from conversations in small groups over the past several decades. The following statements summarize the categories.

"She has the Midas touch."—a voice of Culture via Greek mythology

"Don't we have Good Samaritan laws?"—a voice of Christian Tradition in scripture

"This is a strange place. I have a feeling we are not in Kansas anymore, Toto."—a voice of Culture via the movies to interpret experience

"I believe that all people are good to begin with."—a voice of Position or Personal Belief

"That's how I felt when I fell out of a tree and broke my arm."—a voice of Personal Experience

Each of these statements makes an assertion that states a belief, opinion, or a position. Yet, while the person making the statement expresses a belief, the way to communicate a fuller meaning is to use images or words that pull from other sources. Each statement "borrows" from some other story or experience to flesh out meaning centered on something that mattered.

Faith Tradition, Culture/Society, Personal Experience/Action, and Personal Belief/Position provide a common language for individuals and groups to use as they engage in theological reflection. The vocabulary might feel a bit like jargon; however, the words provide some definition that can guide and clarify the theological discussion, whether it is within a group conversation or an individual's internal conversation.

Faith Tradition: Whenever the language, concepts, terms, or images in a conversation come from the Bible or some other document or story that is part of the Christian lore, then one is drawing from the Christian Tradition source. Words like "creation" or "sin"; images like "Good Shepherd" or "walking on water" come from the Christian scriptural tradition. Concepts such as providence, eschatology, or incarnation make use of the terms used by theologians. In EfM's theological reflection model, the umbrella term "Tradition" more accurately refers to the Christian heritage and is the source that marks the reflective conversation as theological. However, someone *formed* in (not simply having a passing interest in) another faith tradition would hear the voices from *their* sacred writings or stories, their wisdom figures, or their leaders, and the contributions from such connections would enrich the reflection.

Culture/Society: This source of the four-source model refers to a very large body of material. Literature, music, paintings and other artifacts are part of the Culture source. References from a movie or from a novel would be examples of something from the contemporary Culture source. The Culture source also includes traditional social or ethnic norms that might be referenced by "My grandmother used to say . . . ." The Culture source contains both written and oral content, and may have been handed down from one generation to another.

Notice that the Tradition and Culture sources have a common characteristic. They have an objective quality independent from an individual; that is, they are sources "from outside" a person. The material from these two sources resides in the "other." It may be contained in printed material or recorded in a way that can be referenced in much the same way as a footnote in a research paper. The oral content of the Culture source has a less impartial quality. What one's grandmother transmitted (Culture) often gets incorporated in the psyche of the person. Nevertheless, the content of the aphorism distinctly comes from outside the grandchild. Cultural and ethnic messages transmitted within a society are placed within the Culture source of the EfM model. These too have a quality of being embedded from the outside into the individual.

The other two sources in the theological reflection model have a more subjective nature. They can be modified with the pronoun "my" and refer to personal experience; drawing a distinction between them becomes somewhat awkward.

Personal Experience/Action: Behavior and activity define this source; what actually happened that can be communicated using neutral words. For example, a person draws from the Action source when she describes what happened such as, "One Halloween our family attended a city-wide celebration. I went as a pink bunny rabbit with a carrot in hand. I got separated from my siblings and followed the crowd as it left the stadium. My family found me walking along the side of the road. I was crying and felt alone. When they got me into the car, I was told that my rabbit ears had been tied together by someone." This is something that happened within a person's experience and which fostered some learning and viewpoints and attitudes that would continue long after the incident. The experience was formational to some extent and became a source/voice in that person's life.

Personal Belief/Position: Behavior centers on what is seen and heard. Any experience also contains the feelings and thoughts that shape the meaning attributed to the experience. Opinions, beliefs, viewpoints, and convictions held by a person constitute the position pole of the four-source model. A person's position arises out of the mix of behavior, images, feelings, and viewpoints. A person's history and the meaning attributed to the past contribute to the formation of beliefs. Positions rest, however tentatively, on the meaning attributed to behavior, learning, or life events.

The content of theological reflection comes from combining distinctive voices. Human consciousness employs reason, emotion, imagination, and praxis (the practical side of something, rather than its theory) to create meaning and value in life. Theological reflection, individually or with others, is a search for a glimpse of truth and meaning.

Reflection: What and How?

Reflection happens as the mind moves through the four steps of identifying a focus, exploring the focus, connecting to the sources/voices, and applying that focus to ministry. It begins as a topic is identified. Several skills help to arrive at a clear focus for conversation: recognizing that there is something that draws attention such as an experience, a painting, a piece of scripture, and so forth; focusing on the object of attention; discerning where the important consideration needs to center, that is, where the "heart-beat" is of the incident, movie, passage in scripture, painting, and so forth.

Once the topic for reflection is selected, it is possible to begin exploring its dimensions. As the various dynamics are considered, the mind naturally makes connections with other sources, as if each source has a voice that joins in the reflection. As the variety of voices converse, new awareness and insights emerge. Perhaps an individual or group experiences the sensation of being grasped by truth. New understanding leads to considering how insights might be applied. Identifying, exploring, connecting, and applying constitute the movements, phases, or steps of reflection.

Theological Reflection Process Chart[100]

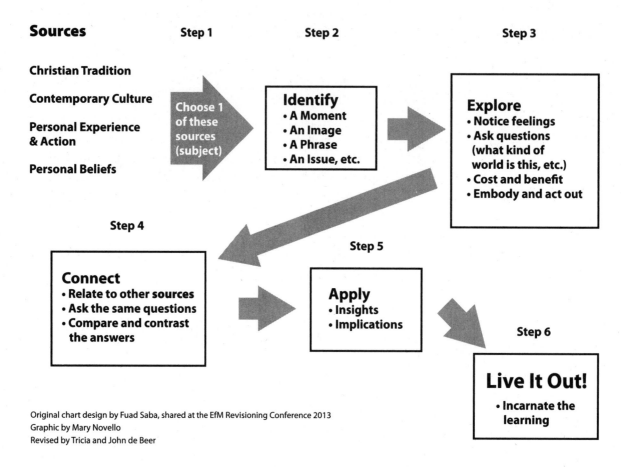

Sources

Christian Tradition

Contemporary Culture

Personal Experience
& Action

Personal Beliefs

Step 1

Choose 1
of these
sources
(subject)

Step 2

Identify
• A Moment
• An Image
• A Phrase
• An Issue, etc.

Step 3

Explore
• Notice feelings
• Ask questions
  (what kind of
  world is this, etc.)
• Cost and benefit
• Embody and act out

Step 4

Connect
• Relate to other sources
• Ask the same questions
• Compare and contrast
  the answers

Step 5

Apply
• Insights
• Implications

Step 6

Live It Out!
• Incarnate the
  learning

Original chart design by Fuad Saba, shared at the EfM Revisioning Conference 2013
Graphic by Mary Novello
Revised by Tricia and John de Beer

TR Process Chart

---

100. Like many of the resources in the EfM program, this one is the product of a collaborative effort. The original process design was developed by EfM mentor Fuad Saba and shared at the Re-visioning EfM conference in Sewanee in July 2013. The graphic presentation was designed by Mary Novello, EfM Coordinator for the Diocese of Western Michigan. Tricia and John deBeer, EfM trainers, further refined the language.

Examples of Theological Reflection

Theological Reflection Beginning with a Social Concern

Philosophical anthropology studies the nature of humankind. Questions of identity, both individual and communal, comprise the field of study. Theological anthropology addresses human nature in relation to God. Both philosophical and theological anthropology address related questions: What is the end (*telos*) of human beings? What does human flourishing involve? What is "the common good"—the actions, values, and policies that allow people to flourish? In theological terminology, what is God's vision for all people? Such questions involve thinking about the meaning of terms such as the Kingdom of God, heaven, and the *eschaton* (end-time).

The following theological reflection outline provides a way to consider philosophical and theological anthropological matters.

Identify a focus.
Develop a list of social concerns that are presently being deliberated in your Culture/society. The items on the list might come from politics, news media, documentaries, current cinema, or advertisements.

For example:

- Environmental concerns

- Universal health care

- National security

- Distribution of wealth

- Economic well-being

Select one topic from the list you create and reflect theologically on that voice from the Culture source. You will have a chance to make additional connections to the voice of Culture when you add the Connect movement to your reflection.

Explore some dimensions of your selected social concern. For example:

- Notice what is revealed about human nature in the identified concern, both individually and corporately. What human values seem to be operating around the social concern? Describe what the identified social concern seems to assert about "the common good"; that is, if the concern you are working with is "economic well-being," how does that concern relate to the common good?

- What characteristics of God are present or absent in that concern? Possibly, a social concern around national security could reflect God's characteristic of protector. What about God's self-emptying?

- Identify the deep hopes that are present or implied in the nature of the social concern.

Connect

Describe various ways the identified social concern gets manifested at the present time. For example, if universal health care is the identified concern under reflection, then identify the ways in which that concern has come to the foreground in the culture/society where you live, such as:

- U.S. news report on congressional action

- Canadian experience of universal health care

- English experience of universal health care

Where do you hear God's voice in your social structure, or your culture?

Learn something new. Find a way to hear the voice of Cultures/societies other than your own, such as how other countries handle the same or similar concern. How do varying cultural groups handle such a matter, perhaps even within the same country? Please resist the temptation to "talk off the cuff" about another place or people; rather, try to talk to someone from that culture or look up information that you could consider authoritative and reliable.

Personal Experience: Name concrete ways in which the issue has intersected your life. For example:

- Retirement brought change in how medical insurance was obtained

- Got ill and had to receive medical attention over an extended period of time

- Health of a friend's parent deteriorated and he/she required extended health care

- Visit to emergency room of hospital and noticing who was there and why

- Change in a person's life that required addressing the need for medical insurance

When have you had personal experience related to that concern or issue? What emotions have you experienced as that concern has intersected your life: fear, frustration, sorrow mixed with gratitude? Name your thoughts and feelings in relation to the focus you have selected.

Personal Belief/Position: What seems to be at stake in the reflection as you have explored and connected to the identified concern? What statements of conviction are you willing to make? What is alive for you in this matter?

- State what you value and hold important that is touched by the identified social concern.

- State your best vision or hope for the world. For creation.

Tradition: Listen to the voice of Christian tradition, especially the way Christian tradition speaks to the questions of God, common good (reign of God), or human nature.

What specific stories from the Christian tradition speak to the concern? Note what scripture stories, perhaps ones you remember from your childhood, give shape to the concern.

As you access the various voices in Personal Experience, Christian Tradition, Culture(s), Personal Beliefs, what rings true for you or seems new to you? Express, as best you can, any intuitive sense of what "should" be, "ought" to be, could be, or "must" be done relative to the social concern. In other words, what matters to you about this?

Describe actions that you could take that might contribute to the reign of God, the common good, in the matter of the social concern on which you reflected.

Apply

Apply the insight and new awareness from the reflection within the context of the social concern you named above.

How do the dimensions of the social concern point to the common good?

In what way does participation in the social concern/issue contribute to a vision of God's reign?

How does human flourishing revealed through the reflective theological conversation point toward action and behavior and practices?

In other words, what are you going to do (ministry) with what you have considered?

What would support you? Where/how will you reach out for that support?

Theological Reflection Beginning with Scripture

Identify

The following passages involve the people of Samaria, a group that fostered strong feelings among the Jews. Carefully read the passages and identify two or three topics common to both.

> When the days drew near for him to be taken up, he set his face to go to Jerusalem. And he sent messengers ahead of him. On their way they entered a village of the Samaritans to make ready for him; but they did not receive him, because his face was set toward Jerusalem. When his disciples James and John saw it, they said, "Lord, do you want us to command fire to come down from heaven and consume them?" But he turned and rebuked them. Then they went on to another village.
>
> *Luke 9:51–56*

> But wanting to justify himself, he asked Jesus, "And who is my neighbor?" Jesus replied, "A man was going down from Jerusalem to Jericho, and fell into the hands of robbers, who stripped him, beat him, and went away, leaving him half dead. Now by chance a priest was going down that road; and when he saw him, he passed by on the other side. So likewise a Levite, when he came to the place and saw him, passed by on the other side. But a Samaritan while traveling came near him; and when he saw him, he was moved with pity. He went to him and bandaged his wounds, having poured oil and wine on them. Then he put him on his own animal, brought him to an inn, and took care of him. The next day he took out two denarii, gave them to the innkeeper, and said, 'Take care of him; and when I come back, I will repay you whatever more you spend.' Which of these three, do you think, was a neighbor to the man who fell into the hands of the robbers?" He said, "The one who showed him mercy." Jesus said to him, "Go and do likewise."
>
> *Luke 10:29–37*

Note: Though the above scripture passages are quoted from the NRSV translation, reading the passages in a variety of translations may increase the sense of meaning.

Focus the passages by considering where the key energy/heart of the passage is, what the passages seem to be about.

Develop an image in words or a drawing that brings the point of the passages into focus.

Explore the image or central idea of the passages, using questions from the theological themes of Creation, Sin, Judgment, Repentance, or Redemption, such as:

- What kind of community does the image-world/theme suggest (Creation)?

- What might get in the way of relationships in that image-world/theme (Sin)?

- What could make those in that world realize there's something wrong; what choices are there (Judgment)?

- What would represent a change of direction (Repentance)?

- What might a new, life-giving creation look like (Redemption)?

Connect

Note: Connecting happens best if some freedom is allowed. Listen to each of the "voices" or "sources" below and let your responses emerge in any order. You may not make a connection in one area; that is okay. That may occur at a later time, or not at all. Mainly, allow your inner life to speak, connecting you to these areas of potential meaning and revelation.

Personal Experience–When has something happened in your life that is like the world of the image/metaphor? For instance, if the image created for the passages is "extending a party invitation," when have you given or sent such an invitation?

Compare your experience with the preceding theological exploration. How do your experience and the image relate to one another?

Contemporary Culture/Society–Who or what has taught you something that is helpful when life is like the image? In our world, how is there opposition to that image? How is there support for it? Where is God extending party invitations in the world in which you live?

Christian Tradition–What other scripture passages or church history events remind you of the image or central point of the passages from Luke?

Beliefs/Positions: What key issues do the metaphor and personal experience and contemporary culture raise? State your Beliefs and Positions relative to those issues.

Apply meaning and purpose to the reflection by identifying learning and clarifying questions.

How do the beliefs and insights of the exploration support you in ministry?

Notice where you might want to make some changes in action or viewpoint about the matter covered in the reflection.

Write a prayer in response to the discoveries in this reflection.

Theological Reflection Beginning with the Culture Source

Identify

Once you have explored another culture in some way, identify a focus, then create an image or metaphor of your limited understanding of that culture, if possible.

Explore the focus from some theological perspectives, such as:

- What beliefs about creation are reflected in the image?

- What is considered sin in the world of your image?

- How does one find forgiveness in that image world?

- What constitutes ultimate fulfillment as that culture understands it?

- What do you regard as the meaning of life for that culture?

- What is the meaning of death?

Connect by listening to other voices. (Reminder: You can do the following in any order.)

Christian Tradition—What passages in scripture or church history come to mind as you explore the image above? Read the passages or material you recall.

Compare and contrast the world you found in the scripture or church history passage with the world you explored with the theological questions.

Personal Experience—What has occurred in your life that provides answers to some of those theological questions?

Compare and contrast your personal experience with the experiences of those in the culture you explored briefly. What differences and similarities are there? What begins to matter to you as you make the comparisons?

Contemporary Culture/Society—How does your culture/society view that of the one you explored? What are the challenges and possibilities?

Personal Beliefs—What beliefs of yours are challenged by those of the other culture? How could that challenge create road blocks? How could it create opportunity? What would you have to give up in order to change your beliefs? What might someone from the culture you explored have to give up?

Apply the reflection by noting your insights and how those insights might make a difference in ministry in your life.

Theological Reflection Beginning with a Personal Position

Identify a focus.

Begin with a focus on the value of music and poetry in worship and prayer.

Explore the focus.

Make a statement or image that reflects a connection between music and poetry and prayer or worship. For instance, someone might express that he only likes a certain type of music in worship because another kind destroys the sense of peace and beauty. Or another person might create an image that depicts people singing or playing instruments and the music notes floating outward towards God and the world.

Explore your statement or image theologically, using a few of the questions provided, or create your own questions for the image:

How does the overall statement or image reflect wholeness or goodness?

What view of the world is contained in your statement or image?

What view of the relationship between God and creation exists in your statement/image?

How would someone experience God in that statement/image?

What might disrupt someone's relationship with God and others in that focus?

What view of restoration to wholeness is contained in the focus?

Connect to other sources.

State your personal belief that undergirds your initial image or statement.

How do your personal belief and the exploration above coincide and how do they conflict?

What troubles you about the comparison? What comforts you about the comparison?

Find one or two scripture references to the place of music and poetry in liturgy and worship. Or, select one or two hymns to connect to. How do those hymns relate to your focusing image or statement and to your position? How do they relate to the exploration?

What view of the world around you is contained in your personal belief statement, in the image, in the hymns you chose?

Apply what is learned to daily life.

Once a person takes a stance or affirms a position, implications for ministry begin to emerge.

What do you see for your ministry as you live day to day?

Close by composing a prayer adapting the structure of Jewish prayers:

Blessed are you, O Lord God, _____
(description of God),

for you _____

and make us _____

through _____. *Amen.*

Theological Reflection Beginning with a Text

Identify a statement in the essay that seems especially strong to you. What kind of a picture could represent the position represented by that statement?

For example, Bishop Charleston's statement, "The great-great-grandchildren of those from the 1960s, 1970s, 1980s, and 1990s will inherit a spirituality that is diverse, multicultural, intimate, and tough," might be pictured using an image of an individual of mixed ethnic features and dress holding hands with someone who looks very different, both of them facing a storm with resolve and hope.

His statement that "The outcome will be watershed reform of Christianity toward the end of the twenty-first century," might produce a picture of a cross (or a person holding a cross) rushing over a waterfall fed by a variety of religious and cultural "streams."

Find an essay statement or idea that you want to reflect on and create an image to capture something of that statement.

What seems to be the essence of the statement and/or the image you developed?

Note: The Explore movement precedes the Connect movement in order to allow the reflection to take on a larger and deeper perspective before making additional connections to the other Source voices. Connections often begin to emerge on their own in the midst of exploring. Trust what emerges and allow it to develop.

Explore the image from one or more theological perspectives based on terms used by Bishop Desmond Tutu: Wholeness/goodness (Creation), Brokenness/separation from God (Sin), Recognition (Judgment), Reorientation (Repentance), and/or Restoration to wholeness (Redemption). Choose any one or more of the following questions to pose to your picture.

What wholeness or goodness does the image or statement reflect?

What demonstrates brokenness in the image/statement?

What represents recognition of the brokenness in the image/statement?

What reorientation is possible in the image/statement?

How would restoration come about for those in the image or statement?

What seems to be at the heart of the consideration at this point?

Connect

Bishop Charleston's essay presents his personal position about the future of spirituality, drawn from his personal experience.

What do you believe about the central matter of the image or statement you chose to explore?

Compare and contrast Bishop Charleston's position with your own. What seems to be "at stake" in the comparing and contrasting?

How does your personal experience connect with the image or statement you are exploring?

What spiritual practices does your faith tradition/background teach that support and sustain your spiritual life?

What do you see or understand in a new way?

Apply

What does your new (or reaffirmed) understanding suggest for your ongoing life in Christ?

In light of the reflection, name some implications for ministry in your life. Think especially of how this reflection contributes to living faithfully in a multicultural world.

Theological Reflection Beginning with a Provocative Word[101]

Identify

Select a word that has impact. For the purpose of this reflection and the practice, try the word "DESIRING."

What revelations on the meaning of the word do you have? Anything it denotes or connotes?

Explore

Next, ask the six "journalist's questions" about the feeling the word conveys:

WHO was involved when you were feeling _____?
(Action . . . tell the stories from your life)

WHAT image comes to mind about the feeling(s) _____?
(Image . . . explore the metaphor–its reflection of wholeness, brokenness, recognition, reorientation, and/or restoration)

Connect

Go to the other sources we use to help explore meaning.

WHERE does this feeling come from and WHERE is it found in society?
(Source/Culture)

WHEN does this feeling come up in the Bible, lives of saints, hymns, and so forth?
(Source/Tradition . . . explore the world of tradition)

WHY is this feeling manifest in our lives?
(Source/Position)

HOW might God redeem any negatives in this?
(Hope in Christ)

Consider insights and implications.

WHAT have you learned for the next time you feel _____?

Apply
Write a collect using the outline:

Dear God . . .	**(naming of God's aspects)**
You . . .	**(connect situation of the image to that aspect)**
We pray that . . .	**(petition of our hearts)**
So that . . .	**(result we desire)**
Amen.	

---

101. Adapted from a design by Patricia Bleicher, EfM mentor.

Theological Reflection Beginning with a Wide-Angle Lens (1)

Why this title? The image of a wide-angle lens is used because this reflection begins with a variety of perspectives, then focuses on a thread/theme/idea/image that connects them. An individual starts by finding the threads or themes present—in this case in something he or she reads or watches. The key for use by an individual requires initiation from something that could produce several themes or ideas (in this case, two or more articles on a topic of interest). In an EfM group, the reflection's beginning point can be themes from the spiritual autobiographies, themes from the week's reading, themes from any on-board time of the group, or some other starting point from which a variety of perspectives can be elicited.

The key is first to list the themes in what is under consideration, then find a thread that runs through the themes.

Identify

FIND A COMMON THEME OR THREAD

Begin with the articles chosen for the Respond section above.

What are the common themes or elements which emerge?

Is there a central question, struggle, or issue contained in the articles?

State the central thread as a simple statement, image, metaphor, or issue.

For instance, a review of several articles could reveal themes of challenge of the *status quo,* support of a particular view, and/or revelation of something new. Asking "What ties some of those themes together" yields a thread that may have run through the articles.

Explore

THEOLOGICAL PERSPECTIVES

Write about what's going on in the image, issue, or statement you created in the Identify step above.

Sit quietly and let the image or statement and your writing rest in you.

What questions does your image or statement raise?

What questions does that image or statement answer?

Identify the perspectives contained in the questions, that is, wholeness, brokenness, recognition, reorientation, or restoration.

Connect

This is the point at which one looks at the various sources in life to help find meaning in matters of daily life and ministry. The object is to find connections between the image, statement, or issue and other aspects of our life that teach us something.

CONNECT TO CULTURE AND SOCIETY

Focus on one or two areas of your culture or society so that the reflection will not be too broad. These connections might come from your local community or the larger world: your work environment, the education system, the health care system, your grandmothers, movies, TV, literature, art, songs, artifacts, architecture, government, or the press, to name a few.

Pick just one area of our contemporary society with which to connect. For instance, what does the world of employment teach you about the theme you have identified? Or, what have you learned from the news media in your culture/society that helps you or challenges you regarding the theme?

How does the selected area of culture/society speak to or about this thread?

CONNECT TO CHRISTIAN TRADITION

- Identify biblical passages or other elements from Christian tradition (scripture, hymn, prayer, church history document) in which this common thread is evoked or brought to mind. Read the passages.

- Select one passage that seems to address the image, statement, or issue.

- Examine the passage:
  - Note how the passage offers insight into the image, statement, or issue you are considering.
  - Note how the passage challenges the image, statement, or issue.
  - What does the passage mean to you?

COMPARE AND CONTRAST CULTURE/SOCIETY AND CHRISTIAN TRADITION

From the perspectives of each, what kind of a world emerges?

Where do these perspectives join or compete? Where do they clash or contrast?

Note what seems to be "at stake" as you compare and contrast your Culture and Tradition connections.

CONNECT TO PERSONAL EXPERIENCE

When have you experienced something that relates to what seems to "be at stake" above?

CONNECT TO BELIEFS, POSITIONS, AND AFFIRMATIONS

What positions or affirmations do you hold in relation to what is at stake?

Identify how that belief formed for you. Was it from personal experience, from something you learned in your faith tradition, or from the cultural messages you have inherited or encountered?

What "gaps" are there for you between what you believe and how you act in relation to the theme considered in this reflection?

Apply

IDENTIFY INSIGHTS AND PERSONAL IMPLICATIONS

What have you learned about coherence of belief and behavior?

What are you personally called to do differently, to affirm, or to change?

What skills did this reflection help you learn in thinking theologically about something you read or watched?

DECIDE ON SOCIAL AND CIVIC CONSEQUENCES

What actions will you take to carry out the implications you have discovered?

Consider how this reflection supports you in living in a multicultural world.

Theological Reflection Beginning with a Wide-Angle Lens (2)

Identify

After describing the gaps in the Respond section above, pick one gap and identify themes or threads that run through that gap.

What kinds of things does that gap seem to be about? Is it about civil disobedience, or punishment, or resistance–or something else?

Choose one thread (theme) as the focus for reflection.

Explore

The theme is descriptive of some kind of world, where "that's how things are." For example, the focus may be about an act of civil disobedience that represents personal behavior in the gap between orthopraxis and personal action. Deepen your reflection on the theme using two or three perspective questions to ask the focus:

- What temptations or dangers are present in such a world (of civil disobedience, or whatever the focus is about in your incident)?

- What is shown about human nature in this gap?

- What would wholeness look like?

Connect

Consider any or all of the following in any order:

What's at the "heart" of the selected gap?

Note your personal positions or beliefs about the matter under consideration. On what ground is your belief resting? What contributed to the formation of that belief?

Identify how the ground of your belief is watered by a faith tradition, by the world around you, or by personal experience.

Apply

What new ideas or understanding do you have now?

What are the implications for ministry in daily life in a multicultural environment?

Journal about how living with your Rule of Life has been going. Where have you encountered God?

Theological Reflection Beginning with a Dilemma

Identify

Describe an incident for reflection—an experience in which you felt pulled in at least two directions over something, and for which there are no decisions pending, that is, the incident is over, though there still may be feelings. For example:

> I had looked forward to my best friend's wedding for months and had my plane ticket and my new outfit. We had plans to enjoy the sights and catch up and just have fun. And then my surviving parent got sick, but told me I could go ahead with my plans. I felt so torn. There was no one else there.

Name the turning point in the incident.

What's the central moment of the incident? Where is the tension greatest? What was happening? What were you thinking and feeling at that moment?

Record the central moment in a short sentence and your thoughts and feelings at that moment.

State the issue.

Try to state what's at stake or what the central dilemma is at the moment of greatest tension.

To help get to the dilemma, list declarative statements about what you wanted at that moment or what interests were at stake at that moment. You may have several.

Record tension statements as "I wanted _____ and I wanted _____." For example:

> I wanted to attend my best friend's wedding and I wanted to stay to take care of my ailing parent.

Select a pair of statements that best represent the central tension.

Record the central dilemma/what's at stake. For example:

> Personal fun conflicting with caring for another. Dilemma: Plans affected by unforeseen circumstances.

Identify another time.

Clarify the dilemma by recalling another time when you experienced a similar tension.

Record your additional experience with the identified tension by completing the sentence: "It was a time when. . . ."

Explore the dilemma.

What is it like to live in that tension? Contrast the cost/promise of the dilemma.

Record your responses to the questions using either cost/promise or theological perspectives:

COST OF EACH SIDE OF THE TENSION	PROMISE OF EACH SIDE OF THE TENSION
Ex., Plans: caught off guard, decisions made that are hard to change	Ex., Know what is coming

OR use one or two theological perspective questions adapted from the Cycle of Gospel Living, developed by Eric Law (and used in Interlude One, Week 15).[102] This cycle focuses around power, loss or yielding up of power, and empowerment, and moves through four phases.

• Give up power, choose the cross—This is a point of entry for the powerful.

• Cross, death, powerless—This is a point of entry for the powerless.

• Empowerment, endurance

• Empty tomb, resurrection, powerful

Here are examples of asking questions of the dilemma or image. Use only one or two when exploring your image or dilemma:

Give up power, choose the cross: What are the power dimensions of the dilemma or image? Who has power? What has to be yielded?

Cross, death, powerless: What sacrifice(s) might be called for? What are the temptations of the cross, of powerlessness? To whom or what is power yielded?

Empowerment, endurance: How is power transmitted to the powerless party? What is required in order to enter the cycle that leads to empowerment? What builds endurance?

Empty tomb, resurrection, powerful: What is left behind in the image or dilemma? How does resurrection occur in the image or dilemma? What is the hope of the power received?

---

102. Law, *The Wolf Shall Dwell with the Lamb*, 74.

Connect

TRADITION

Identify some stories from scripture or church history that relate to the dilemma or image. How or where does the Gospel Living cycle occur in our Christian story in scripture? In the lives of women and men of faith? Or perhaps some prayers or hymns come to mind that relate to this reflection.

DIALOGUE

Compare and contrast what your Christian tradition has to say about that dilemma or image. What choices would the tradition support? Not support? Why?

CULTURE AND POSITION

Where is that tension or dilemma experienced in our culture? Have there been news stories about it? Have you read a book or seen a movie that dealt with that dilemma? Is there a political dimension?

What do you believe about that dilemma? How was your belief in conflict within the dilemma? What do you hope for regarding the dilemma?

Apply

INSIGHTS AND QUESTIONS

What do you see in a new way now? What have you learned about facing this dilemma? What questions do you have about the dilemma in your life?

IMPLICATIONS

What do you want or need to do about this dilemma? Are there social implications? Are there actions you could take? Is there something more to learn? What support would help? Where will you find that support?

Theological Reflection Beginning with a Personal Experience (1)

Identify a focus. Describe a short conversation that you recently had about something that mattered to you. Write it out or make some notes on what was said. Recall the tone, the points made, and the parts of the conversation that have stayed with you. What was it about? What does it mean to you now? Starting from a conversation like this places you in the Action/Experience aspect of your life.

Name the central theme of the conversation (what it was about) and then try to come up with an image that captures that theme. If you could draw a picture of the theme, what would it be? Or, explore by naming the central issue in the conversation. Either image or issue will work as a focus for reflection.

Explore the issue or image focus by asking a question or two, such as:

How does that image or issue express facets that are creative and those that are destructive?

How would God be present in such a matter?

What values are present?

How would grace be represented?

Connect to other areas of your life. Listen for voices that speak from society or **Culture**, that is, from the world around you; from the Christian **Tradition**; and from your **Personal Beliefs**. Connect freely, without trying to do these in any order.

How and where do any of the questions stimulate response from you?

How do people or groups in your **Culture** deal with the image or issue?

How does the Christian **Tradition** (scripture, hymns, prayers, and so forth) speak to that matter?

What do you **Believe** or wrestle with about the theme upon which you are reflecting?

What other times have you had to deal with this matter (**Personal Experience**)?

What are you becoming aware of as you explore and connect to the issue or image? What do you see in a new way?

Apply

What difference, however great or small, does this reflection have for your daily life? What implications for ministry are there?

Theological Reflection Beginning with a Personal Experience (2)

IDENTIFY A FOCUS	RESPONSES

Write a brief description of an incident for reflection.

For this reflection, use something related to "work" in a broad sense. Recording the experience aids in making the identification specific and concrete. Use the criteria of "a piece of your life story which challenged your feelings, values, or way of looking at things."

For instance: Describe one specific incident of parenting, or income-producing work, or a hobby. The criterion is that the incident matters to you.

List the shifts in action in the incident you chose, and choose one shift for the focus.

"Shifts in action" can be physical, emotional, or cognitive movement. Conscious decisions as well as spontaneous responses are listed. Look over your list and choose one. Any of the shifts will serve as a point of departure. Therefore, choose one that holds a certain interest for you.

Example: An incident of creating a garden that was raided by deer might have shifts such as:

- *I walked out to enjoy coffee in my garden.*

- *I saw most of the plants eaten down to the ground.*

- *I saw deer prints.*

- *I sat down and cried.*

One of the shifts in your incident will have the most energy. Choose that one as the focus.

Recapture the feelings and thoughts at the moment of focus.

List three or four feelings and thoughts you had *at the key moment of shift of focus identified above.* Often, there is the temptation to project feelings and thoughts into past situations. Recall as accurately as possible what you actually experienced at that moment specifically.

Thoughts	*Feelings*
Oh no!	Shock
I'm going to set a trap	Anger
All that work gone	Sorrow

IDENTIFY A FOCUS	RESPONSES

Recall another time when you had the same combination of feelings and similar thoughts.

Identifying another time when you viewed life in the same way is important. Metaphors are generated best by comparing two or more incidents. When you recall a past experience, new insights often occur. Briefly record the similar incident, including any insights and awareness.

Similar Incident

Create a metaphor.

Think about both experiences. Allow them to become present again. Consider what they were like. How would you describe them using a single metaphor, image, or simile? List all that come to your mind. Then, choose one to explore further.

Ex.: At the moment of seeing the destroyed garden— Possible images/metaphors that capture what it's like in that kind of moment: "I feel like a wrung-out dishcloth"; "I feel like I've been hit in the stomach"; "I feel like a fallen soufflé."

What images/metaphors reflect what life is like when you had the thoughts and feeling you identified?

Write or draw your metaphor.

EXPLORE THE FOCUS	RESPONSES

Explore the "world of the metaphor."

Explore or question the metaphor from one or more perspectives such as:

"What is life like in the metaphor?" (CREATION)

"What temptations to destroy are there in the metaphor world?" (SIN)

"What brings those in that image up short, takes their breath away?" (JUDGEMENT)

"What changes would be called for?" (REPENTANCE)

"What would be an occasion for celebration?" (REDEMPTION)

These are some of the questions that can be used to develop your understanding of the "world of the metaphor." Don't attempt to give a full account of each question. When your energy begins to slow, take this as a sign that enough work may have been done. Sometimes insights will occur while exploring the metaphor. Write those down.

Ex.: In a world of being hit in the stomach—Creation—what the world/life is like: life is dangerous, needs caution, painful

Sin—what tempts those in this world to be destructive: tempted to seek revenge, to harm in return, to give up because of anger or fear

CONNECT TO OTHER SOURCES OF MEANING	RESPONSES

Bring in the Christian Tradition.

Consider the material that you have been studying as it relates to this reflection. Is there anything from the current reading chapter that comes to mind? Review several of the chapters you have read. Write a few sentences commenting on the part of the TRADITION that connects with the selected metaphor/image.

What stories from the Bible or hymns or prayers come to mind with this metaphor? Ex.: Where in the Bible would there be accounts where someone might feel/think "It was like being punched in the stomach"?

List possible stories and select one. Read it carefully.

Compare and contrast the perspectives of the metaphor and of the piece of Christian Tradition.

Write a short paragraph that compares and contrasts the Christian Tradition with the perspective contained in the "world of the metaphor."

How is the scripture story or hymn or prayer similar to and different from the metaphor perspectives?

Connect to Contemporary Culture/Society and Personal Beliefs.

What examples are there in our contemporary CULTURE of life being like the metaphor you chose? How is God present in those times?

Include any statements or judgments that represent presently held positions or beliefs. How would you state the "truth of the matter" as you see it in this reflection (POSITION/BELIEF)? What does "the truth of the matter" contribute to the relationship of meaningful work and worship?

Record your responses.

APPLY	RESPONSES

Identify insights and questions.

Record insights you now have. Do you have any new questions related to the matters that the reflection brought up for you?

Record your responses.

Decide on implications.

In light of your reflection, what might you do? Are you aware of something you want to change, or study more, or pray about, or talk to someone about? You might want to choose a new way to act out your ministry during the next few days.

Record your decisions.

Theological Reflection Beginning with a Mind Map

This link, http://mindmap.nu/how-to-do-radiant-thinking-based-on-mind-mapping/, provides information on "mind-mapping" or "radiant thinking." You may also want to look at other sources of information on this process.

Identify a focus.

Construct a "mind-map" by making associations with the centering theme. For example, the mind map below starts with the theme "re-formations" placed in the center of paper. As you make associations from your assigned reading over the past few weeks, write those associations around the theme and draw a line between the theme and each association.

After making several associations, study the entire map.

- What images or metaphors express the nature of "re-forming?"

- Select one to explore.

Explore the world of the metaphor/image.

Identify a specific point from which to explore the chosen image. For example, if the image is "jumping into an abyss," then be sure to explore the image from a standpoint such as the person jumping into the abyss. Do not shift to other possible standpoints such as observing someone's jump into the abyss or leading someone to the edge of an abyss.

Develop two or three questions and explore the image through those perspectives. For example, what questions would explore the destructive dimensions of the image (Sin)? What questions explore the nature of the world of the metaphor-image (Creation)? What questions bring in the Judgment dimensions of the metaphor? Or the Repentance and/or Redemption perspectives?

Connect with other areas of life.

Begin connecting with your life by briefly stating when you experienced the world depicted in the image/metaphor. Remember to work from the standpoint previously identified. For example, when have you metaphorically "jumped off into an abyss"?

Connect with other sources, such as contemporary culture and the Christian tradition. You may find that something from your reading over the past few weeks comes to mind.

Bring in your personal beliefs. What do you believe? What do you hold to be true?

Apply to your life going forward.

Notice how what you learn from the reflection applies to your life. For example, what light does this reflection shed on how you engage opportunities for ministry?

Resources for Community Life

The Respectful Communications Guidelines and Mutual Invitation process are from the Kaleidoscope Institute with whom EfM has been in a collaborative relationship since 2011. Learn more about KI at www.kscopeinstitute.org

Respectful Communication Guidelines

R = take RESPONSIBILITY for what you say and feel without blaming others

E = use EMPATHETIC listening

S = be SENSITIVE to differences in communication styles

P = PONDER what you hear and feel before you speak

E = EXAMINE your own assumptions and perceptions

C = keep CONFIDENTIALITY

T = TRUST ambiguity, because we are not here to debate who is right or wrong

(from *The Bush Was Blazing but Not Consumed* by Eric H. F. Law)

I agree to uphold these guidelines for the time we have together.

Signature _____ Date _____

Mutual Invitation

In order to ensure that everyone who wants to share has the opportunity to speak, we will proceed in the following way:

The leader or a designated person shares first. After that person has spoken, he or she then invites another to share. (Whom you invite does not need to be the person next to you.) After the next person has spoken, that person is given the privilege to invite another to share.

If you are not ready to share, say "I pass for now" and we will invite you to share later on. If you don't want to say anything at all, simply say "pass" and proceed to invite another to share. We will do this until everyone has been invited.

We invite you to listen and not to respond to someone' s sharing immediately. There will be time to respond and to ask clarifying questions after everyone has had an opportunity to share.

(adapted from *The Wolf Shall Dwell with the Lamb* by Eric H. F. Law[103])

---

103. Atlanta: Chalice Press, 1993.